TABLE OF CONTENTS

LIST OF EXHIBITS

ACKNOWLEDGMENTS

Indebtedness is acknowledged to numerous persons for their assistance, cooperation, and counsel which made this study possible. Especial gratitude is offered to Dr. Norman X. Dressel, Dr. Catherine E. Miles, and Dr. Jack Blicksilver who provided guidance, assistance, and encouragement throughout the period of study.

Several individuals at the University of Illinois were helpful. Dr. Vernon K. Zimmerman, Director of the Center for International Education and Research in Accounting of the College of Commerce and Business Administration and Associate Dean, graciously provided a substantial amount of material as well as many helpful suggestions. Dr. E. J. DeMaris, Head of the Department of Accountancy, and his office staff, offered additional assistance and extended many courtesies. Biographical files on A. C. Littleton were made available in the Department of Accountancy, the Office of the President, and the Alumni Office. A special vote of thanks is due Mr. Maynard Brichford, University Archivist, for his invaluable assistance in locating material in the library and archives.

Dr. Doris Cash Pruitt, who conscientiously read the various drafts and maintained continuous interest and

and counsel, is due heartfelt gratitude. Barbara Obitz provided invaluable typing assistance in the final stages of the work. Sincere appreciation and gratitude is extended to these and others who have evidenced an interest in the study.

PREFACE

The basic problem of the student of accountancy who
is confronted with reviewing a very large amount of literature to formulate a reasonable and proper perspective concerning the subject prompted the present study of selected
areas of the work of A. C. Littleton. This statement of
selected contributions of one of the prolific writers in the
field of accountancy during the first half of the present
century provides a comprehensive aid to the student. The
areas covered are of major significance in the total work of
A. C. Littleton. The objective of this study is to develop
an integrated synthesis of Littleton's philosophy in the
selected areas. In addition, the evolution of his thoughts
as well as his possible impact and influence upon the development of accounting thought are presented.

Kathryn Current Buckner
Spring, 1975

INTRODUCTION

TO

LITTLETON'S CONTRIBUTION TO

THE THEORY OF ACCOUNTANCY

By

Kathryn Current Buckner

The basic purpose in this study is to consider the
work of Ananias Charles Littleton, Emeritus Professor of
Accountancy at the University of Illinois, to determine his
significant contributions to the theory of accounting and
the nature of those contributions. The study is confined to
consideration and analysis of his additions to the literature of the theory of accounting in selected areas which
are of major significance in his work.

The methodology followed is both historical and interpretive. The historical development of Littleton's views
on the selected areas of accounting is presented, analyzed,
and evaluated. Particular attention is directed toward
Littleton's consistency of treatment of ideas as well as the
evolution of his thoughts in order to develop an integrated

synthesis of his philosophy concerning the selected areas. Emphasis is placed upon selective review and analysis of his publications. His thoughts, as presented in his published writings, are traced chronologically with the objective of evaluating his work for continuity, consistency, and development. Littleton's work is viewed within the framework of the status of development of accounting at the time he entered the profession. In addition, consideration is given to contemporary developments.

This study supports the conclusion that Littleton was a major force in the development of accounting thought during his productive period. His highly articulate writing and his overall work in the field of accounting constitute a significant contribution to the development of the stature of the accounting profession. He was responsive to the needs of business management and addressed himself to the intrinsic problems of accounting in income determination methodology. He believed that income determination is the central purpose of accounting and this is a major theme in his writing. The top objective of accounting is to reflect the results of enterprise actions. The comparison of business effort and accomplishment is implemented via the accounting process of matching cost and revenue. Littleton's continued emphasis upon income determination and the related matching concept as to revenue and cost must be considered as influential in the final acceptance of the concepts which are basic to accounting thought today.

Littleton resolutely defended and promoted the allocation of cost as an essential feature of the matching process in income determination. His emphasis upon the necessity for maintenance of the integrity of cost data for records and reporting is a prime element of his total philosophy. In his advocacy of and adherence to the use of historical cost, Littleton crystallized a goal which became an accepted practice.

Littleton's development of a structure of accounting theory based upon inductively derived principles rooted in experience and action has no doubt had a significant influence on accounting developments during his writing span of some forty years. He stressed the necessity for principles, as headlines of theory, to be interrelated and interdependent. He viewed the coordination of principles as an integral feature of a body of theory.

CHAPTER I

OBJECTIVES AND PARAMETERS OF RESEARCH

The reputation of any discipline of study may depend to a great extent upon the recognized writers in the field. The accounting discipline, as others, has many writers who have been recognized as significant contributors to its reputation. Ananias Charles Littleton is one of the writers who has been so identified with the literature of accounting. This study deals with the literature of accounting; specifically, it deals with the material written by Ananias Charles Littleton in selected areas of the theory of accounting. This chapter is devoted to an introduction of the study. The purpose, nature, scope, and limitations of the study are stated. The literature studied is listed. Finally, a brief discussion of the subject matter and the areas of concern in the following chapters is included.

The Problem

The literature of accountancy is becoming more and more voluminous. The student of accountancy and accounting is confronted with the problem of dealing with this large and growing mass of literature. A study restricted to written materials added to the literature during the present century becomes a tremendous task. It should be noted that, since the early 1900's, a number of writers within the accounting profession have endeavored to develop in written form a theory of accountancy which could provide a framework and foundation for the study of contemporary accounting thought.

The period since 1900 has been recognized as a dynamic one in the long record of the evolution of accounting. During this era of time, accounting has been recognized as a legitimate academic area of study; a professional examination has been developed for a recognized, established, self-regulated profession; the profession has shifted significantly upward on the social spectrum; and electronic data-processing techniques have been introduced into the functions of recording and interpreting economic data.[1]

The work of certain writers predominates in the literature of the twentieth century. If the student chooses to study the work of one of these major writers, he will probably find it necessary to seek out articles published in a variety of periodicals and journals in addition to published books. This will be necessary because the

[1]V. K. Zimmerman, "The Long Shadow of a Scholar," The International Journal of Accounting Education and Research, II, No. 2 (Spring, 1967), 1.

articles written by an individual have not been, in most cases, reproduced in complete collections or in an anthology.

The articles probably were published over a lengthy period of time, may be repetitious, and may be or may not be consistent over the period of years. The articles may reveal a chronological evolution of the writer's thoughts and ideas. Some of the published material may have been pertinent only within a particular time period, or in a particular context, or to an issue of temporary interest. On the other hand, other articles written by the same individual may be of lasting and permanent interest and importance. Some of a writer's work may truly constitute a portion of the foundation and/or framework of contemporary accounting thought. Further, some of the statements or thoughts of the same writer may conflict with those of other notable writers.

Clearly, the task of reviewing the literature and attempting to formulate a reasonable and proper perspective is formidable. There is a need for efforts directed toward the purpose of extracting the essence from the total presented by an individual major writer. A comprehensive condensation of the overall work of an individual could serve a very useful purpose in this area. Specifically, a comprehensive statement concerning the contributions of a particular individual in important selected areas will be a valuable aid to students.

Objectives

Ananias Charles Littleton,[2] Emeritus Professor of
Accounting, University of Illinois, is one of those who has
been prominently associated with accounting history and accounting theory during the past half-century. He has written four books (two of them with coauthors), coedited two
books, and written over 300 articles, reviews, comments,
and editorials for accounting periodicals and journals.
The University of Illinois Press published his Essays on
Accountancy in 1961. This is a compilation by Littleton of
extracts and reprints of his prior publications and a small
amount of previously unpublished material. Littleton was
on the accounting faculty at the University of Illinois
from 1915 to 1952. He is credited with exerting the pioneer effort toward the graduate accounting program at that
institution where the first Doctor of Philosophy in accounting was awarded in the United States. Littleton has been
explicitly recognized as a major contributor to the twen-
tieth-century literature of accountancy.[3]

The basic purpose of this study is to consider
Littleton's significant contributions to the theory of ac-
counting and to determine the nature of his contributions.
The particular concern of this study is confined to

---

[2]Henceforth referred to as Littleton.

[3]James Don Edwards and Roland F. Salmonson, Contributions of Four Accounting Pioneers, Kohler, Littleton,
May, Paton (East Lansing, Michigan: Michigan State University, 1961), Passim, Section II and others.

consideration and analysis of his additions to the literature of selected areas of the theory of accounting. It is intended that the areas selected are of major significance in his work.

Major ideas as presented in his writings have been selected for study to develop insight as to his consistency of treatment, the evolution of his thoughts over the years, and his possible impact and influence upon the development of accounting thought. This study is designed to develop an integrated synthesis of Littleton's philosophy with regard to the selected areas.

A secondary objective is to place Littleton within the context of his time in order to review his role in the evolving professional and academic accounting climate. This involves a presentation of, as background, the general status of development and accounting thought at the time he began writing.

Definitions and Terminology

It is appropriate to specifically define a few of the terms used in this study. In their more general usages, accountancy and accounting are usually used synonymously. Accountancy, of relatively rare occurrence in the literature, generally has reference to the entire field of theory and practice. On the other hand, accounting is restricted to particular areas of reference, especially as an adjective.[4] Accountancy denotes a field of knowledge while accounting means the processes active in that field.[5] This clear-cut distinction between the two terms is not always maintained by Littleton in his writing; however, the intent can be perceived. Because the term accountancy is used infrequently in the literature of the field, while accounting is used in the dual context, this study uses accounting with the understanding that the term means accountancy and/or accounting. Accountancy is used only when it is clearly necessary and in direct quotations. Theory is defined by Littleton as simply thinking that is focused upon doing; it consists of explanations and reasons and, of course, comes in a variety of grades, each with its own usefulness.[6] Additional definitions and discussion of terminology are included in a later chapter.

Scope and Limitations of the Study

The scope of this study is limited to the work of Littleton in the selected areas of accounting theory enumerated later. Emphasis is upon selective review and analyses of his publications. Littleton's thoughts, as

---

[4]Eric L. Kohler, A Dictionary for Accountants, 3rd Edition (Englewood Cliffs: Prentice-Hall, Inc., 1963), p. 10.

[5]A. C. Littleton, Accounting Evolution to 1900 (New York: American Institute Publishing Company, 1933), p. 165.

[6]A. C. Littleton, Structure of Accounting Theory (Menasha, Wisconsin: George Banta Publishing Company for American Accounting Association, 1953), p. 132.

presented in his published writings, are traced chronologically with the objective of evaluating his work for continuity, consistency, and development. In conjunction with this, consideration is given to influences upon Littleton by colleagues, prevailing accounting practices, and other contributors to accounting literature. Although Littleton also worked extensively with professional accounting groups, this study deals with that phase of his activities only as it relates to accounting theory.

Littleton did much study, research, and writing in accounting history. He has been recognized as a major contributor to the literature in this area. His work is of an interpretive nature itself and as such does not come within the scope of this study. While the review of that phase of his work is confined to aspects related to theory development in the areas considered, his eminence in this field is noteworthy. In 1965, the following comment concerning Littleton's Accounting Evolution to 1900 was made: "Although written over 30 years ago, this is still the most important book in English on accounting history by one author."[7]

There has been no intention to cover Littleton's contributions to the area of accounting education except as

---

[7]R. H. Parker, "Accounting History: A Select Bibliography," in Contemporary Studies in the Evolution of Accounting Thought, ed. by Michael Chatfield (Belmont, California: Dickenson Publishing Company, Inc., 1968), p. 391.

they have an impact on the areas of accounting theory studied. Many of his speeches, discussions, and reports for
professional and educational groups were, in fact, published. The American Accounting Association published his monographs and various studies. As editor of The Accounting
Review many of his views were brought to the forefront
through "The Accounting Exchange" column. Biographical
material concerning Littleton is presented in Appendix II.
In addition, a bibliography of Littleton's publications
arranged in chronological order is included in Appendix I.

The Importance of the Study

The student of accounting should have the opportunity to study the work and contributions of those who have
made pioneer efforts toward building the foundation of the
current theory of accounting. As stated earlier, the total
volume of published materials in the field is already so
voluminous that the average undergraduate accounting student probably cannot be expected to obtain meaningful in-
sights as to the work of a particular author. Time con-
straints will in most cases prevent a student from making
an in-depth study of one individual's efforts. This is
especially the case when the material is to be found in
various periodicals and journals covering a time span of
forty years or more. The problem intensifies when the publications contain repetitious material and duplication of
viewpoint. This study will be helpful to present and

future students by providing a carefully derived reference source of manageable proportions based upon intensive, critical, and exhaustive study of selected aspects of the work of Littleton.

Literature Studied

Selected published writings of Littleton have been studied. A selected group of articles from the following periodicals have been covered: The Accounting Review, The Journal of Accountancy, Illinois Certified Public Accountant, The Certified Public Accountant, The American Accountant, Harvard Business Review, The Accounting Forum, College News and Views, Australian Accountant, Proceedings International Conference on Accounting Education, The International Journal of Accounting Education and Research, and various publications of the American Association of University Instructors in Accounting. In addition, the following publications have been included: An Introduction to Corporate Accounting Standards (Coauthor, 1940); Structure of Accounting Theory (1953); Studies in the History of Accounting (Coeditor, 1956); Essays on Accountancy (1961); Accounting Theory: Continuity and Change (Coauthor, 1962); and Significant Accounting Essays (Coeditor, 1965). Related literature has been used as required to establish support for findings. A limited amount of unpublished materials has been used as available and as appropriate to the purpose of this study. The unpublished material is substantially personal and biographical in nature. The sources of this unpublished material are: The Commerce and Business Administration Archives, Library, University of Illinois, and Biographical Files. The Biographical Files are from the following offices at the University of Illinois: The Department of Accountancy, The President's Office, and The Alumni Office. Limited amounts of data have been obtained from colleagues and associates of Littleton by personal interview and correspondence.

Method of Research

An examination has been made of published materials and written records available. An intensive study was conducted in the areas selected. Certain major themes dominate in Littleton's work and determined the selection of areas of study. Material relating to each of the areas was studied to determine the consistency of treatment over the years, the response to contemporary influence, and its logical connections and consistency of treatment in conjunction with other areas of theory.

Copies of substantially all items written and published by Littleton have been obtained for examination. Many of the unpublished items were obtained through primary research at the University of Illinois.

Areas of Research

Certain areas have been selected for intensive coverage. The areas selected are basic approach and views on principles, income determination as the central theme of accounting, and the prestige of historical cost. These areas are closely identified with Littleton's writing. An intensive study has been made of Littleton's work in each of these areas. The development of Littleton's ideas on the topics was traced chronologically. The period covered in this study extends from 1920 through 1966. It is a particular concern of the study to determine evidence of change of viewpoint, consistency of treatment of related aspects, logic of presentation, depth of presentation, and consistency of treatment of one idea.

Development of Selected Areas

The Development of Accounting Theory

The second chapter is devoted to the general stage of development of accounting theory at the time Littleton began to write. The purpose of coverage of the status of accounting at that time is to allow the discussion of Littleton's work within the context of his time. A very brief synopsis of background biographical information on Littleton is included.

The Central Theme of Accounting

A major chapter is devoted to coverage of Littleton's belief that income determination is primary, and therefore is the central theme of accounting. The measurement of enterprise effort and accomplishment, the measurement of cause and effect, is a major feature of the

central theme. Littleton's concept of a pyramid of enterprise principles is illustrated.

Littleton said that the function and purpose of
accounting is to supply information concerning the business
enterprise; to make the results of effort and accomplishment
readable. This viewpoint is discussed as a separate area.

The businessman's and accountant's concept of
profit as Littleton wrote of it is covered. In addition,
the earning power of the enterprise, the reality of profit,
and the matching of revenue and cost are important areas of
concern. The necessity for accruals and deferrals and the
fundamental cost allocation process are presented from
Littleton's standpoint. Finally, the shift to an emphasis
upon income statement information rather than balance sheet
presentations is discussed.

Prestige for Historical Cost

The concept of cost, a predominant feature in
Littleton's writing, is the topic of a separate chapter.
It was Littleton's belief that the prestige of accounting
is founded upon the integration of real and nominal accounts based upon natural costs or historical costs.
Littleton allowed no perversion of this outstanding characteristic of accounting.[8] Littleton's views on the money

---

[8]A. C. Littleton, Essays on Accountancy (Urbana:
University of Illinois Press, 1961), p. 340.

unit assumption, costs attach concept, homogeneous costs, cost terminology, cost recognition, and exchange transactions are all closely related aspects of the historical cost concept and are discussed.

Basic Approach and Views on Principles

One chapter reviews Littleton's basic approach to a theory of accounting and his views on principles. Consideration is given to his basic approach or manner of thinking in this area. His distinction between rules, standards, and principles is stressed. A section is included on definitions and terminology with major coverage on standards and objectives. His concern for objectives and his concept of the interrelationship of objectives are covered. Littleton visualized a pyramid of objectives which are basic determinates of purposeful accounting actions; this pyramid is emphasized and illustrated.

Littleton's observations concerning principles are presented. This topic is closely related to his basic approach. Littleton stressed the interdependence of theory and practice; theory being derived from the distillation of accounting actions. Littleton viewed principles as fundamental truths which are inductive generalizations slowly distilled from actions. His ideas on the inductive and deductive approaches to theory development are presented. Principles are central parts of a body of doctrine, called theory, and are useful aids to clear thinking about real problems. Littleton's emphasis was upon interrelatedness and structural wholeness as characteristics of good theory; a single principle is incomplete if isolated from companion principles.

Conclusions

The final chapter summarizes the results of the research. Conclusions reached as a result of the study as to the nature of Littleton's contribution to the theory of accounting are stated. A final evaluation is made as to his overall consistency of treatment and possible contemporary and lasting impact and influence upon accounting theory. Littleton's philosophy is also summarized.

CHAPTER II

THE DEVELOPMENT OF ACCOUNTING THEORY

Before exploring Littleton's contribution to the
field of accounting, it is desirable to examine several aspects of the nature of the business and accounting world at
the time of his writing. In the first place, the business
scene, because of its dynamic nature, is constantly changing. This was certainly true in the early part of the present century. The sphere of government was being broadened.
Therefore, as a result of its regulatory and taxing powers,
all levels of government required expanded and more realistic information from business enterprises. Accountants were
pressed to assist businessmen to fulfill the demands for
such information.

Accountants met this challenge in a number of ways.
The profession saw the need to provide for formal education
in accounting at the advanced level. Furthermore, professional organizations of accountants emerged at this time.
These organizations provided a means for exchange of ideas
and reflection on accepted accounting practice.

Prior to the early twentieth century, treatises on
accounting were predominantly expositions of practices.
There was, however, during the span of time under

consideration a noticeable emergence of thought concerning the theory of certain commonly accepted accounting practices. Littleton became a prime figure in this development.

The Changing Business Scene and Governmental Regulation

Business conditions and operating methods were changing rapidly during the early 1900's in response to major institutional developments of the period. These changes were in large part caused by the great strides made in industrial achievement, the improvement in distribution methods, and the increasing pressures of governmental regulation. By 1900, statutes permitting incorporation of a lawful business had been passed by the legislatures in nearly all of the states of the Union. The corporate form of business was widely used; the trend toward mergers and consolidation was well established.[1] Conservationists, social workers, and some politicians and journalists were critical of the practices and motives of businessmen at the time.[2]

The expansion of business by various means, as well as the trend toward incorporation of business, created a demand for more disclosure of financial information. The broader base of ownership in the corporate form of enterprise

[1]Eldon S. Hendriksen, Accounting Theory (Revised edition; Homewood, Illinois: Richard D. Irwin, Inc., 1970), p. 50 (Hereinafter referred to as Hendriksen, Theory).

[2]N. S. B. Gras and Henrietta M. Larson, Casebook in American Business History (New York: Appleton-Century-Crofts, Inc., 1939), pp. 730-35.

increased the need for more and better financial information for absentee owners. Businesses which had published limited financial details in the past were pressed to present more extensive reports. Demands for this expanded data came from the government, the public, and investors, as well as owners.

Business expansion and the criticism of some business practices were accompanied by an increase of governmental regulations which created problems of compliance and reporting.[3]

The Interstate Commerce Commission's regulations of 1887 had initiated annual reporting requirements and some specification of accounting controls for regulated carriers. However, the regulations failed to specify, until 1907, any uniform practices for accounting computations; therefore, little uniformity was evident in the reports. Even the regulations of 1907 provided for very little uniformity. For example, the regulations allowed the individual carriers the option of deciding upon depreciation charges against operations after consideration of the company's general financial condition.[4]

The passage of revenue-gathering regulations by the government initiated considerable pressure upon business to maintain more adequate accounting records.

---

[3]Ibid.

[4]Hendriksen, Theory, p. 40.

The Payne-Aldrich Tariff Act of 1909 imposed a special excise tax of 1 per cent on income over $5,000 earned by every corporation organized for profit. The tax, equivalent to 1 per cent of income, was assessed on the privilege of doing business as a corporation. The tax was not on net income. Net income was merely the measure of the indirect tax which, as an excise tax, was valid under the Constitution of the United States without apportionment to the states according to population.[5] Net income was essentially to be measured by deducting from actual cash receipts the actual cash disbursements for expenses, interest actually paid, uninsured losses actually sustained, and a reasonable allowance for depreciation, if any. In addition, the law stipulated that reporting must be upon a calendar-year basis. Many accountants viewed the provisions as impossible to apply and in violation with accepted accounting methods in use at the time.[6] The United States Treasury Department finally issued regulations which allowed the computation of income on an accrual basis for tax purposes.[7]

The requirements of the several revenue acts between 1912 and 1918 caused the implementation of improved reporting by business firms, and regulations were gradually

---

[5]1971 Federal Tax Course (New York: Commerce Clearing House, Inc., 1970), p. 110.

[6]Editorial, "Accounting Errors in Corporation Tax Bill," The Journal of Accountancy, VIII (July, 1909), 213.

[7]Hendriksen, Theory, p. 44.

reconciled to conform with contemporary accounting practices. The Revenue Act of 1915, passed after the adoption of the Sixteenth Amendment to the Constitution, merged the 1909 excise tax with a new and general income tax.[8] Compliance with the provisions of this law led many businessmen to prepare statements of income and expenses although they had not previously done so. In this way, the law encouraged the extension and improvement of accounting records and reports. The 1916 act and the excess profits law of 1917 permitted returns for tax purposes to be based upon regular corporate accounting records if such records clearly reflected income. The wording and the requirements of the statutes made compliance difficult.[9] The 1918 act was the first to actually recognize accepted accounting procedures in the determination of taxable income.[10] Recognition of the best accounting practices of the time was the result of the advice of a lawyer, an economist, and a certified public accountant. The Treasury Department had called on these men for assistance in setting up the regulations of the 1918 act. These advisers were instrumental in helping to draft some of the

---

[8] *1971 Federal Tax Course* (New York: Commerce Clearing House, Inc., 1970), p. 111.

[9] James Don Edwards, *History of Public Accounting in the United States* (East Lansing, Michigan: Bureau of Business and Economic Research, Michigan State University, 1960), pp. 102-5 (Hereinafter referred to as Edwards, *History of Public Accounting*).

[10] Hendriksen, *Theory*, pp. 45-46.

provisions of this act in an effort to make the regulations workable from an accounting standpoint.[11]

The revenue acts and regulations of the Treasury Department indirectly influenced the development of accounting thought. For example, the laws provided an impetus toward improving accounting practices. The provision for depreciation in the acts led not only to the use of systematic depreciation methods; it also promoted the development of better depreciation concepts and more appropriate methods of calculating depreciation cost. In addition, the mandatory use of inventories for income determination provided in the laws stimulated concern about inventory valuation methods. The acceptability of the lower-of-cost-or-market basis for inventory valuation for tax purposes led to much interest on the part of accountants about the concept.[12]

Businesses, therefore, were forced to attempt compliance with the growing governmental reporting requirements. The various income tax regulations focused attention upon the contemporary accounting practices and the need for improvement in them. The tax regulations made it necessary that immediate attention be given to income determination. Furthermore, since income was the basis for tax, much additional concern was concentrated upon a proper and true computation of income. The cost allocation procedures used

---

[11]Percival F. Brundage, "Milestones on the Path of Accounting," Harvard Business Review, XXIX, No. 4 (July, 1951), 73-74.

[12]Hendriksen, Theory, p. 46.

became highly significant and led to much concern for the previously neglected but important question of depreciation expense.

In addition to the reporting requirements of government regulations, there was an increasing demand for fuller disclosure of financial information to other groups of users. These demands were forthcoming from the public and investors. As a consequence of these factors, accountants began to be called upon by businesses more and more frequently for assistance in providing adequate financial information.

Inadequate Financial Disclosure

Inadequate financial disclosure, based upon diverse accounting methods, was presented on an irregular and infrequent basis by the normal business in the early 1900's. Simple balance sheets were usually presented and some information about capitalization and dividends was sometimes disclosed. However, sales and profit figures were seldom released and income statements were rarely published. Certifications by the company or an auditor were very infrequently presented. Financial secrecy was a common characteristic of both large and small companies. This secrecy was based upon owner-manager attitudes, weak state laws, public apathy, and the accepted method of distributing securities, as well as the absence of accounting standards and theory. The concept of depreciation was not understood by many accountants and businessmen. In fact, many firms had never recorded depreciation expense. Furthermore, there was confusion as to the proper accounting for valuation of assets, the consolidation of subsidiaries, and the treatment of unusual charges and credits.[13]

In spite of the growth of business, the demands of critics who viewed the businessman as motivated only by the desire for material gain, the gradual recognition of more managerial responsibility, and the need of the public and investors for more information, the improvement of financial reporting and disclosure came slowly. It should be noted that the New York Stock Exchange, as early as 1900, requested that the application of a corporation for listing of its securities on the Exchange be accompanied by an agreement to publish annual reports to investors concerning the company's financial position and the results of its operations.[14] However, from 1885 onward, the Exchange had maintained a so-called Unlisted Department. Companies which traded securities through this department were not required to furnish the Exchange with financial information concerning an issue. From approximately 1910 onward, when it abolished its Unlisted Department because of growing threats of government regulations, the New York Stock Exchange influenced

[13]David F. Hawkins, "The Development of Modern Financial Reporting Practices Among American Manufacturing Corporations," The Business History Review, XXXVII (Autumn, 1963), 137-44 (Hereinafter referred to as Hawkins, "Development of Reporting Practices").

[14]Hendriksen, Theory, pp. 50-51.

improvements in financial reporting practices of listed companies. The Exchange's efforts to bring about fuller disclosure were successful only in a limited way. There was a recognized need for the assistance and cooperation of accountants. Nonetheless, accountants evidently were less than prompt in their response. The publication of a thirty-five page annual report by the United States Steel Corporation, in 1902, is generally noted as one of the initial steps toward fuller disclosure. The report was accompanied by an audit certificate from Price, Waterhouse and Company.[15] Other companies apparently did not rush to follow this reporting example. In general, it is evident that businesses and accountants moved toward fuller disclosure of financial information slowly.

The Status of the Professional Accountant

It is apparent that prior to approximately 1885 there were relatively few American public accountants. Those who were in practice were considered "expert book-keepers,"[16] "those business ferrets," and/or "financial coroners."[17] The qualifications of the practicing accountant

---

[15]Hawkins, "Development of Reporting Practices," 147-50, and others.

[16]J. Edward Masters, "The Accounting Profession in the United States," The Journal of Accountancy, XX, No. 5 (November, 1915), 349 (Hereinafter referred to as Masters, "Accounting Profession").

[17]T. Edward Ross, "Random Recollections of an Eventful Half Century," The Journal of Accountancy, LXIV, No. 4 (October, 1937), 267 (Hereinafter referred to as Ross, "Random Recollections").

in the United States in the last years of the nineteenth century were simple and limited in scope. Questions relating to costing principles, sinking funds, reserves, earned surplus, capital surplus, fixed and liquid assets, capital and income charges, invested capital, working capital, depletion, amortization, obsolescence, and depreciation were vaguely understood and often not dealt with at all. There was no uniform observance of auditing or of account maintenance throughout the United States as there was in Great Britain.[18]

By the turn of the century there was evidence of a deeper appreciation of the functions of the public accountant. This change was related to the increase in the incorporation of American companies and the sale of their securities to a large number of investors, many of whom were from Great Britain. Accountants from England and Scotland who came to this country to make audits are credited with much of the original impetus toward the establishment of the profession of public accounting in the United States. American public accountants gained new insight into the duties and responsibilities of auditors from those chartered accountants. The

---

[18] James T. Anyon, Recollections of the Early Days of American Accountancy, 1883-1893 (New York: Privately printed, 1925), pp. 9-10, 43-9.

chartered accountants drew upon a background of professional training and affiliation not enjoyed in the United
States.[19] By 1913, the public accountant was in a much
more established position in the American business community and in governmental circles.[20]

The Formation of Professional Organizations

Coinciding with the development of the accounting
profession was the movement toward the formation of professional organizations. This movement was initiated in 1886
with the formation of a group in New York who called themselves the American Association of Public Accountants.[21]
This organization merged with other state groups in 1905,
and by 1915 the membership was approximately 1,100.[22] The
association made concerted efforts to secure legislative
enactment of Certified Public Accountant laws in the
various states. However, in spite of the efforts of the
professional bodies, it was 1924 before all states had
enacted some type of law covering certified public accountants. The requirements for certification in the various
states were not uniform. The association was unsuccessful in

---

[19]Ibid., passim, and Mary E. Murphy, Advanced
Public Accounting Practice (Homewood, Illinois: Richard D.
Irwin, Inc., 1966), pp. 8-12 (Hereinafter referred to as
Murphy, Public Accounting Practice).

[20]Edwards, History of Public Accounting, p. 78.

[21]Ross, "Random Recollections," 268-69.

[22]Masters, "Accounting Profession," 352.

efforts to have Congress pass legislation to recognize and regulate the public accountants on a national basis.[23]

The professional organizations also made concerted efforts in the area of accounting education. Their efforts were closely related to the development of the accounting courses in universities.

Development of Accounting Education in Universities

An important aspect in the evolution of accounting thought was the development of accounting education in the universities. The same factors listed as influential in the evolution of accounting practice were also influential in the evolution of accounting education. The organization of railroads, the growth of other large corporate enterprises, the creation of public regulatory commissions, the efforts of professional accounting associations, and, of course, the enactment of Certified Public Accountant laws all contributed to the pressures which led to the addition of accounting to university curricula.[24] However, the development of accounting courses at the university level was a very slow process prior to 1900. The movement to establish schools of

---

[23]Edwards, History of Public Accounting, pp. 70-73, 110, 224.

[24]Roy J. Sampson, "American Accounting Education, Textbooks and Public Practice Prior to 1900," Business History Review, XXXIV, No. 4 (Winter, 1960), 466.

business was confronted by a great deal of opposition, and this same attitude of opposition adversely affected the development of accounting courses.[25]

Very Early Efforts

Very early efforts to establish schools of business at the university level were unsuccessful in many cases. In 1851, a school of commerce was incorporated in the University of Louisiana but the school was abandoned in 1857. In 1868, the University of Illinois established a School of Commerce which was discontinued by the trustees in 1880. The School of Commerce was established again, in 1902, at the University of Illinois. In 1881 the Wharton School of Finance and Economy was founded.[26]

The public accountants in America had recognized very early that a formal educational program should be adopted to prepare accountants for practice.[27] Because of the impetus to business, there was a growing demand for the services of accountants, and it became evident that there was a scarcity of well-trained accountants. Guiding precedents for accountants were relatively scarce. Prior experience provided the main source of knowledge. Not only

---

[25]Jeremiah Lockwood, "Early University Education in Accountancy," The Accounting Review, XIII, No. 2 (June, 1938), 132-33 (Hereinafter referred to as Lockwood, "University Education").

[26]Ibid., 131-32.

[27]Murphy, Public Accounting Practice, p. 29.

were there no schools of accounting but there were very few
American textbooks. Of course, accounting articles in
journals and periodicals were nonexistent.[28] Members of
the profession felt that action should be initiated to secure the cooperation of some educational institution which
would establish a course in accountancy to train students to
fill future needs for trained assistants. The American Association of Public Accountants started a school of accounts in New York under the authority of the Regents of
the University of New York in 1892 but this effort failed.[29]

First Accounting Courses in Universities

The institutions of higher learning were skeptical
as to the feasibility or advisability of starting accounting schools. Finally, in 1901, after urging by a committee
of the New York Society of Certified Public Accountants, the
first course was instituted at the New York University with
a registry of sixty-three students. Thus was established
the first department of accountancy, as such.[30]

---

[28]Lybrand, Ross Bros. & Montgomery, Fiftieth
Anniversary, 1898-1948 (n. p. : Privately printed by
Lybrand, Ross Bros. & Montgomery, n. d., p. 29 (Hereinafter
referred to as Lybrand, Fiftieth Anniversary).

[29]Richard Brown, A History of Accounting and Accountants (New York: Reissued by Augustus M. Kelley
Publishers, 1968. Originally issued: London: Frank Cass
and Company Limited, 1905), p. 272.

[30]Lockwood, "University Education," 141, and
Edward L. Suffern, "Twenty-Five Years of Accountancy," The
Journal of Accountancy, XXXIV, No. 3 (September, 1922), 177.

In 1902, the Pennsylvania Institute of Public Accountants sponsored the formation of four accounting courses. The classes were held in the offices of Lybrand, Ross Bros. & Montgomery. In 1904, the classes were taken over by the Wharton School of the University of Pennsylvania. The enrollment in the first evening class was 126. One of the conditions under which the Wharton School agreed to offer these courses was that any resulting deficit would be made up by guarantors among the members of the Pennsylvania Institute. However, the project was self-supporting from the beginning.[31]

The growth of accountancy as a practical course of instruction was slow. There were a number of factors which deterred progress; for example, there were very few people who could teach accounting. The instructors, in many instances, knew very little about accountancy, and they also had to teach other business subjects. The burden of these additional courses naturally retarded the development of courses in accounting. However, the development of the courses was accelerated overall by the interest and concern of practitioners of accounting and the growing certified public accountant movement. These factors provided much of the necessary impetus.[32]

---

[31] Lybrand, Fiftieth Anniversary, p. 25, and Ross, "Random Recollections," 272.

[32] Lockwood, "University Education," 134-35.

Lack of Textbooks

The lack of textbooks on accounting was a major difficulty in the development of accounting courses, and teachers were forced to use the lecture system until textbooks could be prepared. In 1900, accounting knowledge in the United States was basically founded upon English procedures and practices. American authors had written extensively but the material covered only bookkeeping techniques for various types of businesses. A few books on corporate accounting, cost accounting, auditing, voucher systems, and certified public accountant examination questions had come into being between 1880 and 1900. Most of these books had been prepared for business colleges and were not suitable for use in the university courses.[33]

The lack of textbooks on accounting and accounting theory placed the burden upon the teachers to develop material for the courses taught. This led to the publication of textbooks based upon material used and tested in the classrooms. It would appear reasonable to conclude that these teachers, through their textbooks, wielded a considerable influence upon accounting instruction and concepts during this period.

---

[33]Ibid., 133-34.

Lack of Accounting Teachers

The lack of teachers of accounting was a very serious problem. Professors who could teach did not necessarily understand accounting. Those who knew accounting were often unable to teach. A prominent accountant and teacher who later wrote one of the important texts of the era (Modern Accounting, 1909) confessed, in 1903, that he did not know the difference between bookkeeping and higher accounting.[34] This confession was made after approximately five years of teaching accounting subjects. The early career of this teacher illustrates somewhat the development of courses, teachers, and textbooks during the period.

In the autumn of 1898, a new course was offered in Railway Accounts, Exchange, and other topics by the Department of Political Economy at the University of Chicago. It was taught by a new instructor, H. R. Hatfield, who had received his Doctor of Philosophy degree in 1897. Hatfield had worked in a bank and bond house for five and one-half years; part of the time he worked on the books. He had never had a course in accounting or bookkeeping. In 1900-1901 he started another new course called "Accounting" which placed emphasis on the interpretation of balance sheets and related problems. Dr. Hatfield later noted that

_____

[34]Dr. H. R. Hatfield, in the Proceedings of the Michigan Political Science Association, February 5-7, 1903, Vol. V, 183, cited by Lockwood, "University Education," 134.

his beginning efforts in the course were feeble. Hatfield took a six-month leave of absence to study in France and Germany. When he returned to the university he continued the same course until January, 1904. Although he used no textbook in the classes, Hatfield followed the text written in 1894, and reprinted in 1901, by Professor J. F. Schär of Germany. Hatfield also taught a variety of other courses at the University of Chicago. When he left Chicago and began teaching at the University of California (1904), he introduced "Principles of Accounting" with emphasis upon the balance sheet and the profit and loss statement.[35]

Another illustration of the need for capable instructors of accounting is found in the early career of Arthur Andersen. Andersen, who had passed the Certified Public Accountant examination in 1908, was instructing evening accounting classes as a lecturer while he was a student himself at the newly organized School of Commerce of Northwestern University. In 1912, when the department head resigned, taking with him his copyrighted lecture material and problems, Andersen was appointed Assistant Professor and Head of the Accounting Department. He had to reorganize the department and develop material for the various courses. Andersen finally received his bachelor's degree in 1922.[36]

---

[35]Lockwood, "University Education," 138-39.

[36]The First Fifty Years, 1913-1963 (Chicago: Arthur Andersen & Co., 1963), pp. 3-5.

Thus, he was an instructor and head of an accounting department long before he had his bachelor's degree.

During the period 1900-1910 there was a gradual but obvious recognition that accounting was an essential subject in our large universities and colleges. This trend increased even more during the years between 1910 and 1916. The lack of accounting instructors continued, however, to be a very pressing problem.[37]

For a number of years following the establishment of the New York and Pennsylvania schools, the schools did not graduate an adequate supply of men to fill the needs of the profession. It was necessary for public accounting firms to establish their own internal training programs.[38]

Status of Instruction in 1916

In December, 1916, the First Annual Meeting of the American Association of University Instructors in Accounting was held. John E. Treleven, University of Texas, presented a paper concerning the status of instruction in accounting at colleges and universities in the United States. His remarks were based upon a comprehensive nationwide survey. He noted that the previous decade had produced a very

---

[37] C. E. Allen, "The Growth of Accounting Instruction Since 1900," The Accounting Review, II, No. 2 (June, 1927), 150-60, and Joseph A. Sterrett, "Progress of the Accounting Profession," The Journal of Accountancy, IX (November, 1909), 16.

[38] Lybrand, Fiftieth Anniversary, p. 47, and others.

noticeable and rapid increase in both the number of institutions in which accounting was taught and in the number of students. Accounting of collegiate grade was offered at 105 institutions. The institutions were classified on the basis of the amount of accounting offered and the purpose for which the instruction was given. The groups are tabulated below:

Group	Number of Institutions
I. Intention to provide professional training -- two full-year courses	51
II. Intention to provide business training -- no professional accounting training	11
III. Accounting included in curriculum because of relationship to economic and governmental problems and/or its business application	35
IV. Accounting offered because of its application in specialized technical professions other than business	8
	$\overline{105}$[39]

Some of the additional conclusions reached were that accounting is distinctly an urban profession; a large proportion of the institutions offering accounting, many of which were in non-urban areas, were publicly supported; the study of accounting as an aid in the interpretation of business is more important than study of professional accounting;

---

[39]John E. Treleven, Papers and Proceedings of the Annual Meeting, December, 1916, I, No. 1 (Columbus, Ohio: The American Association of University Instructors in Accounting, May, 1917), 7-10.

every school of business required study of accounting; and there were many variations in practice and divergence in methods among the different schools. Treleven decided that those differences were not major in view of the fact that the entire development of both professional and general college accounting courses had come within a twenty-year period, with 75 per cent of the growth during the period 1906-1916.[40]

Tremendous progress had been made during a short span of years. The early resistance toward business schools in general had been an obstacle. Later, the shortage of competent accounting teachers held back progress.

The educational efforts of the professional organizations and individual practitioners were very closely related to the development of courses in accounting at colleges and universities. The professional practitioners were very concerned about developing the accounting curriculum because of the needs. The needs were created by the industrial and commercial expansion, the trend toward consolidation and merger, the corporate form of business with its employee management and public ownership, the creation of the Interstate Commerce Commission and other regulatory measures, the passage of tax laws, and the enactment of certified public accountant laws.

---

[40]Ibid., 10-19.

Basic Themes

Accounting ideas and practices in the United States during the early years of the twentieth century were concentrated upon certain basic themes. The proprietary theory of accounts was dominant. Although the entity theory had been used in Europe, it was not introduced in the United States until 1922. William A. Paton wrote of the entity theory in 1922 and thereafter promoted it. The balance sheet received emphasis as the prime financial statement. The pressing question of depreciation emerged in the early years of this period. Depreciation questions brought on further problems as to the use of cost or other valuation bases for assets in the balance sheet. Income statement information was not demanded prior to this period. Conditions of this period created the impetus for recognition of the importance of income statement information and determination. Accounting principles had not become an important issue and very little had been written about them.

Proprietary Theory

The proprietary theory of accounting was dominant during the early twentieth century. The balance sheet was emphasized as the most important financial statement under this theory. The proprietorship theory of accounting can best be associated with the proprietary form of enterprise. The proprietor or partners and the business are so legally inseparable that the accounting for one amounts to accounting for the other. Historically, proprietorship theory appears to lie at the origin of accounting theory. The concept of proprietorship equity seems to complete the concept of accounting and support the necessity for equality of debits and credits.[41]

The proprietor is the center of accounting under the proprietary theory, and all accounting concepts and processes are related to the basic notion of the proprietor's interests. Under this theory there is an emphasis upon the proprietor as the paramount or central feature in the enterprise. The interpretation and reporting of transactions is carried out from the viewpoint of the proprietor. The proprietor owns the assets, the liabilities are his debts, and all revenues and expenses represent changes in his interest. Within this framework income is the net of the proprietor's collective gains and losses. Therefore, distinctions between returns on investment, returns from personal services, returns from risk or other cause are unnecessary. The structure of proprietary theory is summarized and embodied in the concept of proprietorship equity.[42] The presentation of ownership theory in complete form was

---

[41] William J. Vatter, "Corporate Stock Equities, Part I," in _Handbook of Modern Accounting Theory_, ed. by Morton Backer (New York: Prentice-Hall, Inc., 1955), pp. 362-63.

[42] _Ibid._, p. 362.

first made by Charles E. Sprague, Henry Rand Hatfield, and Roy B. Kester in their textbooks.[43] Sprague's presentation did away with personal and impersonal accounts and instituted real (assets, liabilities, and proprietorship), temporary (generators of income), and mixed accounts. Sprague banished the idea that bookkeeping is a mere game of matching debits and credits. The preservation of an accurate record of assets, liabilities, and changes in proprietorship via the double entry system was stressed.

Sprague's system includes the "ME account" to represent the interest of the proprietor. The balance in the "ME account" can be viewed as different from that of any of the other accounts in the system. The "ME account" does not represent property, nor indebtedness, but proprietorship's interest. The account displays the results of income being greater than outlays.[44]

The proprietary interest cannot be treated as a liability as it differs materially from a liability. The proprietor has dominion over assets and power to use them as he pleases, while the creditor's rights are limited to definite sums. The proprietor's right is of an elastic or flexible value. Losses, expenses, and shrinkage reduce the proprietor's interest, whereas profits, revenue, and increases of

---

[43]Hendriksen, Theory, p. 30.

[44]Charles E. Sprague, The Philosophy of Accounts (4th edition; New York: The Ronald Press, 1920), pp. 16-17 (Hereinafter referred to as Sprague, Philosophy).

value benefit the proprietor. These reductions and benefits pertain to the proprietor alone. The business cannot
stand in the same relation to its owners as to its creditors. The business is owned by its proprietors; the business does not own the proprietors.[45] Sprague was firmly
against the entity idea. He could see no benefit in lump-
ing "Due to Creditor" and "Net Worth of ME" accounts together as liabilities. He saw a contradiction in the term
liabilities in that the proprietary account cannot be the
excess of assets over liabilities if the proprietary interest is, in fact, one of the liabilities.[46]

Hatfield, a student of Sprague's writings, also adhered to the proprietary theory in the three editions of
his book. Hatfield elaborated upon Sprague's framework.
The proprietary theory was used to reflect the businessman's
approach to accounting. Hatfield documented his textbooks
with references to other writers, to court decisions, to
rulings of regulatory commissions, and to statutes. In
this manner he reflected the thinking of the period.[47]

---

[45]Ibid., pp. 47-49.

[46]Ibid., p. 18.

[47]Henry Rand Hatfield, Accounting, Its Principles
and Some of Its Problems (New York: D. Appleton and Company, 1909) (Hereinafter referred to as Hatfield, Principles,
1909); Henry Rand Hatfield, Modern Accounting, Its Principles and Some of Its Problems (New York: D. Appleton and
Company, 1915) (Hereinafter referred to as Hatfield, Principles, 1915); and Henry Rand Hatfield, Accounting, Its
Principles and Problems (New York: Appleton-Century-Crofts,
Inc., 1927) (Hereinafter referred to as Hatfield, Principles,
1927).

Kester also followed the basic proprietary approach. He noted that proprietorship is also called Net Worth, and can be shown under such titles as Capital, Investment, Capital Stock, Surplus, Undivided Profits, or Reserves, depending upon the type of organization.[48]

Cole wrote of the structure of the proprietary account. There are three kinds of accounts in proprietorship accounting: (1) Property or claim accounts which represent property in the business or claims of it or against it, (2) force accounts which represent forces of business that cause it to have gain or loss, and (3) proprietorship accounts which represent what the proprietors have invested, plus any profits accumulated but not yet withdrawn.[49]

Balance Sheet

The idea of net worth and proprietorship is illustrated by views on the balance sheet which were dominant at the time. The proprietary concept emphasizes the balance sheet. The balance sheet was considered as the groundwork of all accountancy because it represents the origin and the terminus of every account.[50] The presentation of a correct

---

[48] Roy B. Kester, Accounting Theory and Practice (Second edition; New York: The Ronald Press Company, 1922), pp. 15-16 (hereinafter referred to as Kester, Accounting).

[49] William Morse Cole, Accounts Their Construction and Interpretation (Revised and Enlarged edition; Boston: Houghton Mifflin Company, 1915), p. 55 (Hereinafter referred to as Cole, Accounts, 1915).

[50] Sprague, Philosophy, p. 26.

exhibit of the financial status of the concern at a given moment of time was considered as the essence of accounting. Display of the results of operations during a given period of time was only a secondary function of accounting. The accounting treatment of any transaction was determined by its effect upon the balance sheet.[51] Put in a slightly different way, the balance sheet was visualized as the statement of resources and liabilities or the statement of property and claims which shows the solvency of the business. The balance sheet shows the status of the real accounts at the end of the year. It gives a summary view of the situation at a definite moment of time.[52] The arrangement of the items on the balance sheet should be according to a governing principle which would cause the marshaling of items in a systematic order. Assets should be ranked according to their liquidity, and strict consistency compels the marshaling of liabilities in a similar manner.[53]

Thus, the balance sheet was considered as the statement of prime importance and was given the primary emphasis by the writers of the period. This was the case particularly because of the balance sheet's usefulness in furnishing clues as to a borrower's probable ability to repay short-term

---

[51]Hatfield, Principles, 1909, preface v, p. 54.

[52]Cole, Accounts, 1915, p. 84 and Kester, Accounting, p. 22.

[53]Sprague, Philosophy, p. 32, Hatfield, Principles, 1915, pp. 46-47, and Kester, Accounting, p. 22.

loans. The ability to repay these loans was thought to be more directly related to the conversion of inventory into cash than to the ability to earn a periodic profit from operations.[54]

The balance sheet was clearly given the primary emphasis by the writers and by businessmen. The income statement was considered as somewhat incidental. The usual annual report was quite short and generally included only a condensed balance sheet and perhaps a summarized income statement which was the difference between balance sheets.

Income Determination

As another facet of the view of the balance sheet as the statement of primary importance, the income statement was considered as of little importance as it only provides an elaboration of an item finally incorporated in the balance sheet. The income statement was viewed as a useful summary of information for management's use; however, it was incidental in the reporting process. The income sheet was presented to show the explanation of changes in solvency, so far as profits and losses had produced change, during the year.[55]

---

[54] Hendriksen, _Theory_, _passim_ pp. 29-32, 57-59.

[55] Cole, _Accounts_, 1915, p. 84.

Depreciation

As mentioned earlier, there were various practices used for the computation of depreciation but there was essentially no theory of depreciation during this period of time. Depreciation was not a clear concept in the writings, and it was treated in a haphazard manner by businessmen and accountants. Computation of depreciation expense was not uniform between different companies. Many accountants were uncertain as to the proper treatment of the expense. In addition, treatment was not consistent for succeeding periods in a given company. The debate on the subject of depreciation continued for several decades.

Some of the writers of the period, such as Sprague, gave little attention to depreciation. Sprague did suggest that it is sometimes desirable to separate the account of an asset into two accounts, one to be an offset or adjunct to the principle account. He suggested that a "Depreciation" account be set up to have a credit balance. This account should not be viewed as a liability, but as an offset to the asset, in a correctly constructed balance sheet.[56]

Hatfield included a chapter on depreciation in his earliest books. He noted that destruction is the law of nature and that fixed capital is not exempt from this law.

---

[56]Sprague, _Philosophy_, p. 51

Furthermore, he noted that all machinery is on "an irresti-
ble march to the junk heap." He said that although the
march of the machinery might be delayed by repairs it
cannot be entirely halted.[57]

Hatfield emphasized that the cost of production
must include some allowance for the diminished value of
the fixed assets due to gradual loss of serviceability.
Profits cannot be determined until such allowance for
depreciation has been made. Depreciation is not a disposition of any part of profits; it is an expense without
which income cannot be determined.[58]

Hatfield described three methods of computing the
amount of annual depreciation: (1) charge each year with a
fixed per cent of the original cost, (2) charge a fixed
percentage of the decreasing net value, and (3) a more com-
plicated annuity method which includes consideration of the
amount of capital invested in the asset. He then went on
to say that although there might be uncertainty in each of
the methods, there can be no doubt of the illegitimacy of a
fourth method frequently used at the time. This method
makes the amount annually written off for depreciation expense somewhat loosely proportionate to profits. The use of
this fourth method ignores the fundamental principle involved

---

[57]Hatfield, Principles, 1915, p. 121.

[58]Ibid.

that depreciation is something inexorable and inevitable.
It is an expense to be estimated before it is possible to
determine profits. Practice at the time did not conform to
Hatfield's view of the correct principle. Recognition of
any depreciation was relatively uncommon. The few companies
which recorded depreciation in prosperous profitable years
were inclined to grow faint-hearted when business declined
and profits were small.[59]

In 1927, depreciation was still not given full recognition in general practice. Those who recorded depreciation
did not always compute it according to a correct principle.
However, there was a closer adherence to the recommended
procedures which Hatfield credited to the income tax laws.[60]
Depreciation should be computed so as to cover all decline
in value due to the use of productive assets.[61] The recording of excessive depreciation, as a conservative policy,
is as offensive a practice as recording too little depreciation. The effect of excessive depreciation is to conceal
profits and thereby create a secret reserve. The presence
of the depreciation allowance account signifies the substitution of something new, presumably some floating asset, in
place of part of the value of the fixed asset. The account

---

[59]Ibid., pp. 127-36.

[60]Hatfield, Principles, 1927, pp. 130-40.

[61]Ibid., p. 142.

implies the presence of new assets of equivalent value, except in a balance sheet showing a net loss. Whether these new assets would furnish the means of replacing the old asset depends upon their nature and general market conditions.[62] Hatfield's coverage of depreciation expense clearly reflects the best approximation of what have become the accepted concepts. His exposition was clear and detailed. Other writers did not have the same complete, clear, and cohesive presentations.

Kester defined depreciation as the loss from wear or other causes. He determined it as the difference between the present appraised value of the asset and its former cost or appraised value. He said the recording of depreciation expense and the entry into a depreciation reserve related to the asset consists of nothing more than separating the expense element from the asset element, both of which have been carried currently under the asset title. He said that the reserve account is an integral part of the asset record and must always be considered in connection with the asset account. This is necessary in order to determine the value of the asset.[63]

It has been noted that by the beginning of the twentieth century depreciation was widely accepted as a

---

[62]Hatfield, Principles, 1915, pp. 131, 139, and Hatfield, Principles, 1927, pp. 130, 140-45.

[63]Kester, Accounting, pp. 102-4, 123.

valuation concept, but the concept was not completely understood. Depreciation was still thought of as a valuation process and a means of providing funds for replacement or funds for payment of dividends to investors.[64] William Morse Cole's coverage of depreciation in 1908, and again in 1915, indicates this common misconception. He explains the writing off or allowing for depreciation as simply a process that replaces a former book valuation with another new and smaller valuation.[65] Cole devotes little space to discussion of depreciation expense. The discussion which he does present fails to provide a clear idea of depreciation concepts to the reader. He refers to a depreciation account with a credit balance which represents the amount by which the real value of the property is overstated in the property account. Cole's discussion of reserves and funds appears likely to confuse the uncertain student:

> . . . we see that both the assets which are meant as provision for depreciation and those which constitute profits withheld for general purposes of safety are set aside in separately labeled funds; that the depreciation fund [he meant expense] is taken out of product for the replenishment of worn-out real estate and plant, and that the reserve fund is a setting aside of profits.[66]

The problems involved in calculating depreciation expense were still unresolved in 1922. Paton suggested

---

[64]Hendriksen, Theory, p. 37.

[65]Cole, Accounts, 1915, p. 95, and William Morse Cole, Accounts, Their Construction and Interpretation (New York: Houghton Mifflin Co., 1908), p. 79.

[66]Cole, Accounts, 1915, pp. 112-15.

the possibility of calculating depreciation on expected
cost of replacement rather than on original or actual
cost. In a period of either rising or falling prices, he
said, the original cost does not express true value nor
provide a good basis for depreciation expense charges. Extended arguments for and against his suggested proposition
are presented by Paton.[67]

It is apparent that the problem of depreciation expense existed during the early 1900's. In addition, it is
clear that the problem was not only unsettled, it was not
completely understood. There was no consensus as to concepts involved or as to proper treatment in the accounts
and financial statements. The Interstate Commerce Commission regulations of July 1, 1907, which discussed depreciation as a question of values, and the provision for depreciation included in the 1909 and subsequent income tax
acts, provided motivating impetus for improvements. The
regulations eventually gave rise to the use of systematic
depreciation methods, the search for better depreciation
concepts, and more appropriate methods of calculating depreciation cost. The discussion of and debate concerning
depreciation was to continue over several decades. The
issues were principally related to the question of whether
or not property consumption should be measured currently

---

[67]William Andrew Paton, _Accounting Theory_ (Chicago:
A. S. P. Accounting Studies Press, Ltd., 1962, reprint),
pp. 424-25.

by a depreciation provision or only upon retirement, and
whether the provision for depreciation should be based upon
original cost or estimated cost of replacement.[68]

Cost and Valuation

The basis for valuation of assets in the balance
sheet was an unsettled issue. There was no complete, general agreement as to the proper basis for valuation of assets in the balance sheet. The liquidation value, of significance to the creditor, was often used. The replacement
value was considered by many as the most significant value
basis. The emerging going concern viewpoint created increased emphasis upon the problem. The value of assets to
a going concern was determined to be their use value, not
their liquidation value. There was an increased stress upon
the going concern view which included these additional aspects: Changes in market value of fixed assets are not to
be recorded and depreciation is always to be recorded each
period.

Accounting Principles

The first period of time in which there was particular and noteworthy interest in accounting principles has
been set forth as falling between 1930 and the beginning of

---

[68]Percival F. Brundage, "Milestones on the Path of
Accounting," Harvard Business Review, XXIX, No. 4 (July,
1951), 73, and Hendriksen, Theory, p. 46.

World War II.[69] It should be noted that the surge of interest in and literature pertaining to principles probably
was rooted in events and the development of ideas which took
place during the preceding years. It is apparent that
little had been formalized in the way of principles of accounting during the early 1900's.

Terminology

Terminology questions had appeared also. Terms
were not used in a uniform way by accountants and confusion
about the meaning of terms was common. Certainly, it was
evident that some study should be made regarding accounting
terminology. There was a committee on terminology formed
by the American Institute of Accountants in 1920. The
formation of this committee illustrates the awareness of
the terminology problem.

Summary of Development Prior to Littleton

In the early years of the nineteenth century it appears that accounting was based more upon rules than upon
basic principles. In turn, the rules were primarily based
upon implicit assumptions and objectives. Within this context, accounting practice placed few restrictions upon
industrial management. However, environmental and institutional changes had been taking place on the economic front.

---

[69]Reed K. Storey, The Search for Accounting Principles (New York: American Institute of Certified Public
Accountants, Inc., 1964), p. 3.

As a result, a trend had become evident of a change of objective for the preparation of accounting information. This shift of objective involved an increased emphasis upon information for investors and the public rather than upon information for creditors and management. This trend, of course, reflected the growth in number and size of incorporated businesses and the broadened base of ownership in businesses.

The new objective of financial statements led to changes in accounting ideas. The prior emphasis upon liquidation and solvency in a statement of values, the balance sheet, was replaced by an emphasis upon the going concern view that the business will continue to operate on a more or less normal basis. This going concern view placed an emphasis upon the balance sheet only as a link between income statements. Full disclosure as a goal was contrasted with the former goal of business secrecy.

The passage of the income tax acts had created a necessity for income determination which had not been faced by many businesses before. The determination of income for tax purposes highlighted cost allocation problems. The cost allocation problems included the one of computing depreciation expense which many businesses had not considered before, at least not on a consistent basis.

The new emphasis upon the income statement called for more uniform concepts of income determination.

Consistency became an important goal to be reflected in the income statement. Attention was thereby focused not only upon the character of accounting allocations and accruals but upon their effect on income.

Littleton and Accounting

Thus, Littleton entered the profession during a period of change and development. There was a developing awareness of the need for more meaningful accounting statements. This need provided an impetus to Littleton's active and perceptive intellect.

After graduation from high school at Bloomington, Illinois, in 1905, Littleton had worked as a telegrapher for two years on the Chicago and Alton Railroad to obtain funds for college.[70] Although English literature and composition were his favorite subjects in high school, Littleton entered college to study railroad administration. His father and uncle had both worked in railroading. However, after his freshman year a chance association with two students from Chicago brought to his attention the relatively new certified public accountant statute of the State of Illinois and the attractions of public accounting as a career. Persuaded to give up railroad administration, the

---

[70]Newspaper clipping, "Littleton Has Birthday Today," December 5, 1925, Biographical File of A. C. Littleton, Alumni Office, University of Illinois, Urbana, Illinois.

field of accounting became the area of pursuit.[71] During

1911-1912, while a student, he did bookkeeping work for the

University Club and its supervising architect. Littleton

received a Bachelor of Arts degree, with majors in account-

ing and economics, from the University of Illinois in 1912.

He worked as a practicing accountant until 1915 when he

accepted a teaching position at his alma mater.[72]

Littleton's work in public accounting practice with

Deloitte, Plender, Griffiths & Company in Chicago was under

the guidance of Hiram T. Scovill, a 1908 graduate of the

University of Illinois, who was a senior accountant with

the firm. Littleton served his apprenticeship under Scovill

and two accountants from Great Britain. Valuable first-hand

knowledge of the English and Scottish application of ac-

counting and auditing practices was provided by this expe-

rience.[73]

Littleton returned to the University of Illinois in

1915 to work as an accounting instructor under H. T. Scovill,

then the head of the accounting department. Littleton

---

[71]V. K. Zimmerman, "The Long Shadow of a Scholar," The International Journal of Accounting Education and Research, II, No. 2 (Spring, 1967), 2-3.

[72]"Request for Personnel Information," August 16, 1915, Biographical File of A. C. Littleton, Office of President, University of Illinois, Urbana, Illinois.

[73]H. T. Scovill, "Sound Theory is Necessary," un-published article, April 25, 1956, Biographical File of A. C. Littleton, Department of Accountancy, College of Commerce and Business Administration, University of Illinois, Urbana, Illinois.

taught at the university for 37 years. In the meantime, in 1918, Littleton received his Masters of Arts degree in Economics from the University of Illinois. In 1919, he received his Illinois certificate as a Certified Public Accountant. In 1931, Littleton also received his Doctor of Philosophy degree in Economics from the University.

Littleton became an accounting teacher soon after the first courses in accounting were offered at the university level. His work in the areas of income determination, historical cost concepts, and accounting principles are of particular importance.

Littleton became a firm advocate of emphasis upon the income determination aspects of accounting. His attention was focused upon the prime importance of the proper determination of income. Related to his concern for proper income determination was his belief in the integrity of original transaction data which is reflected in the accounts and the resulting reports by historical cost. Historical cost is used to match properly the revenues and expenses of the entity. The allocation of costs, as an integral feature of income determination, is dependent upon the retention of original costs in the records. The injection into the records of any data related to transactions to which the entity is not a party was strongly opposed by Littleton.

Littleton's concern for principles of accounting continued throughout his writing period. His reflections upon the problem of principles led to his conviction that inductively derived principles must form the framework for accounting theory. Inductively derived principles can be then tested by the deductive method.

CHAPTER III

THE CENTRAL THEME OF ACCOUNTING

Littleton viewed income determination as the most important area of concern in accounting. This seems not to have been the popular consensus at the time Littleton entered the profession. The pressures upon business firms to present income information had brought about a recognition of some problems in this area of financial reporting. However, in spite of this developing need, there was only a limited amount of literature available related to income determination problems. Littleton's stress of this feature of accounting was of an innovative nature. This theme was consistently emphasized by him. He believed, in fact, that the calculation of profits has been the central theme of accounting from its beginning and that all of the slowly accumulated knowledge of accounting bears directly or indirectly upon profits.[1] This position was based upon the assumption

---

[1]A. C. Littleton, "Dividends Presuppose Profits," The Accounting Review, IX, No. 4 (December, 1934), 304, reprinted in A. C. Littleton, Essays on Accountancy (Urbana, Illinois: University of Illinois Press, 1961), p. 261 (Hereinafter referred to as Littleton, Essays). Many footnotes referring to Littleton's works indicate duplicate or multiple sources of quoted material. "Reprinted in" indicates reproduced verbatim, almost verbatim, or paraphrased without change of content. Punctuation, capitalization,

that the primary and central problem of business has always

been and continues to be the production of income. Such a

foundation calls for a methodology business entities can

use to compute the income produced. It was obvious to

Littleton that the methodology needed to accomplish this

computation is provided by accounting. For this purpose he

defined accounting as a reasonable, realistic, convenient

method of calculating profits by expressing quantitatively

a great diversity of actual business transactions.[2]

Littleton emphasized that the income produced by a firm, not

its capital in use, is the core of accounting, and as such

is the focal center of the business enterprise.[3] His view

of income determination as the central determinant of ac-

counting is supported by his treatment of the related as-

pects of this outlook. This theme includes what he consid-

ered the foundation of accounting, namely, enterprise effort

and accomplishment. In addition, tangent areas include a

concept of profits, the matching of revenues and costs,

the importance of earning power, cost allocation, and the

increased emphasis on income statement information. All of

---

use of italics, and hyphenization may have been the only
change(s) from the original. Paraphrased material contains
only minor revisions by the original author without change
of content or idea.

[2]A. C. Littleton, "Contrasting Theories of Profit,"
The Accounting Review, XI, No. 1 (March, 1936), 15 (Hereinafter referred to as Littleton, "Contrasting Theories"),
reprinted in Littleton, Essays, p. 295.

[3]Littleton, "Contrasting Theories," 13, reprinted
in Littleton, Essays, p. 209.

these facets are closely interrelated and overlapping.
This interdependence necessitates further discussion.

Enterprise Effort and Accomplishment

The idea of enterprise efforts and accomplishments
and their measurement is an important aspect of Littleton's
total view of the central theme of accounting. Management
initiates enterprise efforts, which result in costs, to
produce accomplishments in the form of revenues greater
than the costs incurred. Littleton wrote repeatedly of
enterprise efforts and accomplishments and the role of accounting in their measurement and the related quantification of profits.

According to Littleton, business practice has always
favored and continues to favor the income and expense concept of profit. This income statement view recognizes
profit of an enterprise as the differential between revenue
derived and costs and expenses assignable thereto.
Littleton looked upon management's role as a vital one in
this explanation of profit. However, he pointed out, it is
necessary to look to economics for the forces which generate profit or loss. Business management must anticipate
economic conditions, adjust to circumstances, and in general
expend energies to keep selling price and cost apart in order to create a profit. Management's main concern is to
search out, locate, and accept opportunities and then deal
with them intelligently to produce a profit. Profit,

said Littleton, is the outcome of work directed toward keeping selling price and cost apart.[4]

Littleton's educational background included a degree in economics and this training evidently made him particularly conscious of and concerned about the economic surroundings of the business enterprise. He carefully supported his views about accounting by providing a sound economic foundation as a framework. He discussed accounting problems with a constant awareness of the economic framework. It is evident that Littleton regarded the business enterprise as basically more of an economic unit than a legalistic creature. This conforms to the accepted accounting definition of an economic unit as any person or group of persons having a name, common purpose, and transactions with outsiders.[5] Littleton considered a business enterprise as an economic unit carrying on economic activities with outsiders. He stated that the economic nature of the business enterprise is signified by the fact that financing is secondary to the primary economic activity of producing an output acceptable to customers. This led him to the conclusion that it is the economic condition, not the financial position, which is of prime importance to the business

---

[4]A. C. Littleton, "What is Profit?" The Accounting Review, III, No. 3 (September, 1928), 280, 283-86 (Hereinafter referred to as Littleton, "What is Profit?"), reprinted in Littleton, Essays, pp. 206-7.

[5]Eric L. Kohler, A Dictionary for Accountants (3rd Edition; Englewood Cliffs, New Jersey: Prentice-Hall, Inc., 1963), p. 196.

enterprise. The economic condition, a relationship between income derived and the cost of producing it, is, in turn, a foundation to financial condition. Net income, therefore, is the clue to the concept of economic condition.[6]

Littleton asserted that revenues are a relatively passive element in the production of net income because management has little direct control over them. On the other hand, costs are controlled by management decisions as to timing of outlay, quantity of outlay, and distribution of outlay. Costs, therefore, represent solidified choices made intentionally by management. Costs, in this sense, are quantitative expressions of management's policies translated into action.[7]

Littleton pointed out that the demand for and sale of goods and services offers the opportunity for a business concern to earn a profit. The opportunity for profit arises when the customer accepts that good or service which is offered; however, the acceptance by the customer does not assure profit. To an important extent profit realization depends upon how successfully the costs have been kept below the revenues. It follows, reasoned Littleton, that the

---

[6]A. C. Littleton, "Concepts of Income Underlying Accounting," The Accounting Review, XII, No. 1 (March, 1937), 16-18 (Hereinafter referred to as Littleton, "Concepts of Income"), reprinted in Littleton, Essays, pp. 212-13, and A. C. Littleton, "Business Profits as a Legal Basis for Dividends," Harvard Business Review, XVI, No. 1 (Autumn, 1937), 58.

[7]Littleton, "Concepts of Income," 18-19, reprinted in Littleton, Essays, pp. 213, 217.

costs of input and the revenue from output are the most important data for the guidance of management in making its present and future decisions. Accounting provides this necessary data. The cost data, because it is more directly under managerial control and more expressive of causal factors in prior planning, is the most useful to management. In general, the creation of service or goods output by a business enterprise is not a chance result of a speculative adventure but the result of efforts deliberately undertaken to create such goods and services by the expenditure of other goods and efforts. Money income is not realized as a result of chance events and lucky circumstances but as a result of the prior planned expenditures.[8] The impact of management's efforts and influence, stressed so purposefully by Littleton, is an important feature of the total view of accounting today. The control of cost is accepted as an important means of increasing profits. It is widely recognized that costs are more responsive to managerial influence in many instances than are revenues.

The net income expressed in terms of homogeneous money price reflects the waxing and waning influences of revenue and cost flows. These revenue and cost movements are the active representations of the inflows and outflows of enterprise services. This vigorous feature of business, according to Littleton, dictates that accounting also must be

---

[8]Littleton, "Concepts of Income," 17-19, and reprinted in Littleton, Essays, pp. 212, 217-18.

62

primarily dynamic. Based upon this premise, it follows that the income statement view should take precedence over the static balance sheet approach. He claimed that it is the same forceful continuous side of business which creates a need for the calculation of interim income via accrual accounting. Provisional income calculation is necessary because the reality of income will be finally determinable only upon ultimate liquidation of the business.[9] Littleton wrote as follows regarding the reality of profits or loss:

> . . . the fact is that figure calculations do not make profit or avoid loss; accounting can only reveal profits and disclose loss. Reality lies behind the figures, not in them. . . .[10]

The reality of the enterprise is an important element of Littleton's total view of income determination based upon the principle of periodic matching of revenues (accomplishments) and costs (efforts). Littleton developed four enterprise principles which form essential support for, as well as a foundation for, the matching principle. In 1953, in his Structure of Accounting Theory, Littleton wrote of the four enterprise principles[11] which make up the

---

[9]Littleton, "Concepts of Income," 20-22, reprinted in Littleton, Essays, p. 194.

[10]Littleton, Essays, p. 381, reprinted from A. C. Littleton, "High Standards of Accounting," The Journal of Accountancy, LXVI, No. 2 (August, 1938), 101.

[11]In a footnote, Structure of Accounting Theory, p. 23: "A principle is a crystallization of ideas into a clear verbal statement of a significant relationship. Thus a principle serves accounting in very much the same way as a mathematical equation serves science."

concept of the enterprise. These principles are (1) the
principle of enterprise service, (2) the principle of enterprise entity, (3) the principle of enterprise periodicity,
and (4) the principle of enterprise effort and accomplishment. Littleton's discussion of these principles follows:

> The principle of enterprise service . . . :
> Business enterprises are accepted and used because
> they perform effective economic functions in sup-
> plying goods (for living) and employment (for
> earning).
> . . . .
> The principle of enterprise entity . . . :
> Each business enterprise is treated in our indus-
> trial society as if it were a cohesive economic
> entity in its own right, or a self-contained and
> impersonal operating unit, rather than a grouping
> of persons.
> Accounting-wise, a distinction between an
> enterprise and the persons concerned is inescap-
> able. . . .
> . . . the principle of enterprise periodicity:
> In the functioning of a business enterprise there
> is a rhythm of seasons and activities, a cycle of
> events, which furnishes a framework for compress-
> ing the flow of enterprise data into comparable
> time-segments.
> . . . .
> The principle of enterprise effort and accom-
> plishment is the most important of the four: The
> data of primary significance to all parties shar-
> ing in the proceeds of enterprise or in control-
> ling enterprise operations are those facts which
> express enterprise efforts made and accomplish-
> ments attained. Many parties have an interest in
> a given enterprise: Creditors . . . , workers
> . . . , customers . . . , managers . . . , stock-
> holders . . . , government. All of these are con-
> cerned about the continued success of the enter-
> prise with which they are associated. It is
> important to all interests that the enterprise
> continue to be financially healthy and economi-
> cally productive. The facts most directly keyed
> into these conditions are the ones that make pos-
> sible an intelligent comparison of enterprise
> efforts with enterprise accomplishments. These
> are the cost-and-revenue facts which accounting
> presents in the income statement. The balance
> sheet has its place--a place of importance for

some uses--but it cannot come as near being all things to all men as can the income statement.[12]

Littleton summarized the four enterprise principles into an enterprise principles pyramid supporting the central purpose of accounting. A progressive sequence of layers form the pyramid. The bottom layer represents the reason for enterprise existence; the top of the spire is the effort and accomplishment element which points the arrow directly toward accounting. This places the total concept[13] of the enterprise directly in support of the central purpose of accounting.[14] Littleton's pyramid is illustrated in Exhibit I.

Littleton stated the central purpose of accounting in the form of a hypothesis[15] to be rephrased into a

---

[12]A. C. Littleton, Structure of Accounting Theory (Menasha, Wisconsin: George Banta Publishing Company for American Accounting Association, 1953), pp. 24-26 (Hereinafter referred to as Littleton, Structure).

[13]"Concept," or "proposition" or "assumption," as used by Littleton, may be incompletely defined as a mental pattern of related ideas which grow into an integrated complex idea as more and more relevant instances become known. Concepts are much more inclusive than principles or definitions. (Littleton, Structure, p. 148).
"Concepts" are ideas which are essential to understanding accounting functions and limitations.
(A. C. Littleton, "The Significance of Interrelated Concepts in Accounting," The International Journal of Accounting Education and Research, II, No. 1 (Fall, 1966), 28-29.)
"Concepts" are discussed at greater length in the chapter on basic approach and views on principles.

[14]Littleton, Structure, p. 26.

[15]Littleton defined hypothesis as an unsupported belief stated as a basis for investigation. (Littleton, Structure, p. 22). This idea is discussed at greater length

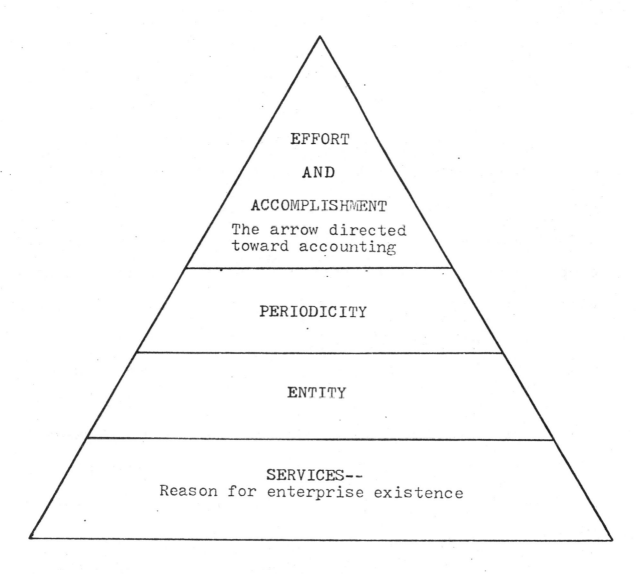

EFFORT

AND

ACCOMPLISHMENT
The arrow directed
toward accounting

PERIODICITY

ENTITY

SERVICES--
Reason for enterprise existence

EXHIBIT I.   THE ENTERPRISE PRINCIPLES PYRAMID

Adapted from: A. C. Littleton, Structure of Accounting Theory (Menasha, Wisconsin: George Banta Publishing Company for American Accounting Association, 1953), pp. 24-26.

principle. The hypothesis states that the extensive need for dependable determinations of periodic net income makes the income statement the most important product of enterprise accounting. The hypothesis was then rearranged into a principle which follows:

> For many uses the most important data from accounting are the revenue charges and the revenue credits by means of which enterprise efforts are periodically matched against enterprise accomplishments.[16]

Littleton avowed that the concept of an enterprise as disclosed in his pyramid is closely related to and supports the central purpose of accounting. He saw accounting as the means of making the mass of enterprise effort and accomplishment activities understandable. The principal service of accounting, as a quasi-statistical methodology, he said, is to arrange the facts about the extensive and diversified economic activities of an enterprise in a manner designed to make the activities more understandable.[17] The classification, compression, and simplification of masses of raw data highlights the significance of enterprise facts and makes them more understandable.[18] The need for careful

---

in the chapter on basic approach and views on principles, under the caption, "Theory is Thinking Focused Upon Doing."

[16]Littleton, Structure, pp. 22-23.

[17]Ibid., p. 26.

[18]Ibid., p. 8. The same idea is found in A. C. Littleton and V. K. Zimmerman, Accounting Theory: Continuity and Change (Englewood Cliffs, New Jersey: Prentice-Hall, Inc., 1962), p. 3.

separation of unlike transactions in the classification

process was pointedly stressed by Littleton as follows:

> . . . It is fatal to good classification to
> squeeze transactions into accounts where they meet
> stranger transactions. Probably no other feature
> of system is more sensitive to transaction changes
> than accounts, and probably more unsuspected dis-
> tortion of the classified facts comes from crowd-
> ing unlike elements into the same account than
> from any other fault. The chances are good that
> the accounting information is not altogether re-
> liable in a growing concern that does not expand
> its list of different accounts as it grows.
> . . . .
> . . . only by using "unmixed classes" can we avoid
> a high risk of introducing misrepresentation.
> . . .[19]

Closer adherence by accountants today to Littleton's

position with respect to the classification process would no

doubt prove beneficial in the reporting process. Observance

of Littleton's rules could only lead to more valid and mean-

ingful information in financial statements. Proper disclo-

sure would be promoted by correct attention to this

suggestion. It would appear in many instances that conden-

sation of heterogeneous transactions and accounts has been

extended to such a point that meaningful information is ob-

scured and disclosure is less than adequate. There is a

reasonable doubt in some cases as to whether the reality of

the enterprise transactions has been presented in the

financial statements.

---

[19]Ibid., pp. 45-46. This also relates to Littleton's
principle of homogeneous data. Transactions must be classified so that account categories contain only homogeneous
data stated in terms of money price. (Littleton, Structure,
p. 192).

68

The basic task of accounting is to present information in such a manner that enterprise effort and accomplishment can be compared intelligibly. Accounting provides for this comparison by representing effort as expense figures and accomplishment as revenue figures. Accounting is only an instrument; it does not make expenses nor incomes what they are. Expense is generated by business effort, and revenue is generated by business accomplishment. The goal and objective of accounting and the resulting financial statements are to provide a real understanding of the relation of effort and accomplishment.[20] Littleton was consistent in the development of the effort and accomplishment idea over the period of years during which he wrote. In 1966, he continued to discuss enterprise transactions as representations of enterprise effort and accomplishment. He repeated that accounting has been dedicated to making possible the analytical study of enterprise undertakings in order that next decisions can be aided by interpretation of prior experience. He worked out a structural representation of accounting concepts. These concepts are ideas essential to understanding accounting functions and limitations based upon a foundation of enterprise transaction experience. Littleton visualized a layer of operational elements resting upon the transaction foundation. In Exhibit II these

---

[20]A. C. Littleton, "Fixed Assets and Accounting Theory," The Illinois Certified Public Accountant, X, No. 3 (March, 1948), 14, reprinted in Littleton, Essays, p. 312.

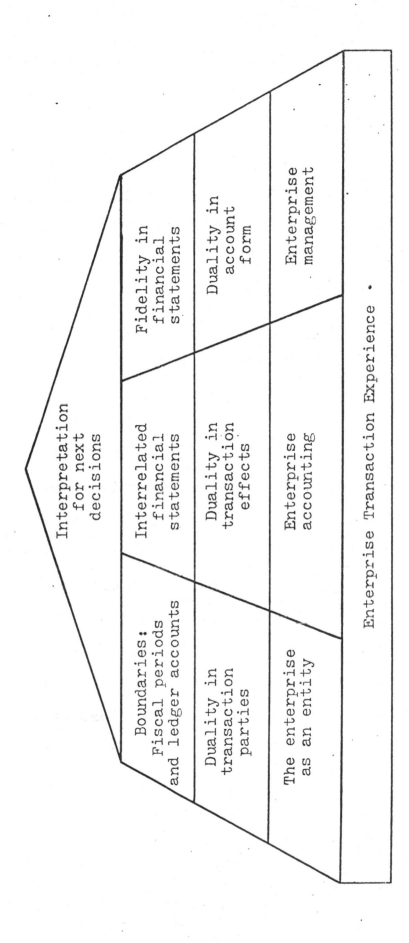

EXHIBIT II. ACCOUNTING CONCEPTS

Adapted from: A. C. Littleton, "The Significance of Interrelated Concepts Accounting," The International Journal of Accounting Education and Research, II, No. 1 (Fall, 1966), 26.

70

elements are shown as the enterprise entity, enterprise accounting, and enterprise management. The enterprise as an entity is seen as a boundary. The business enterprise is a self-contained operating unit whose transaction experience is limited by the decisions and acts of its management. Littleton specified that only those transactions to which an enterprise has been a participating party can provide appropriate experience data for the enterprise accounts. Violation of the limits can grossly distort the meaning which lies within the records based upon actual experience.[21]

Thus strict limits are established for transaction experience which is allowed to be recorded in the accounts of the enterprise. Outside economic events, changes in price levels, or transactions between outside third parties (even though of a nature related to the enterprise) do not qualify to be recorded in the accounts. These transactions do not qualify because decisions or acts of the enterprise's management have not been and are not involved.

Throughout the lengthy period during which Littleton wrote he maintained his original viewpoint. The efforts and accomplishments of the enterprise, as manifestations of management decisions, represent the transaction realities which must be portrayed by accounting. Enterprise

[21]A. C. Littleton, "The Significance of Interrelated Concepts in Accounting," The International Journal of Accounting Education and Research, II, No. 1 (Fall, 1966), 27-29 (Hereinafter referred to as Littleton, "Interrelated Concepts").

management is the human factor whose decisions and actions
initiate the items of enterprise transaction experience.
The major function of management is to generate a satisfactory relationship between efforts and accomplishments.
Accounting, as the connecting link between management and
the business entity, is necessary to organize data from
the transaction events generated by management's decisions
and to make the prior experience readable.[22]

The useful information provided to management about
prior enterprise transactions provides the basic justification for accounting, according to Littleton. This
justification provides, in turn, the foundation for other
accounting ideas and concepts. These ideas draw significance both from their relationship to the enterprise transaction experience foundation and to each other. The entity
idea excludes from consideration any transactions to which
the enterprise is not a party. The management idea encompasses the view of managerial responsibility for originating entity transactions and thus attaches to the entity
idea. Management responsibility and the entity are closely
related to each other and are connected by accounting.
The major emphasis is upon the feature of accounting as
the connecting link.[23]

It is Littleton's belief that the accounting
discipline evolved as a means of analyzing and recording

---

[22]Ibid., 28.

[23]Ibid., 29.

enterprise transactions and presenting the results of the prior experience in such a manner as to provide a helpful base to users for future decisions. The results stated in terms of income provide the meaningful information needed.

The Function or Purpose of Accounting

The notion of a single function or purpose of accounting is based upon Littleton's conception of enterprise effort and accomplishment. In 1938, Littleton said he conceived of accounting as built about a single function, one central purpose, one primary function. The effective performance of this service provides dependable, relevant information about a business enterprise. This all-embracing function is efficiently fulfilled, within the framework of a coordinated body of theory, by the proper collection, recording, testing, summarization, and reporting of relevant information about the efforts and accomplishments of the enterprise.[24]

There is a tendency in discussions of function, cautioned Littleton, to confuse central purpose with possible uses. Accounting data have many uses, but these uses do not constitute functions of accounting. The unique function of accounting, according to Littleton's firm belief, is to supply dependable relevant information about the bargained prices of transactions between an enterprise and outsiders,

---

[24] A. C. Littleton, "The Relation of Function to Principles," The Accounting Review, XIII, No. 3 (September, 1938), 235 (Hereinafter referred to as Littleton, "Function to Principles").

and to match these costs to revenues within fiscal periods.[25] Littleton continued his stipulation that the central purpose of accounting is to make possible the periodic
matching of costs (efforts) and revenues (accomplishments).
Clearly, he said, there are secondary, derivative uses of
accounting data; however, it must be remembered that these
uses do not alter the basic function of the data. The
basic function must establish accounting procedures.[26]
The same primary accounting purpose, said Littleton, must
form the center and nucleus of accounting theory. He emphatically set forth his view, in detail, as follows:

> The center of accounting theory is not a
> pin-point axis with all the rest of accounting re-
> volving about it. The center must be concerned
> with accounting purpose. But purpose is not a
> single idea or a simple center point. Accounting
> purpose, like a golf ball, is built up of succes-
> sive layers. The top layer--broad purpose--is to
> supply certain significant information about the
> economic activities of an enterprise. This infor-
> mation (derived from enterprise transactions) is
> collected, recorded, classified, reclassified, com-
> pressed, summarized, tested, reported. Such work
> is done with reference to a coordinated body of
> theory and by means of an extensive array of
> experience-derived techniques.
>
> . . . .
>
> But deep under the outer layers is the central
> purpose, the main objective, the continuing in-
> tention. . . . The central purpose of accounting
> is to make it possible for men to reach a calcula-
> ted judgment of the success of the enterprise in
> rendering its services. Without being the whole
> of accounting purpose, this is the heart of account-
> ing, and therefore the center of the structure of
> accounting theory. . . .[27]

---

[25]Ibid., 235-37.

[26]Littleton, Structure, p. 30.

[27]Ibid., pp. 34-35.

Littleton adhered to his view of accounting as a technology whose service is focused upon aiding men to understand a business enterprise and its management. The mission of accounting, he said in 1961, rests upon the broad objective of supplying information which will allow management to make decisions based upon knowledge and understanding of prior experience. The contemporary development, as well as the early development of accounting, asserted Littleton, was brought about to supply indispensable information concerning the outcomes of management created exchange-priced transactions of the past. Decisions concerning the present and the future rest upon an understanding of the present and the past.[28] This particular view is set forth more than frequently in the accounting literature today.

The role of accounts and financial statements in the communication of information regarding enterprise transactions was carefully discussed by Littleton as an important feature of the function of accounting. He emphasized that the accounts merely reveal the enterprise realities of relationships among transactions. Enterprise capital is at work in the transactions of the enterprise and management's use of capital produces results whether accounts are maintained or not. Accounts convert the inherent integration of capital in action and the income produced by that action into

---

[28]A. C. Littleton, "Mission and Method," The Illinois Certified Public Accountant, XXIII, No. 4 (Summer, 1961), 1-2.

intelligible communications. Financial statements represent an integration of capital and income. In this manner they reflect and report upon the interrelations among the judgments, decisions, and actions of management.[29]

Littleton remained steadfast in his view of the function or purpose of accounting. He repeatedly and continuously stressed the idea that accounting information must be based upon the reality of transaction experience. He insisted that the goal of accounting is to present compact, dependable, and relevant data about the enterprise. Based upon transaction experience, the accounting information becomes a relevant portrayal of enterprise events which can be relied upon by management and other users. However, accounting information cannot reveal everything which has happened to the enterprise. In addition, the interpretation of the information is a separate nonaccounting function.

The Central Theme

Littleton reaffirmed over and over his belief that the central theme of accounting has always been concerned with the problem of calculating profits. The basis of this is the belief that income production is the primary and central problem of business and therefore its determination is the central problem of accounting and finance. It follows, according to Littleton, that the central purpose of accrual accounting, which has evolved as a result of refinements

---

[29]Ibid., 4-5

of original methodologies, is to reveal the contrast between inflowing services received and used with the related outflow of services rendered. In other words, its purpose is to contrast the expenses and costs of producing goods and services with the revenues received from their sale. The matching process of accrual accounting is used to perform this essential task in order to determine the profits from enterprise transactions. Based upon this proposition as a concept of profit, Littleton set out the following:

> . . . Profit (net income) is the result of pro-viding an output of economic services (thereby causing an in-flow of gross revenue) which ser-vices are valued by the purchaser at an amount higher than the input of economic factors (brought about by an out-flow of expense) required to pro-duce the services put out.[30]

This concept of profit led Littleton to the conclusion that accrual accounting makes it possible to compare goods or services rendered with the disservices or costs of preparing those goods or services. Accrual accounting, from Littleton's viewpoint, is a means of refining the analysis of things given and things received which leads to a comparison of utilities given and received. The utilities are represented in accounting by costs and selling prices. If the producer's economic services have proven acceptable in the market the comparison of exchange prices will reveal the presence of profit. On the other hand, if loss is revealed by the comparison it indicates lack of

---

[30]Littleton, "Contrasting Theories," 13, reprinted in Littleton, Essays, p. 198.

success in the provision of economic goods and services desired by others at a price acceptable to them.[31]

Littleton believed that the increasing recognition of the importance of the income calculation had been long delayed. He was highly gratified that the primacy of income determination was being recognized again. In 1937, he noted that the emphasis given in publications by the American Institute of Accountants to the importance of correct income determination and to the isolation of earned surplus indicated a return to basic first principles. Profit, said Littleton, has always been the focal center of business enterprise and the focal center of accounting. It had drifted into relative obscurity in much of the accounting literature because of the tendency to stress the balance sheet almost to the exclusion of the income statement. This had evolved primarily as a result of balance sheet audits for credit purposes. However, said Littleton, the fundamental vitality of the principles upon which accounting rests finally brought about a reaffirmation of the fundamental truth that income _is_ primary.[32]

In the determination of income under the accrual accounting system the matching process is fundamental, and must be recognized as such. In 1939, Littleton discussed

---

[31]Littleton, "Contrasting Theories," 13, reprinted in Littleton, _Essays_, p. 198.

[32]Littleton, "Concepts of Income," 15, reprinted in Littleton, _Essays_, p. 210.

the important matter of matching. He wrote at length, as
follows:

> The central problem of accounting is to bring
> into association, in the present, the revenues
> identified with the present and their related
> costs, and to bring into association, in the fu-
> ture, the revenues identified with the future and
> their related costs. In solving this problem
> those who use accounting are, in effect, matching
> enterprise efforts and accomplishments. Some
> efforts are effective in the present; they are
> measured by the costs (effort) currently deduc-
> tible from revenue (accomplishment); they are the
> revenue costs of the present. Other efforts are
> expected to be effective in the future; they are
> measured by the costs that are deferred as being
> revenue costs of the future (assets). Some ef-
> forts prove ineffective in the present and are
> judged unlikely to be effective in the future;
> they are measured by the costs that must be cur-
> rently deducted from revenue as recognized losses.
> The fundamental problem of accounting therefore
> is to cut through a continuing stream of costs and
> correctly assign portions to the present and to
> the future. . . .[33]

W. A. Paton and Littleton, in their 1940 monograph
sponsored by the American Accounting Association, stated
that in writing the monograph they considered that effort is
measured by costs and accomplishment is measured by revenues. They recognized that the layman, as a rule, inter-
prets costs and expenses as cash disbursed, and revenues and
income as cash received. They carefully stressed that the
accounting concept of matching goes far beyond this shallow
interpretation of the accounting matching concept as a

---

[33]Littleton, Essays, p. 201, reprinted from
A. C. Littleton, "Suggestions for the Revision of the Tentative Statement of Accounting Principles," The Accounting
Review, XIV, No. 1 (March, 1939), 60 (Hereinafter referred
to as Littleton, "Suggestions of Accounting Principles").

comparison of disbursements and receipts. The service of the concept is to match: (1) enterprise efforts and accomplishments, (2) goods and services acquired and goods and services rendered, and/or (3) acquisition price-aggregates and disposition price-aggregates. Paton and Littleton emphasized that the terms cost and revenues and accrual accounting comprehend all of these matching terms.[34]

Whereas the economist views the sales price of a good or service as equal to the costs of the marginal producer, the position taken by the accountant involves a different view. The economist is primarily interested in the total cost of production which includes all elements which the sales price must cover if production is to continue. Inherent in this view of cost is the inclusion of the profit for the marginal producer. Paton and Littleton noted that the accountant has adopted a different position. The accountant's outlook is that accounting is primarily a means of computing a residual balance which is the difference between costs and revenues for an individual enterprise. This residual balance is the accounting profit.[35]

The nature of revenue and its affect upon the assets of the enterprise were also discussed by Paton and Littleton. The revenue accounts are designed, they set forth, to

_____

[34]W. A. Paton and A. C. Littleton, An Introduction to Corporate Accounting Standards (Chicago: American Accounting Association, 1940), pp. 15-16 (Hereinafter referred to as Paton and Littleton, Standards).

[35]Ibid.

reflect and gauge the augmentation of resources resulting from operational sales and service activities without deduction of costs. It must be noted that enterprise assets are augmented in various ways, not all of which reflect the emergence of revenue. A part of the process of income determination is the separation of asset increases which reflect revenue from those which do not.[36] The increase in assets caused by the flow of productive accomplishment, the furnishing of goods and services, constitutes the only source of revenue to be recognized.

As a result of the joint publication of Monograph No. 3, a number of inquiries and criticisms were received by the authors. Littleton answered one question concerning the possible abandonment of either the income statement or the balance sheet in the following way:

> . . . If you were to choose the one which contained ideas that lie closest to the heart of business--and therefore closest to the heart of accounting--how could you possibly choose the snapshot of a moment rather than the picture of events extending over a period?[37]

It is evident that Littleton had no hesitancy in making his choice between the two statements. He voted for the income statement which to him presents a proper picture of events over a period of time. He clearly preferred the income

---

[36]Ibid., p. 47.

[37]A. C. Littleton, "Questions on Accounting Standards," The Accounting Review, XVI, No. 4 (December, 1941), 333 (Hereinafter referred to as Littleton, "Questions on Standards").

statement as the one which depicts the vital aspects of business operations.

Littleton was convinced that the emphasis upon balance sheet information and solvency data had been a mistake as well as a perversion of the essential purpose of accounting. He reasoned that this mistaken emphasis was brought about, at least in part, by early auditing literature and procedures and statutory and case law. He examined the situation as follows:

> Yet income determination rather than determination of solvency has always been the central feature of double entry, the very heart and soul of the system, the sine qua non since the fifteenth century. Think what double entry bookkeeping would be if income determination were omitted. . . .
> . . . .
> From the historical evidence it must be concluded that income determination by matching cost and revenue has for 500 years been the central feature of double entry.[38]

Littleton's strong belief in the primacy of income determination as the primary theme of accounting was a permanent element of his view of accounting. He reiterated the same views many times. The essence of enterprise accounting, according to Littleton, had often been by-passed but this does not change the fact that the matching of costs and revenues is the true focal center of accounting. He found little evidence in the early history of bookkeeping

---

[38]A. C. Littleton, "The Accounting Exchange: The Indispensable," The Accounting Review, XX, No. 3 (July, 1945), 351 (Hereinafter referred to as Littleton, "The Indispensable"), reprinted in Littleton, Essays, p. 6. Also found in Littleton, Structure, pp. 26-27.

pointing to an emphasis upon balance sheet data. Income data, he found, were clearly compacted in every ledger that had a profit and loss account, but it was a long time before solvency data were assembled into a balance account.[39] Littleton emphasized certain basic thoughts connected with this view. To Littleton the determination of income had continued to be the focal point of accounting because initial evolution of accounting resulted in the design of certain characteristics. It is the basic patent of double entry, the integration of real and nominal accounts, which makes possible and allows the products of accounting to be widely useful. As a result, said Littleton, emphasis upon any feature other than income determination as the focal feature is in error. Littleton reiterated repeatedly that the central purpose of accounting, in the midst of its many other uses, is to periodically match costs and revenues. This, as the nucleus of accounting theory, forms a benchmark point of reference in the discussion of accounting. It is only reasonable, he said, that the central purpose should control the ordering of accounting procedures. Other uses of the data are clearly secondary and/or derivative uses. It is to be expected that these secondary uses may require some modifications of the original data. However,

---

[39]Littleton, Structure, pp. 28-30.

any change made is a change _from_ basic data; the change does not produce something basic.[40]

Littleton was thorough in his treatment of the central theme. He looked carefully at possible alternate or conflicting concepts. He examined the concepts of financial statements, assets, and capital as possible basic focal points of accounting which could override income determination. He argued that financial statements are displays of assets but are not the unique concept of accounting. Financial statements are in essence tabulations to summarize the extensive accumulation of a particular kind of classified quantitative data. He discarded assets as the pivotal point because solvency is not the primary concept of accounting. Assets are the principal means used to carry on enterprise activity, however, accounting is not essential to the existence of assets. Assets can exist independent of a system of accounting. Capital is closer than an asset to the center of accounting as it tends to direct thought toward property in productive use. However, capital is not as fundamental as income since an understanding of production and income is a necessary antecedent to an understanding of property or capital used to produce income. Moreover, capital is initially saved income; and capitalized income

---

[40] A. C. Littleton, "The Accounting Exchange: Balance-Sheet Prominence," _The Accounting Review_, XX, No. 3 (July, 1945), 353-54, reprinted in Littleton, _Essays_, p. 114. Also found in Littleton, _Structure_, pp. 30-31.

is a primary basis for judging property value.[41] Continuing to build his case for the central theme, Littleton
analyzed the protective value of assets as distinguished
from their productive value. He carefully illustrated that
the production of income is unquestionably the dominant
characteristic of the enterprise:

> It is evident that most uses of the balance
> sheet involve people who are protection conscious.
> They tend to view assets as protective values.
> Assets do have this usefulness, but only in the
> last analysis. At all other times--which means
> most of the time--assets are productive factors.
> . . . The information of vital concern most of
> the time to all parties, therefore, is to be found
> in the series of income statements. Income infor-
> mation is vital right up to that critical moment,
> often long deferred and perhaps never faced, when
> some phase of solvency is in question. . . . But
> as long as the enterprise is a going concern, sol-
> vency is a purely hypothetical question; earning
> capacity is the truly critical question. The in-
> come statement pictures capital busy at the work
> of earning a return. Here is the basis for making
> timely judgments about the protective aspects of
> the enterprise situation. If the enterprise is
> recognized as a productive mechanism, it will be
> easily seen that the best protection for all in-
> terests lies in doing everything possible to keep
> the mechanism productive.[42]

Based upon the above type of reasoning, Littleton
concluded that the central importance of earning power is
implicit in the needs of creditors as well as others. The
ability or inability of a going concern to produce net income is of vital concern to the creditor. Income _is_ the
primary concern of all users.

----

[41]Littleton, _Structure_, pp. 18-19.

[42]_Ibid._, pp. 89-90.

He compared the income statement and the balance sheet with assurance. To Littleton, the income statement is the report of critical importance because it speaks of the results of efforts. The balance sheet speaks only of the remaining means to future results. The balance sheet is not dynamic enough to report upon the central theme of the enterprise. The balance sheet cannot suggest the trying for results and the getting of results, both negative and positive, as does the income statement.[43] In this manner, Littleton made his case that income determination is the central theme of enterprise accounting. Enterprise accounting is designed to tell of results of enterprise transactions for the guidance of management toward decisions. Results are displayed in the earning power information contained in the income statement. Related to the problem of income determination is the tangent idea of a concept of profit.

A Concept of Profit

The concept of profit, referred to in the previous section, was considered of prime importance by Littleton. It appears as a dominant theme in his earlier articles. In 1936, he wrote of a number of contrasting theories of profit which are held by various groups of people. Some aspects of this have been mentioned earlier in the discussion of the contrast between the economist's and the accountant's

---

[43]Ibid., p. 35.

concept of profit. He wrote the following concerning the profit aspect of barter and the intangible nature of such profit. This quotation is an illustration of Littleton's careful, analytical method of building background for the expression of his views. Concerning the profit side of barter he reasoned as follows:

> Here then, in primitive barter, is the basic concept of profit: Profit is an individual's opinion of the increase of total utility, usefulness, or value-in-use that is his as the result of an exchange.
> From this it will be noted that a concept of profit does not need to be associated with money or accounts or formal calculations of any kind. Expected profit from consumption is simply a judgment of relative usefulness read into the goods received in barter, and accomplished profit, the test of the prior judgment, is the excess of consumptive satisfactions flowing out of the use of the thing received. . . .
> . . . .
> In this analysis of barter certain characteristics of profit appear without the intervention of money or accounts. The first of these is that profit is a highly intangible, inconclusive element, depending for a trader upon an almost unending chain of events for its validity. Profit is not a thing in itself, nor is it a specific condition among things; it is an intellectual concept only and varies from person to person and from time to time.[44]

Littleton also wrote at length concerning various features of and viewpoints regarding profit concepts. Concerning the characteristics of a concept of profit he said that the clue to the existence of profit is relative utility. He explained that any conclusion concerning relative utility requires that judgment be applied to a comparison

---

[44]Littleton, "Contrasting Theories," 10, reprinted in Littleton, Essays, pp. 191-92.

of things received and things given in exchange. The exchange of one good or service for another good or service involves differing ideas of relative utility on the part of the transacting parties. The idea of relative utility introduces a concept of profit which leads to the need for a method of computing profit quantitatively. Profit stated quantitatively is the excess of money price received in an exchange over the money prices previously spent. This development of the concept of profit led to several conclusions by Littleton. These conclusions are further indication of the thorough coverage made of the topic:

1. A uniform money of account (not to be confused with money having a stable value) can be used to render diverse elements quantitative and homogeneous so that comparison and summation becomes possible.
2. Bookkeeping is an instrument of "quantification." In order to render profit estimates quantitative, bookkeeping systematically records the bargained prices, in terms of a standard money of account, of things given and things received.
3. The use of these two processes does not change the illusive nature of profit or make its inconclusive characteristics more definite. Caution in accepting profit figures is still as necessary with money of account as it was in judging the utilities involved in direct barter-exchange.[45]

Finally, after building up the general foundation of a concept of profit, Littleton wrote of enterprise profit. He said that there is, in fact, a concept of profit which is usually considered as the underlying basis of enterprise accounting. The following presentation

---

[45]Littleton, "Contrasting Theories," 12, reprinted in Littleton, Essays, p. 193.

88

represents Littleton's total grasp of the many factors

underlying the problems of the enterprise and its accounting

system:

> Profit is the result of providing an outflow
> of economic services valued by the purchaser at
> a price higher than the cost of the input of
> economic factors required to produce the output.
> This phrasing of the concept rests upon the
> following ideas:
> (1) Receiving and giving (exchange) are
> basic to economic activities.
> (2) The basic purpose of double entry is
> systematically to bring into comparison the
> money price of the things received and given
> by a specific enterprise.
> (3) Enterprise accrual accounting is a re-
> finement of double entry techniques by means
> of which cost and revenue are periodically
> and sharply associated much as if cost rep-
> resented enterprise effort and revenue rep-
> resented results of effort.
> (4) By referring to data from his accrual
> accounting an enterpriser is able to compare
> cost given (incurred) with revenue received
> (earned) and consequently is in a position to
> judge the satisfaction with which his services
> have been accepted and the skill with which
> he has kept his costs below the price the
> market would pay.
> Thus it is evident that there has been an inner
> consistency in the traditional views of profit
> even though time has brought modifications and re-
> finements. Business custom, reaching backward far
> down the centuries, has consistently made use of
> original, outlay costs as the basis for profit
> calculations. Five hundred years of bookkeeping
> practice reflect this theory of profit because
> bookkeeping employs the ideas of businessmen. . . .[46]

At approximately the same time, in 1937, Littleton

wrote that accountants and businessmen are sometimes accused

of having a vague concept of profit. He defended the

---

[46]Littleton, Essays, p. 293, reprinted from
Littleton, "Contrasting Theories," 13-15.

businessmen and accountants against the charge. He stated
that there is an accounting and/or business concept of profit.
The businessman's concept of net income emerges from his
productive activity and his inability to defer decisions.
Decisions must be made prior to ultimate liquidation which
will authenticate the reality of profits.[47]

The discussion of a concept of profit, as such,
does not appear explicitly as a dominant theme in later
materials written by Littleton. However, it is apparent
that the basic idea is implicit in the make-up of his total
view of the function of and the central theme of accounting.
His concern apparently had been to distinguish between the
economist's and the accountant's view of profit and to
make the point that accountants do not ignore profit in
their total scheme of accounting.

The Earning Power of the Enterprise

As a part of his total view of the primacy of income determination, Littleton concluded that the information
concerning the earning power or earning capacity of an enterprise comprises the important information needed by various
users. The potential earnings to be derived in the future
from the use of the assets of an enterprise is the vital information to management, investors, and others. The earnings to be expected in the future, added Littleton, can be

---

[47]A. C. Littleton, "Business Profits as a Legal Basis for Dividends," Harvard Business Review, XVI, No. 1
(Autumn, 1937), 59, and Littleton, "Concepts of Income," 22.

projected best by looking at the earnings of the past. He strongly believed that trustworthy knowledge concerning true earning power was far more important than information concerning probable ability to pay debts. Littleton maintained that little helpful information regarding earning power could be gleaned from a balance sheet without an accompanying income statement. The necessity for payment of debts in a liquidation situation is not expected in the normal continuing business enterprise, and assets are to be used in the efforts to produce income, not to pay debts.[48]

Littleton noted with satisfaction that the American Institute of Accountants in the 1934 Audit of Corporate Accounts stated that the earning capacity of any large business enterprise determines the real value of the enterprise's assets. The Institute publication further noted that intelligent investors on a whole probably recognize that earning capacity is the fact of crucial importance in the valuation of the enterprise, and that therefore the income statement is far more important than the balance sheet.[49]

In 1940, Littleton re-examined the objectives of the income statement with special concern for the question of whether, under modern conditions, the statement can serve as

----

[48]A. C. Littleton, "Dividends Presuppose Profits," The Accounting Review, IX, No. 4 (December, 1934), 311, reprinted in Littleton, Essays, p. 262.

[49]Littleton, "Concepts of Income," 14, reprinted in Littleton, Essays, p. 209.

both a report of earning power and a report of managerial effort. He set forth that assets are a focus of interest because they represent investment, the means of operating the enterprise, and the means of discharging the enterprise's obligations. Finally, the objective of enterprise activities and the hope of the investor is to increase the assets. Some would probably conclude, therefore, that a report which displays the changes in assets from the beginning to the end of the period would be enough. Littleton pointed out very clearly that this is not the case:

> Some people might be content with such a reporting; but others of a more inquiring turn of mind would wonder which of the changes that were so readable in the comparative asset table were due to additional investments or withdrawals by stockholders and creditors, which to appraisal write-up or write-down, and which to the active administration of the assets in the midst of current business conditions.
>
> Assets and changes therein are indeed the central interest of all concerned, but a reporting of assets alone would be quite inadequate to the user's need, because the results of various differing causes would be indistinguishable.
>
> Each asset, in spite of careful classification by type, arises out of a variety of antecedents. The person with an inquiring turn of mind will want supplementary figures which will help him to isolate and judge the different kinds of asset changes. He will wish to view the assets in the light of diverse interests of the various parties who have contractual rights in them, and he will like to have the means of viewing the assets in a manner designed to give him some insight into the effectiveness with which the assets have been acquired, manipulated, and exchanged under the direction of management.[50]

---

[50]A. C. Littleton, "The Integration of Income and Surplus Statement," The Journal of Accountancy, LXIX, No. 1 (January, 1940), 32-33.

The balance sheet and the income statement each display special kinds of information designed to serve specific purposes. The balance sheet conveys information regarding (1) the relationship of various equities to each other, and (2) the relationship of the equities to the assets which support them; the income statement supplies information regarding (1) the corporation's earning power as indicated by recurring transactions, and (2) the total results of the efforts of management to employ the capital of the enterprise in an effective manner. Each statement serves in a dual capacity; and both roles must be reflected in each statement. This is necessary in order that the full purpose of each statement may be achieved.[51] In other words, the balance sheet must reflect not only the relationship of owners' and creditors' equities to the assets but also the relationship of the owners' and creditors' interests to each other. In the same vein, the income statement does not fulfill its purpose if it fails to reflect not only the earnings from regular enterprise transactions but also the results of other nonrecurring events. It should be noted that Littleton's view of the income statement requires that income information be presented under the all-inclusive concept. Gains and losses from nonrepetitive, nonoperating transactions must be disclosed in the income statement. This presentation conforms to his belief that

_____

[51] Ibid., 32.

all events should be disclosed and that such disclosure is of prime importance.

To Littleton it was evident that earning power was both the blood stream of the enterprise and the basis of most judgments about the value of the enterprise. In addition he identified the reflection of a variety of interests in the income statement data. The varied interests may, of course, be in conflict at times. Littleton observed that because of this difference of interest and viewpoint different parties would tend to record transactions and prepare financial statements in different ways. This tendency would probably produce biased results without the moderating influence of the various other interests which must be recognized and represented in the final figures.[52]

The emphasis upon the earning power of the enterprise, as the notion of a concept of profit, was not explicitly evident in the materials initially written by Littleton after the 1940's. However, the idea of the earning power of the enterprise was an important implicit feature of his total view and was reflected in his presentations.

[52]A. C. Littleton, "The Accounting Exchange: Claims Upon Income," The Accounting Review, XIX, No. 4 (October, 1944), 452-53 (Hereinafter referred to as Littleton, "Claims Upon Income"), reprinted in Littleton, Essays, p. 214. Also found in Littleton, Structure, pp. 31-32.

The Reality of Profit--
Recognition and Realization

Littleton was concerned about the difference between the reality of profit, or realization, and the earning process. Littleton identified profit as an extremely
illusive element. He wrote of this particular problem as
early as 1936:

> . . . Reality of profit should not be read into a
> situation too soon or upon inadequate evidence.
> This is the basis of the so-called "realization
> principle." When an objective test has verified
> a personal hope, conviction of reality may safely
> follow but not before. Anticipated profits are
> mere opinions and therefore subject to individual
> bias and mistaken judgment. Realized profits on
> the other hand have met an objective test, under
> conditions by which the utility of the goods has
> been further attested by the independent judgment
> of a subsequent receiver in exchange. But even
> such "realization" may prove to be an incomplete
> test of reality because today's gains may be con-
> sumed by tomorrow's losses if the goods last re-
> ceived prove useless.[53]

Paton and Littleton also wrote of this problem in
the same manner. The importance of distinguishing between
earning and realization was stressed. They noted that the
dominant view holds that revenue is realized upon the receipt of new liquid assets. The two tests implicit in this
view are the conversion through legal sale or similar process and validation of the sale through the acquisition of
new liquid assets. It was emphasized that revenue may be
considered as earned by the entire process of production
but revenue cannot be measured and recognized prior to

---

[53]Littleton, "Contrasting Theories," 10-11, reprinted in Littleton, Essays, p. 192.

completion and disposition of the product. The amount of revenue is uncertain and realization does not occur until production is completed, the product is transferred to the customer, price is objectively determined, and new assets appear.[54]

In 1953, Littleton wrote that _every_ revenue transaction is based upon a transaction supplying a customer with chosen goods and/or services. Performance of the service or the supplying of goods is an enterprise action which objectively determines the time of the transaction. The transaction supports a well-established convention of accounting that profit is realized when the sale is made, and not before. If no sale occurs, no realization of revenue can be recognized.[55] It seems to follow, if realization cannot occur until a sales transaction takes place, that the sale is the end toward which all efforts are directed. Paton and Littleton also designated the sale as the capstone of all enterprise actions. The completed sale, stated in financial terms as revenue and supported by new and dependable assets, is the decisive step in the stream of enterprise activity. Therefore, the completed sale is the best test of the realization of revenue.[56] Revenue is not only the evidence of sale and the capstone of enterprise

---

[54]Paton and Littleton, _Standards_, p. 49

[55]Littleton, _Structure_, pp. 201-2.

[56]Paton and Littleton, _Standards_, pp. 53-54.

activity, it is also the clue to costs. Littleton formulated a principle of revenue recognition based upon this idea.
He wrote of it as follows:

> It will be evident that revenue is more often
> the leading clue to the assignment of applicable
> costs, expenses, and losses than the latter are
> clues to the recognition of revenue. It will also
> be noted in the following statement of principle
> that recognition, not realization, is the key
> word of the objective:
> Revenue Recognition: Objective evidence of
> services performed and benefits received in return
> . . . afford the only acceptable basis for perio-
> dically assigning revenue to the present or of al-
> ternatively deferring recognition into the
> future.[57]

Realization marks the point at which the reality of
profit is recognized for the business enterprise and therefore it is the recognition point in the accounting system.
Without a sale there is no realization of revenue and no
possibility of profit. The following statement made by
Littleton in 1953 summarizes his opinion concerning
realization:

> Late in the eighteenth century a direct
> statement was made in Adam Smith's Wealth of
> Nations to the effect that profit could arise
> only if "goods changed masters." This idea we
> now call the realization principle; it seems as
> reasonable under the new name as under the old
> phraseology. By inference both expressions in-
> clude the idea that unrealized value change does
> not generate profit or loss. Before realization,
> price change only hints that profit or loss may
> eventually materialize. . . .[58]

---

[57]Littleton, Structure, pp. 202-3.

[58]A. C. Littleton, "Variety in the Concept of Income," The New York Certified Public Accountant, XXIII,
No. 7 (July, 1953), 421, reprinted in Littleton, Essays,
p. 289.

In this statement Littleton again ties realization to the completed exchange transaction, the sale. His comment on the unrealized value change was designed to forestall any suggestion to recognize profit or loss because of the change in price of assets held, but not yet sold. The reality of profit is finally determined when an actual sale is made and thus revenue is recognized as realized. Profit realization, of course, depends upon the total amount of costs which are matched with the recognized revenues.

Matching of Revenue and Cost

The matching of revenues and costs has been set out as the focal center of accounting and an integral part of accrual accounting. Income determination involves the careful and objective matching of revenues and costs. Littleton wrote about the matching process as early as 1937. He noted that net income is the result of a favorable or unfavorable relationship between revenue and cost.[59] This association of costs and revenues creates the matching problem. It is important that the matching of costs with revenues be objective. If nonobjective influences are reflected in the matching process the bias will be reflected, in turn, in the resultant net income. Bias in the cost figures may influence the profit considerably. The assignment of costs to the present is reflected in the income statement, whereas

[59]Littleton, "Concepts of Income," 18, reprinted in Littleton, Essays, p. 213.

the balance sheet reflects the assignment of unamortized acquisition cost to the future.[60] In other words, both the income statement and the balance sheet reflect the results of the matching process. Bias toward income computation is correspondingly reflected in the balance sheet figures.

Paton and Littleton also discussed the matching process. They said that the essential task of accounting consists of the rational matching of costs incurred with resulting revenues. An objective and rational attitude is implicitly necessary to the matching process. Cost, they said, is accounted for in three stages. The stages are: (1) determining and recording costs as incurred, appropriately classified; (2) tracing and reclassifying costs as to operating activity; and (3) assigning the costs to the revenues. It appears that the crucial stage from the standpoint of periodic income determination is the third one. The third stage, the matching stage, encompasses most of the difficult problems of accounting analysis. They stressed that more than careful procedure and accurate compilation are required to match costs and revenues. Efficient clerical processes coupled with close observation in the recording of cost inflows tends to eliminate the bulk of the problems of the two first stages. However, recording the outflow of costs for which revenue is recognized is essentially a matter of judgment and interpretation. It is

---

[60]Littleton, "Suggestions of Accounting Principles," 60, reprinted in Littleton, Essays, p. 201.

essential to always remember that the cost of any factor utilized in activities of an operation can be charged to revenue only as the resulting product is recognized as having produced revenue. The matching process forces an accountant to seek bases for the satisfactory association of costs and revenues. It is necessary that the bases be reasonable and dependable. Reasonableness in light of all pertinent conditions is the essential test of a matching basis.[61]

As a follow-up to his expression of the principle of periodic matching[62] Littleton elaborated upon the matching process and the problems inherent in it. He stressed the difference between capital and income, as follows:

> The word "matching" is not a part of traditional terminology and perhaps deserves comment. As used here it means more than setting two elements side by side and more than comparison of size or calculation of difference. It means the mating of related data; it carries the implication that bases have been found to indicate that the data belong together. In connection with income determination, matching means associating revenue credits and their proper charges; it means associating revenue charges and their proper credits.
>
> The proper matching of costs and revenues involves all that is contained in the problems of distinguishing capital and income--and more. . . . The action of matching treats capital as a means, income as an end. Thus capital (as a means) is in intention and in effect an advancing of costs, an investment for the future, and as use takes place it converts into a measure of efforts made. And gross income is in part a recovery of costs advanced, a fruition of a future

---

[61]Paton and Littleton, Standards, pp. 59, 69-71.

[62]Supra, p. 66.

now become the present, a measure of accomplishments secured.[63]

It is necessary that there be no confusion between gross income and net income. Littleton spent some effort to distinguish between the two terms. He specified that net income is merely a plus or minus result of subtracting costs from revenues. As such it does not have a clear-cut quantitative significance as do the revenue and cost figures themselves. If only the net income figure were needed, he pointed out, it could be as easily determined by comparing ownership figures at two different dates. The balance sheet, as a connecting link between successive income statements, provides this information. Littleton aired his conviction that the real message conveyed by the income statement lies in the kinds and relative amounts of investments made compared with the kinds and relative amounts of proceeds derived. The real story of the income statement lies not in the final net figure but in the costs advanced in making efforts and in the revenues received for accomplishments.[64]

The focal center of accrual accounting thus rests upon the proper and objective matching of revenues and costs. The final income which is determined is the outcome of the process and will reflect any bias exerted by non-objective influences. Rational procedures must be used in the assignment of costs to revenues.

---

[63]Littleton, Structure, p. 23.

[64]Ibid., pp. 23-24.

Accrual and Deferral

Accrual and deferral as accounting processes are an integral part of the matching process. It is difficult to try to separate the topic of matching from the topic of accruals and deferrals. Nominal accounts and accruals constitute the essence of the accrual basis of accounting, said Littleton in 1934. Objective judgment is required to attempt to identify all those costs, and only those costs, which in reality were incurred in the production efforts aimed toward the resulting revenues. The proper association of the revenues received for service performed with the cost of rendering that service is the essence of the accrual accounting system.[65] It seems to be clear that accrual accounting is concerned more directly with the calculation of correct income and expense for a given period than with securing refinements for the balance sheet. This is true although the two results always appear together.[66]

The relationship of accrual accounting to the time period is significant. There are two important aspects of the time period problem. The first is the distinction between expense and disbursement and between income and receipts. The second relates to the careful separation of assets and expenses. Both of these elements of accrual

---

[65]A. C. Littleton, "The Accounting Exchange: The Income Approach," The Accounting Review, IX, No. 4 (December, 1934), 343-44.

[66]Littleton, "Concepts of Income," 15, reprinted in Littleton, Essays, p. 210.

accounting involve the allocation of costs and revenues between time periods.[67] Therefore, consideration of time periods is a necessary aspect of accrual accounting. The typical business is a continuing process and income is a stream which must be broken up into convenient and arbitrary time segments. This breakdown of the continuing process is necessary for purposes of measurement and reporting.[68] The motivating force behind this break up into time periods is management's need for information prior to the ultimate and unplanned liquidation of the continuing business enterprise.

Periodic reclassification of initial accounting data by year-end adjustment entries for accruals, deferments, provisions, and reserves is a part of the matching process. This reworking of account facts is not done according to wish and will, but according to the nature of the transaction data to be handled and their known relationship to a given fiscal period or operating process. The reclassified facts still must be as dependable as the original facts; therefore, the matching must be of elements which are relevant to each other. There _must_ be a relationship between the costs and the revenues realized during the period. The general objective of making adjustment entries becomes one of assigning costs and revenues suitably to successive

---

[67]Littleton, "Concepts of Income," 20, reprinted in Littleton, _Essays_, p. 194.

[68]Paton and Littleton, _Standards_, pp. 66-67.

fiscal periods. The objective of accrual accounting is to make the calculation of periodic net income nearer to the truth. The assignment of costs means the costs must be divided between periods according to service accomplishment or revenues achieved in a given period. A suitable assignment of costs will be in accordance with their relevance to service efforts made during the period to produce enterprise revenue.[69]

The periodic reclassification of expenditures necessitates attention to accruals and deferrals. Deferral or delay of recognition of costs indicates that a means of making an effort to produce revenue has been provided earlier than the means can be effectively used. In order to conclude that postponement of a cost is needed, it must have been determined that a means of performance exists unused.[70] All costs incurred prudently which can reasonably be associated with future production are subject to deferment.[71] The deferral of a cost indicates that the charge represents a factor from which a future benefit or contribution can reasonably be anticipated. An accrual differentiates between effort made and cash disbursed, and between performance accomplished and cash collected. Accrued charges are those costs which have been incurred, in the

---

[69]Littleton, Structure, passim, pp. 57-58, 63-67.
[70]Ibid., p. 69.
[71]Paton and Littleton, Standards, p. 74.

process of expending efforts, for which no cash has been disbursed.[72]

Accruals and deferrals are used, therefore, to make more precise the measurement of enterprise efforts and accomplishments. In short, the accruals and deferrals make it possible to match efforts with accomplishments, costs with revenues.

Littleton developed principles relating to accruals and deferrals which are as valid today as they were when they were developed. His discussions are clear and detailed. There is no possibility of misunderstanding his meaning. No doubt his discussions contributed to a better understanding of the concepts involved.

Cost Allocation

The accrual and deferral reclassification calculations made in the matching process involve cost allocation, another area of concern in the study of income determination. The propositions of matching of costs and revenues and of adjusting for accruals and deferrals are inseparable from cost allocation as a fundamental process of the accrual accounting system. The cost allocation idea, in turn, is based upon adherence to historical cost, consideration of which is deferred to the following chapter. Because money price can be used to represent the mental concept of use value at the time of the exchange of goods or

---

[72]Littleton, Structure, p. 69.

services it can also represent cost in the matching process necessary to determine profit. The use of money price aids in the quantitative measurement of cost.[73]

In conjunction with a discussion of income determination by accrual accounting methods, Littleton stated, in 1937, that it is no doubt an acceptable generalization to say that cost allocation is the fundamental process of accounting. He elaborated by saying that it is clearly recognized that original outlay costs can be deferred as assets, amortized as expenses, or abandoned as losses. Littleton asserted that it is the duty of accounting theory to lay down rules and reasons for making the distinctions between these possibilities. The relationship of a particular cost cause to its corresponding revenue source is a better clue for allocation than its connection to a time period. Relationship to a time span is the least desirable basis for a cost allocation. Littleton avowed that original outlay costs should be treated as deferred costs only when they may appropriately be considered as causally related to future revenue sources. On the other hand, they should be handled as amortized costs only when they may judiciously be determined to be directly connected to current revenue causes. Expended costs should become abandoned costs only when they may advisedly be regarded as unlikely ever to generate the production of revenue. From this,

---

[73]Littleton, "Contrasting Theories," 11, reprinted in Littleton, Essays, pp. 192-93.

Littleton concluded that if reasonable causal connections
can be established between revenue sources and cost causes,
the allocation of costs and revenues to equal time periods
can be an incidental feature rather than a controlling one
in the calculation of net income.[74]

In 1939, Littleton wrote that the fundamental
problem of cost allocation for income determination is to
cut through a continuing stream of costs and correctly
assign portions to the present and to the future. The income statement and the balance sheet are the mediums for
reporting this division. The income statement reports the
costs assigned to the present. The balance sheet reports
the unamortized, residual acquisition costs to be assigned
to the future.[75] Since the cost allocation process has a
significant effect upon both statements it must be carried
out objectively and without bias. The use of values other
than cost in the statements would introduce such bias. It
is evident that Littleton did not favor the use of market
values for the display of assets. He believed this would
affect both statements in an undesirable manner.[76]

The homogeneous nature of costs is reflected in the
cost allocation process. In this process all costs are

---

[74]Littleton, "Concepts of Income," 21, reprinted in
Littleton, Essays, p. 195.

[75]Littleton, "Suggestions of Accounting Principles,"
60, reprinted in Littleton, Essays, p. 201, and found in
Paton and Littleton, Standards, p. 67.

[76]Littleton, "Suggestions of Accounting Principles,"
62.

viewed as homogeneous and of equal rank as to matching with revenues. All costs are equally significant and any attempt to assign costs through a ranking procedure will tend to be misleading. Paton and Littleton were very eager to assure that there would be no misunderstanding regarding the ranking of costs. All costs, they said, become homogeneous upon entry into the accounts and therefore become an inseparable total of costs of a particular classification. Under this view, all costs, regardless of origin, are of equal impact upon the final cost figure, and as such must be applied to revenues upon a relative basis.[77] The homogeneous nature of costs is represented in the accounts by the use of prices in terms of one money system.[78]

Paton and Littleton used an interesting analogy to illustrate the fallacious results achieved by any form of cost ranking which overemphasizes last increments of costs or differential costs. They wrote as follows:

> . . . The problem of allocation here is somewhat akin to that represented by the old story of the straw and the camel's back. Is the last straw to be held responsible for the result (unfortunate in the classic example) or is the outcome to be considered the effect of the entire load? The more reasonable answer is that the last increment contributes no more to the total accomplishment than its fellow straws; it is decisive in that its incidence precipitates action but this condition depends upon the support of the other factors. . . . this line of thought . . . suggests the conclusion that in income reporting each element of revenue--whatever its origin in time or the special

---

[77]Paton and Littleton, Standards, pp. 67-69.

[78]Littleton, Structure, p. 192.

conditions affecting the price of the particular lot or class of product--should be deemed to
carry that portion of total costs which seems to
be appropriate when the revenues of the period
are viewed as a whole, rather than an estimated
differential cost.[79]

Short-term assignments of costs to revenues create
difficult problems of allocation. However, the cost allocation process must not be used to implement any device or
carry out any policy designed to create an artificial
smoothing of fluctuations caused by varying business for-
tunes over a period of years. Short-term approtionment
should not obscure business trends but should bring interim
statements into harmony with existing conditions. Lean
years and fat years in business operation should be revealed by accounting, not concealed.[80] The tentative nature of
interim short-term assignment of costs to revenues was also
emphasized. Short-term reports, said Paton and Littleton,
should be recognized as tentative because they are based
upon estimates that are likely to be proven erroneous.[81]

Increased Emphasis on In-
come Statement Information

Littleton wrote at various times specifically about
the change taking place which reflected a shift of emphasis
from the balance sheet information to the income statement

---

[79]Paton and Littleton, Standards, p. 69.
[80] Ibid., pp. 76-77.
[81]Ibid., pp. 92, 95.

information. He was much concerned to demonstrate the
reasonableness of this change. In 1938, he predicted that
investors would eventually learn that the history of a corporation's earning power was significant to them. A statement of the book value of their securities does not properly
satisfy their needs.[82]

In 1944, Littleton stressed the fact that there is
a large community of interests behind an income statement.
Consumers, workers, investors, management, and government
interests must all be considered when reporting upon the results of the activities of a large modern corporation. He
wrote that business management faces the challenge of attempting to maintain enterprise equilibrium in the midst of
complex, interacting, constantly changing forces and conditions. If a condition of imbalance does develop, it is
difficult for an untrained eye to discern the situation from
a series of balance sheets. Littleton was emphatic in his
belief that a series of income statements offers the best
information to any interested group.[83] Revenue and cost
figures are the best indicators of the results of varied
economic forces upon the well-being of an enterprise.[84]
Littleton explained the ascendancy of the income statement

---

[82]Littleton, "Function to Principles," p. 237.

[83]A. C. Littleton, "The Accounting Exchange: Interacting Forces," The Accounting Review, XIX, No. 4 (October,
1944), 453, reprinted in Littleton, Essays, pp. 215-16.
Also found in Littleton, Structure, pp. 33-34.

[84]Supra, pp. 58-59.

as the primary enterprise statement. He reasoned that the mounting recognition of the income statement could be explained by the failure of the balance sheet to report upon the sharing of enterprise revenue in any except the simplest conditions. The balance sheet does not furnish adequate information to reflect the claims of government, workers, customers and creditors. Furthermore, a single balancing figure to the assets, liabilities, and capital does not reveal sufficient information regarding the net change in equities.[85] Littleton noted that although awareness of the importance of income determination was recent, the importance is as old as double-entry bookkeeping.[86] The income statement has long existed in the shadow of the balance sheet, but it has never ceased to be of prime importance. Modern conditions have simply led to the perception that income statement data are of higher significance than balance sheet data.[87] One of the reasons for this recognition is the modern emphasis upon income of the enterprise rather than upon its solvency. This suggests that management's stewardship is better reported through the income statement because it tells something of what is being done to make the owner's investment productive. The balance

---

[85]Littleton, "Claims Upon Income," 453, reprinted in Littleton, Essays, pp. 214-15. Also found in Littleton, Structure, p. 32.

[86]Littleton, "The Indispensable," 350, reprinted in Littleton, Essays, p. 6. Also found in Littleton, Structure, p. 26.

[87]Littleton, Structure, p. 90.

sheet only reports the forms in which the entrusted investments stand at a moment of time.[88] This modern emphasis had also been fostered by improvement in cost accounting techniques soon after 1900 and the progressive use of income taxation for governmental fund raising. Littleton also considered changes in American corporation law which permitted issuance of no-par stock, the growing practice of creating surplus by revaluing enterprise assets, and a shift after the 1920's to long-term financing via the sale of stocks and bonds as additional contributory factors leading to increased emphasis upon earnings information.[89]

Littleton believed strongly that income determination has always been a dominant purpose of accounting. Therefore, he viewed the renewed emphasis upon earning power and income statement reports as merely a long delayed but inevitable change. He supported his conviction by historical evidence and was gratified by the acknowledgment of income primacy by the accounting profession and various groups of users.

Summary

Littleton's views of income determination as the central theme of accounting was indeed a dominant theme in his writing. This core idea, and its prime features, as

---

[88] Ibid., p. 21.

[89] Ibid., pp. 90-91.

set forth in this chapter can be stated in summary
form.

The business unit is first of all an economic unit
set up for the purpose of providing goods and services to
customers for a profit. Management, operating within the
economic framework, guides the enterprise efforts toward the
production of revenues through the sale of product and service accomplishments. The economic condition of the enterprise is of major concern because it reflects the relationship between the revenues (accomplishment) and the costs
incurred (effort). The clue to economic condition is indicated by the net income earned. Accounting information is
needed to make the enterprise and the results of its transactions understandable to interested groups.

The primary function of accounting is to reflect in
a quantitative manner the enterprise transactions in order
to provide relevant information to be used by management and
others for present and future decisions. Accounting costs
become the quantitative expressions of management policies
translated into action. The accounting information presents
the prior transaction experience of an entity for review and
evaluation of past efforts and accomplishments. This, in
turn, provides guidance for making future plans.

The realities of business are behind the accounting
figures. The cost and revenue figures of accounting are
based upon the transaction facts. Since business is dynamic
and a continuing process, and since ultimate liquidation is

unplanned and long deferred, interim accounting information is necessary. The need for periodic provisional accounting reports covering arbitrary time periods calls for accrual accounting procedures in order to match current efforts with current accomplishments.

Since profit is the ultimate goal of the business enterprise, it follows that the central theme of accounting, its focal point of concern, must be the calculation of profit. Accrual accounting contrasts via the matching process the service accomplishments of the business enterprise with the efforts it has expended. The mating of costs (things given) and revenues (things received) produces reports which reflect the earning power of the enterprise. If management has guided the enterprise efforts successfully and kept costs below revenues, net income will be reflected via the matching process which is necessarily the nucleus of accrual accounting.

Revenues are recognized as realized when a sale of goods or services takes place through a bargained-price exchange with an outsider. The sale, therefore, is the basic signal for identification of revenue realization. It then is necessary to match all costs incurred (efforts expended) to earn the revenues which have been obtained. The largest problems encountered in this area are in the establishment of relevant and reasonable bases for allocation of the proper costs to the revenues. This association process involves, by necessity, judgment and interpretation. The time period is used sometimes as an allocation basis, however, it is the least desirable footing for spreading costs. The allocation of costs is expedited by the use of cost and revenue accruals and deferrals. The matching of costs and revenues is, in fact, made possible through the use of these accruals and deferrals which are the essence of accrual accounting.

Thus, accrual accounting, via the matching process which uses accumulation and postponement adjustments in the fundamental cost allocation plan, results in the presentation of reports based upon the earning power of an enterprise. This is the information needed by management and external groups in making present and future decisions concerning the enterprise. The earning power report, the income statement, is the vital communication because it speaks of the results of efforts expended and outcomes accomplished.

Littleton, armed with his basic understanding of economics and his public accounting experience under the guidance of accountants trained in English and Scottish methods, began his career as an educator and writer. He displayed a penetrating insight concerning the information needs of business management and other groups of users. He sensibly recognized the developing and growing requirements for information about the earning capacities of enterprises. He responded to this manifest need and expended his efforts and talents to clarification and resolution of the problems.

CHAPTER IV

PRESTIGE FOR HISTORICAL COST

The concept of cost, as a vital feature of the matching process used for income determination, had become an important concern to accountants. Consideration of cost is a predominant feature of Littleton's writing. The cost element is both explicit and implicit in his discussions. Littleton stipulated that the periodic matching of <u>cost</u> and revenue for the determination of enterprise income is the focal center of accounting. The income statement, produced by the techniques of accounting, is the report of critical importance which makes it possible for men to reach a calculated judgment concerning the success of the enterprise in rendering its services.[1] Cost is an <u>essential</u> aspect of this all-important matching process. Cost, as a fundamental element in the matching process, constitutes the basic subject matter of accounting.

---

[1]A. C. Littleton, <u>Structure of Accounting Theory</u> (Menasha, Wisconsin: George Banta Publishing Company for American Accounting Association, 1953), <u>passim</u>, pp. 30-35 (Hereinafter referred to as Littleton, <u>Structure</u>).

Value or Cost

The choice between cost and value as a basis for recording and reporting an entity's productive expenditures, profits, and assets constituted a significant contemporary problem. Littleton believed that there are sound and logical reasons for adherence to cost prices for accounting and financial statement purposes. In 1928, he said that accountants have strong justification for the support of cost rather than value. Cost is a definite quantitative fact which is unchangeable. As such, cost becomes a basis for the calculation of profit as soon as a sale has been made. On the other hand, value is indefinite and changeable. Therefore, value can never be the starting point for profit computation.[2] Littleton elaborated upon this topic. He said that value is the result of a subjective estimate of an individual as to the relative importance of an article or service. A value, in fact, may exist as a tentative price in the mind of one person only. On the other hand, cost price (to the buyer) is a fact established by a closed exchange transaction, after compromise, between two contending parties.[3]

---

[2]A. C. Littleton, "What is Profit?" The Accounting Review, III, No. 3 (September, 1928), 287, reprinted in A. C. Littleton, Essays on Accountancy (Urbana, Illinois: University of Illinois Press, 1961), p. 207 (Hereinafter referred to as Littleton, Essays).

[3]A. C. Littleton, "Value and Price in Accounting," The Accounting Review, IV, No. 3 (September, 1929), 149 (Hereinafter referred to as Littleton, "Value and Price"), reprinted in Littleton, Essays, p. 227.

Littleton carefully distinguished between value, price and cost. The final disposal _value_ of a good or service at a bargained price, asserted Littleton, is determined by its basic scarcity in conjunction with the consumer's needs and demands. The _past cost_ of the goods to the businessman actually has little or no influence upon the price set. However, Littleton noted decisions made in the present are significantly influenced by the expected future costs of goods or services. Furthermore, prior to the sale of the goods at their real value, as established in the market place, incurred costs should be viewed as a temporary investment.[4]

Littleton believed that cost price is neither a value nor a determinant of sales price, but it is a means of establishing the amount of profit or loss derived from a sale. Cost does not represent value in the accounting records of the business. Cost describes a refusal price which signifies the point at which profit or loss begins. Although cost data does provide necessary information for price setting, it cannot determine sales price. In view of this, Littleton concluded that the calculation of profits is the primary reason for the businessman's concern about cost.[5]

---

[4]Littleton, "Value and Price," 152, reprinted in Littleton, _Essays_, p. 222.

[5]Littleton, "Value and Price," 153, reprinted in Littleton, _Essays_, p. 223.

In 1929, Littleton devoted his attention to the confusion created at the time by the frequent revaluation of assets by adjustments up or down to reflect changes in business conditions and/or price levels. Momentary changes in value, said Littleton, are too subjective to be represented by recorded accounting figures. The attempt to reflect such temporary values results in a perversion of the proper recording function of accounting. The accountant's balance sheet, said Littleton, is never really a statement of values but of cost prices. Perhaps Littleton was not yet fully committed to strict adherence to cost. At any rate, he was not as emphatic, in 1929, as he became later, as illustrated in the following quotation:

> . . . The presentation must be a statement of prices--just what prices however is still a subject of debate, perhaps the most central subject of debate in modern accountancy.[6]

By 1953, Littleton was more positive in his view that the display of cost and not value is the proper function of accounting. His outlook on the issue had solidified and he stated quite positively, as follows:

> . . . Trying to make financial statement figures tell of _value_ (for value is subjective, differing from man to man and day to day) would not produce a dependable basis for accounting. The data would lose their prior significance every few days.[7]

---

[6]Littleton, "Value and Price," 153, reprinted in Littleton, _Essays_, p. 220.

[7]Littleton, _Structure_, pp. 210-12.

He also pointed out that most of the property held by an enterprise is not, in reality, kept for exchange. For this reason, its value in terms of possible current selling price is not constantly an issue, and it is not usually a primary concern.[8]

In 1935, Littleton continued to write of value or cost and the continuing debate among accountants because of lack of agreement concerning the problem. He recognized the need for a united front among the spokesmen of the profession, whom he thought would do well to advocate original cost or value for use. In general, Littleton supported and advocated adherence to original outlay cost. He stipulated that original cost should be used in preference to any of the values such as conservative value, replacement value, capitalization-of-earnings-value, insurable value, or security-for-loan-value.[9] These alternative valuation methods have no place in Littleton's scheme of accounting.

In March, 1936, Littleton pled the case for the use of bargained prices in the accounts. Statistical analysis and other uses of accounting data are dependent upon information concerning the results of business operations.

---

[8] A. C. Littleton, "Variety in the Concept of Income," The New York Certified Public Accountant, XXIII, No. 7 (July, 1953), 423 (Hereinafter referred to as Littleton, "Variety of Income"), reprinted in Littleton, Essays, p. 292.

[9] A. C. Littleton, "Value or Cost," The Accounting Review, X, No. 3 (September, 1935), 269-72, reprinted in Littleton, Essays, pp. 227, 231-32.

120

There is a basic need for the original data to be recorded and reported first in terms of bargained prices as they transpired. Later, the basic reported bargained-price data can be rearranged, analyzed, criticized, and interpreted in various ways. For example, replacement costs can be added to the data or price-level adjustments can be made.[10] It is interesting to note the reprint of the 1936 article contained the following supplementary footnote which reaffirms Littleton's faith in the cost concept:

> Twenty years have passed since the above was written and more than twenty-five years since I expressed similar views in Accounting Review, September, 1929. Continued price inflation has greatly stimulated argumentation critical of continued use of historical cost. Although I have followed the recent literature closely, I still believe there is merit in a clear separation of "the techniques of computing and of criticizing."[11]

In 1939, Littleton suggested the presentation of supplementary information in conjunction with the financial statements. This suggestion was made as a desirable alternative to the elimination of cost figures by the substitution of new figures. He said:

> If "values," whether by appraisal, the cost-or-market tradition, or by index-number adjustments, are brought into the statements by account-keeping processes, the ultimate result is likely to be the complete submergence of the only

---

[10]A. C. Littleton, "Contrasting Theories of Profit," The Accounting Review, XI, No. 1 (March, 1936), 15, reprinted in Littleton, Essays, p. 296 (Hereinafter referred to as Littleton, "Contrasting Theories").

[11]Littleton, Essays, p. 296.

> objectively determined quantities that accounting
> has to work with--unamortized historical costs.
> However, if such "values" are brought to atten-
> tion by interpretative action, the objectively
> determined quantities are preserved, with
> illuminating additions.[12]

Littleton also supported his advocacy of the use of
cost price by reference to historical usage. Price, he
said, has been the traditional keynote of orthodox accounting. The record was always made of prices paid or received
in the past or of prices to be received in the future.[13]

Littleton, in 1938, wrote of historical cost, using
the term price-aggregates, as the vital information for investors. He stated emphatically that these facts represent
the pertinent data for investors:

> The information in question (for investors)
> needs to be based upon objective, verifiable
> facts in order to be dependable. The most suit-
> able objective, verifiable facts are price-
> aggregates of specific transactions between
> independent parties (historical costs). . . .
> There is only one price which meets these
> conditions: historical cost, including in the
> term both the price of acquiring services and the
> price of selling services. "Value" should there-
> fore be a term honored by complete omission from
> statements of accounting principles.[14]

---

[12]A. C. Littleton, "Suggestions for the Revision of
The Tentative Statement of Accounting Principles," The
Accounting Review, XIV, No. 1 (March, 1939), 60 (Herein-
after referred to as Littleton, "Suggestions of Accounting
Principles"), reprinted in Littleton, Essays, p. 202.

[13]A. C. Littleton, review of Henry W. Sweeney's
Stabilized Accounting, in The Accounting Review, XI, No. 3
(September, 1936), 298, reprinted in Littleton, Essays,
p. 303.

[14]A. C. Littleton, "The Relation of Function to
Principles," The Accounting Review, XIII, No. 3 (September,
1938), 237.

Paton and Littleton repeated the defense of cost in 1940. They asserted that the recognized inadequacy of recorded original cost or net book value as an expression of market value on a continuing basis should not cause anyone to conclude that values should be substituted for cost in the accounting records. The calculation of periodic income via the matching of revenues and costs was again stipulated as the most important and initial purpose of accounting. This standard scheme of income determination would necessarily require radical modification if estimated current market values were used to replace historical recorded costs. If market values were substituted, the periodic net income would reflect the effect of all write-ups and write-downs of the cost factors instead of the amount of revenues in excess of attaching costs[15] incurred.[16]

Paton and Littleton, repeating Littleton's earlier views, said that the substitution of opinion based current values for the objectively determined recorded cost data would result in less reliable and less dependable income figures. The substitution of values from appraisal, application of the cost-or-market rule, or the application of index numbers for recorded costs would result in the

---

[15]"Attaching Costs," Supra, pp. 137-40.

[16]W. A. Paton and A. C. Littleton, An Introduction to Corporate Accounting Standards (Chicago: American Accounting Association, 1940), pp. 123-26 (Hereinafter referred to as Paton and Littleton, Standards).

suppression of the most objectively determined and dependable data, the cost incurred. However, they viewed the presentation of such value data in a supplementary manner as an illuminating procedure. Cost was viewed as a necessary basing point for such supplementary presentations.[17] The very close similarity between the views expressed here by Paton and Littleton and the earlier statements by Littleton is noteworthy.

Littleton continued his argument for the use of cost rather than value in accounting and asserted that original costs must be maintained in the accounts. Cost is the starting point for the calculation of profit and any alternative to cost will conceal facts. He declared, for example, that the writedown of inventory values to market should not be allowed to submerge the cost figures related to the inventory. If costs are written down, all of the facts must be fully disclosed in order that the reader shall not be misled. The cost facts, Littleton stressed, must not be concealed.[18] All in all, Littleton persevered in his advocacy of cost. The following quotation is an emphatic illustration:

> How far can the wind of current conditions be permitted to change the established facts of accounting record? Little, if at all. Shall we

---

[17]Ibid.

[18]A. C. Littleton, "Questions on Accounting Standards," The Accounting Review, XVI, No. 4 (December, 1941), passim, 335-40.

124

> bury our heads in the sand of recorded trans-
> actions so we can ignore the wind? That is not
> a reasonable alternative.
>   We can hold to the established facts of actual
> enterprise transactions as recorded in the ac-
> counts; we can hold fast to cost until the counter-
> pressure becomes irresistible. When that time
> comes--that is, the time of real full-tide infla-
> tion--no accounting record will be useful, not
> even if it had been remolded daily by any scheme
> men can devise, or if it were left wholly un-
> touched in terms of transaction cost.[19]

In 1952, Littleton again acknowledged the possible

benefit to readers of financial statements of presentation

of supplementary data along with the data based upon cost.

In line with his view of the presentation of information to

management as an all important aspect of the function of

accounting, Littleton favored the use of any supplementary

or interpretative analyses which will aid in its fulfill-

ment. However, he strongly believed that substitution of

index number adjustments for cost in the statements is not

beneficial.[20]

In conjunction with general purpose statements

Littleton emphasized, as an important aspect of the account-

ing service function, the presentation of reports based

upon cost. He stressed that objective, verifiable invested

---

[19]Littleton, Essays, pp. 312-13, reprinted from
A. C. Littleton, "Fixed Assets and Accounting Theory," The
Illinois Certified Public Accountant, X, No. 3 (March,
1948), 14-15 (Hereinafter referred to as Littleton, "Fixed
Assets").

[20]A. C. Littleton, "Significance of Invested Cost,"
The Accounting Review, XXVII, No. 2 (April, 1952), 168
(Hereinafter referred to as Littleton, "Significance of
Cost"), reprinted in Littleton, Essays, p. 323.

cost information is vital to management and, therefore,
accounting has an obligation to provide the information.
It is vital, said Littleton, for management to be able to
look over and analyze its past efforts and invested cost is
the best measure of these efforts. To management the cost
is an investment, and as such, it is a calculated risk which
must be kept constantly in view as a basis for the retrospective judgment of the wisdom of the risk. The backward
look at prior decisions based upon objective data, said
Littleton, is an influential factor in decisions for the
future. Management is handicapped without this information.
The accounting service function also includes the duty to
guard the integrity of the cost data against internal modifications which might undermine objectivity and review-
ability. Littleton recognized that outside facts are, indeed, important to management. However, these outside facts
should not be allowed, by entry into the records, to distort
the statistical and historical recorded facts. Littleton
believed the explanation behind the development of standard
costing and budgeting procedures is that they allow and
stimulate analyses which compare actual invested costs with
estimated costs.[21] Littleton persevered in his emphasis of
these ideas. In summary, he specified that facts outside
the enterprise, transactions to which the entity is in no

---

[21]Littleton, "Significance of Cost," 168, 171, reprinted in Littleton, Essays, pp. 323, 326.

126

way a party, cannot properly induce a change in the facts already classified in the accounts. Until the entity has itself bought again, the prior purchase cost, the historical fact, must remain unchanged.[22]

In 1952, Littleton discussed the long existing and unsolved dilemma which faces accountants, the dilemma of cost and value. His statement demonstrates his constancy regarding the topic. He summarized his views as follows:

> In essence the issue behind any discussion of the significance of invested cost will always involve the dilemma of cost versus value as the clue to accounting function. . . . In the 1920's and 1930's appraisal write-ups and write-downs expressed the same dilemma as that being faced today. The dilemma was not broken; the same accounting choice again is, cost or value. There are new overtones now, but they do not change anything basic. Perhaps some action may soon be agreed upon. But it cannot constitute a solution since the word dilemma means that a choice among alternatives is to be faced. Whatever the choice expressed in a solution, it is likely to be temporary in effect, unless complex circumstances other than the choice selected shall make recurrence of the old dilemma impossible.
> Surely there is little probability of circumstances appearing that will permanently separate, or combine, cost and value. . . . Cost and value must somehow continue to live together.[23]

The necessity for maintaining the integrity of invested cost in the accounting data was clearly of deep concern to Littleton. He said the dilemma of choice between value and invested cost is a continuing problem

---

[22]Littleton, Structure, p. 48.

[23]Littleton, "Significance of Cost," 172-73, reprinted in Littleton, Essays, pp. 320-21.

which he believed probably defies a permanent solution. He concluded that it will be necessary to continue to deal with both cost and value in order to fulfill all of the needs of management. Value information is needed in the contemplation of the future as a supplement to the necessary invested cost data.

Cost in the Structure of Accounting Theory

In Littleton's Structure of Accounting Theory it is apparent that adherence to the cost concept is assumed. His view of cost is basic in the entire presentation. In a discussion of income determination as the center of gravity of accounting, he spoke of the real message found in the income statement which is based upon cost figures. The real story, he said, lies not in the final, net figure but in the kinds and relative amounts of investments made and in the kinds and relative amounts of proceeds derived.[24] The essence of enterprise accounting, the focal center of accounting, is the matching of these costs and revenues. This periodic determination of revenues and costs assignable thereto measures enterprise efforts and accomplishments.[25] Finally, historical cost is seen as an eminently logical basis for achieving the objectives of enterprise accounting.[26]

---

[24]Littleton, Structure, p. 24.

[25]Ibid., pp. 28, 34-35.

[26]Ibid., p. 210.

Historical Cost

The use of historical cost is implicit in Littleton's presentations, and he considered its use as very logical and dependable. He attributed the survival of the historical cost idea to its continued usefulness and not to its age.[27] He drew upon history to support its use; the Italian double entry procedures made use of historical cost not for anyone's convenience but because cost represents money capital invested and risked. The measured money outcome of the enterprise ventures were compared originally with historical cost in order to judge, after the fact, the wisdom of having taken the prior investment risk.[28]

In 1955, Littleton wrote that the prestige of historical cost is not dependent upon its relationship to the double entry system, because, in fact, the double entry system gains from its dependence upon historical cost. The original or paid costs, the invested costs, have always represented prices paid in business transactions. Historical cost enjoys prestige because it is a natural cost and is a figure representation of a known fact which has been recorded and associated with other known facts. The double entry process has gained prestige from its centuries of association with historical cost. The effectiveness of

---

[27]Littleton, "Significance of Cost," 171, reprinted in Littleton, Essays, p. 32.

[28]Littleton, "Variety of Income," 420, reprinted in Littleton, Essays, p. 288.

double entry as well as its acceptance is due, in large measure, to its useful and dependable classification of established, reviewable, quantitative facts in historical cost terms which are needed by enterprise management and/or owners.[29] The importance of historical cost for evaluating prior decisions was stipulated as follows:

> Historical cost, after all, only means "prior invested money price." By using this sort of basic record all parties at interest are better able to see, after the fact, the measure of prior decisions. If that backward look is denied them, as by the substitution of external current events not active within the enterprise, the essential function of accounting will have been negated and its outstanding characteristic will have been perverted.[30]

Littleton maintained and continued his stand against the introduction of price-index adjustments into the accounts as a substitute for historical cost. In 1956, he continued to insist upon the necessity for maintaining the unaltered historical record. He emphasized that use of price-index adjustments or any money prices other than invested costs related to the transactions would result in the insertion of irrelevant data into the record. This would allow an unethical element of misrepresentation into the accounts. In addition, said Littleton, verification of

---

[29]A. C. Littleton, "Prestige for Historical Cost," The Illinois Certified Public Accountant, XVII, No. 3 (March, 1955), 23 (Hereinafter referred to as Littleton, "Prestige for Cost"), reprinted in Littleton, Essays, p. 338.

[30]Littleton, Essays, p. 340, reprinted from Littleton, "Prestige for Cost," 25.

information is simplified if entries are restricted to those representing transactions of the enterprise. Transactions or economic events to which the enterprise is not a direct participant should not be recorded in the accounts of the enterprise. He declared that the businessman must of necessity concern himself with the actual price of goods purchased--not with the factors of causation behind the price. Supply and demand as causal factors are to be considered by the businessman; however, statistics reflecting change in supply and demand do not in fact modify the invested costs.[31]

Littleton believed that the essence of the cost basis of accounting is contained in two ideas which he stated as principles. These ideas are expressed in the principle of homogeneous data and the principle of objective determination. The first indicates the necessity of assuring that the data entering the accounts of an enterprise are homogeneous figures in terms of one money system. The second requires that data entering the accounts shall have been objectively determined and stated in prices resulting from bargaining of independent parties in contact with the enterprise. These principles, in Littleton's words, follow:

> Homogeneous Data. Accounting transactions
> derive their homogeneity . . . in part from the

---

[31]A. C. Littleton, "Choice Among Alternatives," The Accounting Review, XXXI, No. 3 (July, 1956), 367, reprinted in Littleton, Essays, pp. 355-56.

use of prices in terms of one money system and in part from the relevance of transactions to a given enterprise and its objectives.

Objective Determination. Transactions committed to the accounting record that have not been determined by the bargaining of independent parties in contact with the given enterprise . . . may make a report deceptive for lack of objective determination of all the raw data.[32]

Because historical cost is the prior invested money price, it is closely related to the money unit assumption. A few specific references to this assumption are appropriate at this point.

The Money Unit Assumption

The historical cost assumption rests in part upon the money unit assumption which is an important element of the accounting framework. In 1936, Littleton pointed out that a uniform money of account, which must not be confused with money having a stable value, is used to convert diverse elements into a quantitative and homogeneous form so that comparison and summation are possible.[33] Paton and Littleton stressed that accounting uses money price only because it is a convenient common denominator for expressing bargained exchanges involving diverse objects and services in homogeneous terms.[34]

---

[32]Littleton, Structure, p. 217.

[33]Littleton, "Contrasting Theories," 12, reprinted in Littleton, Essays, p. 196.

[34]Paton and Littleton, Standards, p. 13.

The explanatory statements made by accountants relating to the stable money unit assumption are frequently misinterpreted as representations of a limitation of accounting. Littleton, disturbed by these misunderstandings, endeavored to clarify the assumption and its basis in economic fact. Littleton pointed out, in 1948, that accountants' statements concerning the stable value of money of account are intended as a warning of the limited power of accounting figures to express value. He alleged that these assumptions had been misunderstood and skeptics had concluded that accounting figures are undependable because of the fact that prices do change. Littleton maintained that accountants must clarify the fact that money price is used to represent the diverse goods and services transactions of business. In addition, accountants must be prepared to illustrate that the money limitation is not an assumption but an economic fact fully supported by experience. Littleton said: "Money price does acceptably represent physical goods in our computations and our thinking. And that's all money price means in accounting."[35]

Littleton asserted that the belief that accounting money price is based upon an erroneous assumption of a stable dollar arises outside of accounting. He concluded that it is a falsification of the function of accounting to allow anyone, skeptic or not, to assume that accounting is

[35]Littleton, "Fixed Assets," 15-16, reprinted in Littleton, Essays, pp. 313-14.

a system for maintaining transactions facts in the records in tune with economic values.[36] It must be understood that the subject matter of accounting is inescapably economic and specific economic transactions are recorded by accountants in terms of money price.[37]

Littleton emphasized that the use of money price by accountants is a reflection of the relationship of many exchange conditions which make it impractical to separate the results of managerial efforts from the impact of economic change. Littleton argued convincingly that accountants do not assume a stable money situation. However, they have another assumption, which he wrote of as follows:

> To say someone assumes that the dollar has a stable value implies that he does not realize how money and goods are tied together, goods being the purchase price of money and money the purchase price of goods. Accountants and businessmen may not be economists, but they do not need any special kind of education to know and allow for this relationship. They do not assume stability; they know that neither money nor goods have stable value or unchanging prices.
>
> . . . .
>
> Accountants however do have an assumption. It is not that the value of the dollar is stable; it is not that managerial action is wholly responsible for the calculated amount of enterprise net profit. Accountants know that profit results from the interactions of management action and economic change. Their assumption is that an attempted separate calculation of the two causative forces is unwarranted. No suitable methodology is available for convincingly making such calculations. The application of index numbers to

---

[36]Littleton, "Fixed Assets," 16, reprinted in Littleton, Essays, p. 314.

[37]Littleton, Structure, pp. 8-9.

invested cost is presumed [by critics of accounting] to effect a true separation measurement of the two causes. Yet the separate results probably would not be more factual than those from a judgment-directed dividing of the final net profit figure into two parts estimated to reflect respectively the contribution of management and the effect of price change. [emphasis supplied] [38]

In 1963, Littleton reiterated his firm view and understanding that the use of money price as a common denominator to express exchange transactions is based upon business fact and usage. He pointed out that the quantities measured by money price come to accounting ready made. He positively stated his case that money price is not used to measure but to reflect market determined facts. He said:

Money is indeed a common denominator . . . but it is not accounting that makes it so. [emphasis supplied] Use of money is a necessity of trade, whether accounts are kept or not; accounting looks upon money price as a fact, not as a measurement function. It is confusing to speak of money of account as if account figures tell of measured value. Money price and the dollar sign are used in accounts to indicate a service rendered by a medium of exchange. [39]

Thus, the money unit assumption is an inherent element of Littleton's total concept of accounting. It

---

[38] Littleton, Structure, pp. 220-21, reprinted in A. C. Littleton, "Principles Under Challenge," The New York Certified Public Accountant, XXIV, No. 1 (January, 1954), 26-27, reprinted in Littleton, Essays, pp. 405-6.

[39] A. C. Littleton, book review of Robert T. Sprouse and Maurice Moonitz's A Tentative Set of Broad Accounting Principles for Business Enterprises, Accounting Research Study No. 3 (1962), in The Accounting Review, XXXVIII, No. 1 (January, 1963), 221.

underlies his conviction that recorded invested costs are the basic subject matter in accounting.

Basic Subject Matter--Cost

Cost, as the basic subject matter of accounting, is one of the recurrent themes evident in Littleton's work. Paton and Littleton also wrote of measured consideration or price-aggregates in the same context. The primary data of accounting, according to this view, is the measured consideration resulting from exchanges involving services acquired (costs, expenses) and services rendered (revenues, income). Measured consideration is better than value for representation of the quantification of exchanges. The buyer's and seller's mutual valuation determined at the time of exchange is expressed by the consideration named or the price-aggregates. It follows from this, that the price-aggregate records value at the moment of exchange and although the economic value might change afterwards the recorded price-aggregate does not change.[40] Paton and Littleton stipulated:

> The concept of accounting subject matter as price-aggregates resulting from exchanges thus becomes a much needed device for coordinating a number of related concepts. Instead of appearing as a confused mixture of elements--costs, assets, revenue, liabilities, investments, surpluses--accounting can be viewed as dealing with various aspects of a single subject matter. The

---

[40]Paton and Littleton, _Standards_, pp. 11-12.

unity of subject matter thus achieved harmonizes perfectly with the unity of purpose. . . .[41]

Paton and Littleton deplored lack of preciseness on the part of accountants in the use of various terms and recommended the consistent use of cost. They viewed cost as more meaningful and precise, as well as more useful, than any of the various terms which were being used. A good case was presented to support this conclusion and recommendation. They wrote as follows:

> "Cost," "expense," and "asset" are terms which have acquired traditional meanings that are not always helpful in expressing their underlying kinship. In the income statement the revenue deductions that are associated with inventoriable elements, and are viewed as attaching closely to the product, are often called "costs," while those revenue deductions that are viewed as less directly connected with the technical process of production and with the physical product are usually called "expenses." The factors acquired for production which have not yet reached the point in the business process where they may be appropriately treated as "costs of sales" or "expense" are called "assets," and are presented as such in the balance sheet. It should not be overlooked, however, that these "assets" are in fact "revenue charges in suspense" awaiting some future matching with revenue as costs or expenses.
> The common tendency to draw a distinction between cost and expense is not a happy one, since expenses are also costs in a very important sense, just as assets are costs. "Costs" are the fundamental data of accounting, and the term should therefore be used in its broadest sense. The word "cost" is substantially the equivalent of "price-aggregate" (unit price times quantity) or "bargained price." [emphasis supplied][42]

---

[41]Ibid., pp. 12-13.

[42]Ibid., p. 25.

Cost, viewed as the basic subject matter of accounting, is closely akin to the idea of the homogeneous nature of costs. Costs, as representations of classified exchange transactions, attach to a good or service and become indistinguishable from other costs related to the good or service.

Costs Attach--Homogeneous Costs

The costs attach concept of homogeneity of costs based upon objective, verifiable factual exchange transactions is also a dominant theme which is implicit in Littleton's total perspective. In 1929, Littleton wrote of the need for cost figures and referred to the flow of these costs in the recording process. The function of accounting, said Littleton, in all cases except that of credit granting, is to record all cost prices entering the business, to follow their course within the enterprise, and record their final exit from the business via sale or loss. This results in a balance sheet made up of ledger account balances of cost prices to be carried forward to future periods. Littleton adhered to this idea for which he gave W. A. Paton credit.[43]

The tracing of the flow of costs through the accounting records is visualized as a basic service of accounting under the costs attach concept. Accounts, said

---

[43]Littleton, "Value and Price," 154, reprinted in Littleton, Essays, p. 221.

138

Paton and Littleton in 1940, serve as adjuncts to the
economic process. The movements and conversions of goods
and services that take place constantly within the enterprise are recorded in the accounts by cost transfers.
Accounting uses price-aggregates or costs of exchange transactions to represent the materials and services of productive activity. They asserted that it is a basic concept of
accounting that costs can be marshaled into groups because
costs cohere when properly classified. This concept of co-
hesion of costs merely expresses the regrouping and reas-
sembling of costs to represent production effort. Costs
are assembled, by products or time intervals, to express
portions of the total effort exerted to bring about an
eventual advantageous sale.[44]

The idea of attaching cohesive costs is supported
by the idea of cost homogeneity. Paton and Littleton said
that all costs are homogeneous and rank abreast when viewed
in their essential relation to both revenues and assets.
The development of a reasonable scheme of matching costs
and revenues relies upon this total idea. Costs are not
recovered from revenues or matched to revenues in preferential order; all costs have equal rank in their relative
effect upon the total. Any overstressing of distinction
between various types of costs constitutes a questionable
ranking of costs. All costs necessary to the accomplishment

---

[44]Paton and Littleton, _Standards_, pp. 13-14.

of production or service of the business are on a common level of general significance. The type or kind of cost does not provide any basis for its ranking with other costs. Furthermore, all costs must be covered before any net income appears. Net income must be considered as the result of the entire range of operating activity, and it cannot be imputed to segments of revenue producing activity.[45] The tendency to improperly rank costs and to stress cost differentials was illustrated by Paton and Littleton with the story of the straw which broke the camel's back.[46]

The objective of attaching costs to a commodity or service, according to Littleton, is to allow a subsequent calculation to determine if revenues produce a profit. The function of accounting is distorted if a new cost is substituted for another in order to provide a normal profit expectancy in a later period when sale occurs; as, for example, the substitution of a new amount for an inventory cost during a period of sagging prices. In such a situation, instead of providing information as to profit on the sale, accounting only reflects whether profit is as it was previously planned to be.[47] It is clear that Littleton was

[45]Ibid., pp. 121-22.

[46]Supra, pp. 107-8.

[47]A. C. Littleton, "Correspondence: Inventory Pricing," The Journal of Accountancy, LXXXI, No. 4 (April, 1946), 334.

not in favor of injecting substituted cost prices into the accounts.

Accounting costs represent transactions of the enterprise in homogeneous money price terms. Costs are attached to accounts for products and services as they are received into the enterprise and follow those goods and services through the production process to ultimate disposition through sale. All of the homogeneous costs are of equal rank, not distinguishable from each other, and must all be covered before any net income can materialize.

Cost Recognition

Although there are three steps involved in accounting for cost, the recognition of cost is probably the most important as it significantly influences the effects of the other steps. The three stages are (1) initial recognition, measurement, and classification, (2) tracing subsequent regroupings and internal movements, and (3) final matching with the revenue of the present or some future fiscal period. The results of the initial cost recognition process materially influences the later treatment of the costs, particularly the crucial process of assignment to revenue. Paton and Littleton devoted a considerable amount of discussion to the cost recognition stage, because the effects of cost recognition standards extend beyond the initial application.[48] The first stage and the final stage, in which cost is matched with revenue of a given period, are the essential stages. Cost is first an acquisition price and later, after intermediate conversions, a deduction from revenue.[49] Until such time as revenue has been generated by the effort expended, costs merely accumulate and represent an investment. The cost recognition phase is distinct and has a definite impact upon revenues; therefore, the significance of particular costs must be perceived in the beginning in order that they may be soundly classified. The integrity of the classification must be maintained in order that the final matching can be error free.[50] The problem of cost recognition in cases of barter transactions may be especially difficult. In the case of barter, the amount of money implicit in the cash sales price of the goods exchanged establishes the cost to be recognized.[51]

Paton and Littleton were also concerned about the effect of discounts and allowances upon cost recognition. They said that discounts and other allowances must be deducted from cost in order to avoid overstatement of costs. They said fundamental concepts conflict with the practice

---

[48]Paton and Littleton, Standards, p. 25.

[49]Ibid., p. 66.

[50]Ibid., pp. 31-32.

[51]Ibid., p. 27.

142

of interpreting discounts taken as earned income. They
stipulated that income cannot be realized through the buy-
ing process; in general, cash discounts must be cost
adjustments.[52]

Paton and Littleton pointed out that the use of
cost to represent bargained prices applies to liabilities
as well as assets. It also applies to stock equity at the
time of original sale. In other words, the standard of
recorded cost must be applied to both the asset and equity
sides of the balance sheet.[53] Cost recognition as a procedure must be applied to all exchange transactions. The term
is all-inclusive and applies to liabilities and owners'
equities as well as to assets.

Exchange Transactions

The exchange transaction is the basis for accounting records and as such is an important aspect of the foregoing presentation regarding cost. The exchange transaction
is a part of the foundation of the historical cost concept.
In 1952, Littleton summarized his view of the interrelationship of the exchange transaction and historical cost as
follows:

> . . . it is beyond dispute that the data furnished
> to management by accounts over a great many gene-
> rations were data which we have come to call his-
> torical costs (or invested costs) meaning data

---

[52]Ibid., p. 29.

[53]Ibid., p. 37.

drawn from actual transactions of a given enterprise acting in open bargaining exchanges with
other people or other enterprises.[54]

Accounting transactions, Littleton said, are related to and based upon economic activities of a specific
enterprise which is performing economic services under
operating management. Therefore, it follows that conditions
outside of the enterprise, such as price changes, labor
supply, and competition, cannot be the basis for accounting
transactions. The economic transaction must have actually
transpired as a form of exchange by agreement between independent parties (one of which is the enterprise) in order
for it to provide support for an accounting entry. It was
clear to Littleton that unilateral determinations, such as
self-appraisal valuations, cannot be a basis for objective
accounting entries.[55] Accounting records must be confined
to transactions to which the enterprise is a bargaining
party. This provides records which reflect the results of
an indicated individual entity alone. Littleton succintly
expressed this idea in the following statement:

> If and whenever accounting for a given enter-
> prise loses contact with market-determined facts
> in situations relevant to that enterprise, it has
> lost its primary tie to objective reality in the
> accounting sense.[56]

---

[54]Littleton, "Significance of Cost," 169, reprinted
in Littleton, Essays, p. 324.

[55]Littleton, Structure, p. 48.

[56]Ibid., p. 182.

Financial statements are meaningful only if they are reflective of the individuality of the given enterprise. This is the important service of accounting, that is, to present information about one distinct entity.[57] Littleton was concerned with this aspect of accounting when he discussed the principle of homogeneous data and the principle of objective determination. He said that homogeneity of accounting transactions is derived from the use of one money system for pricing and from the relationship of transactions to a particular enterprise and its objectives.[58] Littleton said accounting reports may be deceptive if the transactions upon which they are based have not been determined objectively. It is necessary, he said, for recorded transactions to be based upon bargained transactions between the enterprise and outside independent parties.[59] These two necessary goals are the need to assure that the data in the records are homogeneous and the need to limit such data to that based upon unbiased conclusions. Littleton said that the essence of accounting based upon cost is found in these two objectives. Those who question the means of attaining these ends present a challenge to the cost basis, said Littleton. The objectives are challenged if the

---

[57]Ibid., p. 216.

[58]Littleton, Structure, p. 217, reprinted in Littleton, Essays, p. 408; Supra, pp. 130-31.

[59]Littleton, Structure, p. 217, reprinted in Littleton, Essays, p. 408.

figures for bargained transaction prices in terms of one money system are subject to doubt. In other words, if the money price attached to a closed transaction is doubted, and if current dollars or replacement prices as equivalents are suggested as substitutes, then the stated objectives are challenged.[60]

Remaining firm in his views, Littleton wrote, in 1963, concerning some of the postulates set out by another writer in Accounting Research Study No. 1.[61] Littleton was concerned about the postulates relating to market prices, exchange, and the unit of measure.[62] Littleton noted that the essence of the three postulates was directed toward (1) the idea that account data are based upon exchange-priced transactions, and (2) the idea that the transactions are stated in the common denominator of money price. He pointed out that accounting as we know it would be eliminated if the foundation for account categories were removed.

---

[60]Littleton, Structure, pp. 217-18, reprinted in Littleton, Essays, pp. 408-9.

[61]Maurice Moonitz, The Basic Postulates of Accounting, Accounting Research Study No. 1 (New York: American Institute of Certified Public Accountants, Inc., 1961).

[62]The postulates discussed: B2 Market Prices. Accounting data are based on prices generated by past, present, or future exchanges which have actually taken place or are expected to. A2 Exchange. Most of the goods and services that are produced are distributed through exchange, and are not directly consumed by the producers. A5 Unit of Measure. Money is the common denominator in terms of which the exchangeability of goods and services, including labor, natural resources, and capital, are measured.

146

In other words, account categories are based upon and inseparable from antecedent enterprise entities, antecedent enterprise management, and antecedent exchange-priced transactions. Without transactions, which reflect management's prior decision actions, there would be no substance for accounting. It is the transaction effect, not the money symbols, which become the experience of the enterprise; money merely symbolizes the transactions.[63]

In 1964, Littleton continued and extended his discussion of exchange-priced transactions. The following quotation exemplifies his final as well as his continuing view:

> At the heart of accounting is the nature of the exchange-priced transactions of business enterprises. Such events have several significant characteristics; because of these, accounting is what we know it to be: (1) the facts are realistic and actual because of the independence of the initiating parties, (2) the events are made quantitative by a price agreeable to the parties involved, (3) both the event and the agreed price have legal status, and (4) the transaction expresses managerial decisions initiated by separate parties, and thus provides, in summary with other transactions, a basis for reviewing the results of such managerial actions.[64]

Clearly, Littleton viewed the exchange transaction facts as the basis upon which accounting records must rest.

---

[63]A. C. Littleton, "The Heart of the Matter," The Illinois Certified Public Accountant, XXV, No. 4 (Summer, 1963), passim, 3-6.

[64]A. C. Littleton, "Integrity," The Illinois Certified Public Accountant, XXVI, No. 3 (Spring, 1964), 6-7.

He considered the bargained money price, the invested cost or historical cost, as the only proper amount to record as a reflection of the exchange transaction. Such invested cost is supported by an actual transaction event with a party outside of the business entity, and this, said Littleton, is a necessary characteristic of a quantitative entry.

Cost Terminology

It is evident that invested cost, or historical cost, was designated by a variety of terms in the articles written by Littleton through the years. It seems appropriate at this point to emphasize in summary form some of the views and ideas expressed by him over the span of years.

Cost Price

In 1929, as mentioned earlier, Littleton spoke of cost price as a refusal price. He said that the cost price results from a closed transaction and is an ascertained fact of pertinence in the later calculation of profit following actual exchange. The recorded cost price is not intended as a representation of value but as an investment cost outlay. The worth of the goods or services depends more upon future circumstances than upon past production acts.[65]

---

[65]Littleton, "Value and Price," 151-52, reprinted in Littleton, Essays, p. 222.

Recorded Costs

Littleton wrote, in 1929, of recorded costs and the effects of subsequent price changes upon them. Price changes which occur subsequent to entry of costs in the records cannot justify change in the accounting presentation of recorded costs. Until a sale of the goods has been made, there is no justification for a change in prior recorded costs.[66]

Measured Costs

Littleton stipulated that both revenues and costs must represent bona fide exchange transactions between independent parties and must be _measured_ by definite objective standards in order that accounting data may be dependable and relevant. Cash disbursed is not the objective test for measured cost; for example, the credit system may provide goods and services prior to payment. Unsupported judgment cannot form the basis for cost measurement; the best obtainable objective evidence must be used. An objective test for revenues will result in the same figure as the figure used for cost by the bargaining party.[67] In 1940, Paton and Littleton also emphasized these points. In addition, they spoke of the flow of costs as quantitative expressions or

[66]Littleton, "Value and Price," 152, reprinted in Littleton, _Essays_, p. 223.

[67]Littleton, "Suggestions of Accounting Principles," 59, reprinted in Littleton, _Essays_, p. 200.

measures of exchange transactions which represent business activity. Accounting must make truthful and significant measurements of the continuous flow of business activity through the allocation of costs and revenues between the present and the future. A systematic tracing of costs (attached) places business effort and accomplishment in contrast.[68]

Measured Consideration

Paton and Littleton used measured consideration in some cases instead of measured costs; however, the intent was the same. They set forth that measured consideration is more appropriate than value to indicate the type of information which makes up the subject matter of accounting. In the same vein, they said that the recorded price-aggregate is the best means for representing in homogeneous terms the measured consideration of varied transactions.[69]

Price-Aggregate

Paton and Littleton continued the discussion of measured consideration by asserting that price-aggregates rather than costs best represent the measured consideration. Cost was passed over because it is not as functional for sales as for purchases. They sought a word which would cover both directions of an exchange. Cost is inadequate as a means of saying the same thing about a purchase and a

---

[68]Paton and Littleton, Standards, pp. 10-11.

[69]Ibid., pp. 11-12.

sale; on the other hand, price-aggregates has wide usefulness.[70] They advocated the use of objectively determined price-aggregates as representative of the judgment of two bargaining parties motivated by self-interest. The ideas expressed are very similar to the ones set forth by Littleton in March, 1939.[71] The vital point is to recognize the importance of the mutual acceptance of a price-aggregate by all parties to an exchange as the quantitative representation of an objectively determined and agreed upon price. In 1953, Littleton elaborated the same view of price-aggregate and its relationship to money price. Price-aggregates are expressions which can represent either a sale or a purchase in terms of unit price multiplied by the number of physical units in an exchange transaction.[72]

Measure of Actual Cost and Implied Cash Cost

Measured actual cost and implied cash cost were used by Paton and Littleton in connection with the sale of capital stock, the discovery of natural resources, the receipt of a donated asset, or some similar transaction. The proper measure of actual cost in cases of enterprise exchange in which a cost price is not stated is the amount of money which would have been raised through a bargained-price sale.

---

[70]Ibid., p. 12.

[71]Ibid., p. 26.

[72]Littleton, Structure, p. 9.

An implied cash cost may be used in some such cases;
however, the suggestion to use implied cash cost is not intended to encourage the insertion of hopes, expectations,
and estimates into the asset records. The suggestion is
made only for the instance in which a dependable starting
point is required for resources acquired under extraordinary
circumstances, such as donation or discovery, which have a
clear cut commercial value.[73]

Aggregate Bargained Price, Invested Cost, Historical Cost and Original Cost

Littleton's topic, in 1952, was invested cost. He
discussed a number of possible phrases to represent the
settled amount of a bargained exchange or the amount of actual cost incurred. He suggested aggregate bargained price
as a definitive term. He noted that historical cost and
original cost each indicate accomplished events and tend to
negate any idea that accounts represent current or future
values. He designated invested cost, which signifies bargained price, as the best phrase to fulfill the requirements. He asserted that when invested is attached to cost,
it signifies several thoughts; it indicates that there has
been a meeting of the minds between two negotiating parties
and that each was satisfied as to the advantage derived
from the exchange. He said it also represents a quantitative dollar amount which justifies initiation of a new

---

[73]Paton and Littleton, _Standards_, pp. 27-29.

entry is each party's accounts. In addition, invested cost can represent a liability or income as well as an asset or an expense.[74] In 1953, Littleton elaborated upon the same idea. Historical costs, based upon actual exchanges of the past stated in commonly understood dollar terms, are meaningful to investors, creditors, and management. The dollars of cost involved in past bargained exchanges is of benefit to interested parties because these represent investment of capital savings for production to the investor, creditor, and management.[75]

Cost Dollars

Littleton related the need for information in terms of dollars concerning the facts of the enterprise to the going concern idea of the entity. The entity as a groundwork idea of accounting creates a need for accounts representing only events to which the enterprise has been a transacting party. This rules out the use of any costs other than those resulting from enterprise transactions. Secondly, the going concern idea stipulates that the business is expected to continue; therefore, dissolution because of liquidation or bankruptcy is not planned. Thus, a distinct entity which is a going concern produces a requirement

---

[74]Littleton, "Significance of Cost," 171-72, reprinted in Littleton, Essays, pp. 321-22.

[75]Littleton, Structure, p. 173.

for records based upon cost dollars.[76]   Cost is used in the
sense of a purchase price, invested cost, historical cost,
original cost, or bargained exchanges expressed in money
prices.

The same viewpoint as to cost is evident throughout
the period during which Littleton wrote. Variations in
terminology do not reveal any change of viewpoint. An apparent effort was made to support the cost view by elaboration of terminology and explanations of meanings.

Summary

Cost is, indeed, a predominant theme in Littleton's
writings. He stipulated that the matching process, the
basic purpose of accounting, depends strongly upon the use
of cost figures. Cost is an established fact and is definite and unchangeable. Cost information is vital for
management to take a backward look at prior risks taken and
efforts made in order to make a retrospective appraisal.
For retrospective appraisal management needs data which are
objective, verifiable, and definite. Cost data fulfill
these requirements in terms of prior invested money prices.

Littleton considered the exchange transaction as
the basis for accounting transaction entries. The exchange
transaction, he said, represents the realities of the business entity; it is based upon economic acts and facts. The

---

[76] Ibid., pp. 207, 210

verification of information is simplified if only enterprise transactions are recorded.

He attributed the survival of historical cost to its continued usefulness as the basis for recording business transactions. He said historical cost had always been management's basis for evaluating prior investment risk; as such, historical cost has continued to be useful to management. Cost is useful because it is a quantitative expression of and measure of exchange transactions which represent business activity. Cost signifies the meeting of minds between two parties, each of whom is satisfied with the determined and quantified dollar amount.

Littleton used various terms for cost over the period during which he wrote although his viewpoint conveyed was consistent. In some discussions he used measured consideration and/or price-aggregate resulting from exchanges. He spoke continuously of invested cost. He also wrote of the costs attach concept to represent the homogeneous nature of costs based upon dependable, objective, verifiable, factual exchange transactions. All of these homogeneous costs are considered as equal in rank for charges against revenues; costs cannot be given any rank or preferential treatment in the matching process. In all discussions of cost he spoke of it as basic to the process of matching revenues and expenses. In fact, he said, the essence of accounting based upon cost depends upon costs being not only objectively determined but also homogeneous.

Littleton stated that although historical cost is the logical basis upon which to maintain accounting records, there is a continual dilemma of cost versus value which is probably unsolvable. He said that the choice among alternatives (between cost and value) is to be faced constantly. He believed that there is no way to combine the two or to separate them; therefore, the dilemma is continuing and unsolvable. Littleton believed that value is dependent upon supply and demand and other factors of the market place and is, therefore, undependable. Value should be omitted from the discussion of accounting and accounting principles. It should also be omitted from accounting records because accounting has a record function, not a valuation function. Accounting is concerned with value in use, or cost, and not with value in exchange. Furthermore, value is not supported by an exchange transaction. Value can be reflected in the accounting records only by injecting transactions of a nonentity nature into the records. This involves recording economic factors, such as price-level adjustments, which are completely outside the experience records of the business enterprise. In other words, transactions to which the entity is not a transacting party must not be recorded. In short, Littleton believed accounting records must be confined to the function of reflecting entity transactions.

He believed that in order for the records to reflect objective reality the transactions must be recorded at cost.

Finally, Littleton said that a money price is used to record cost because it reflects market facts and business facts. Money price is not an accounting assumption but a common denominator used to express exchange transactions. This common denominator is based upon the facts and usages of business. The quantities expressed by money prices come to accounting ready-made in the form of business transactions between bargaining parties.

CHAPTER V

BASIC APPROACH AND VIEWS ON PRINCIPLES

There was little accord among accountants during the early twentieth century concerning principles of accounting. In fact, very little had been written about accounting principles or theory. The paucity of published materials in this area indicates that little concern about principles had been demonstrated. However, there was an awareness developing of the need for reflection upon the problems of accounting. It appears evident, as indicated by materials presented in Chapter II,[1] that Littleton entered the profession at a time when there were rapidly growing demands for more income information and more adequate financial disclosure. In addition, it is apparent that there was also a need for more uniform agreement about acceptable practices. There was an equally pressing need for the development of some guiding precepts for accounting.

Littleton's work reflects his recognition of many of the prevalent problems of his era. Littleton confronted the needs by devoting serious attention to the discussion of and development of a theory, as well as principles, of

---

[1]_Supra_, pp. 15-23.

accounting. He also recognized the need for clear thinking about accounting terminology, objectives, and practice.

Littleton's basic approach or ideology and his related views on principles are the areas of concern in this chapter. These two areas are closely related and each area influences the other; Littleton's views on principles are closely connected with and influenced by his basic approach. The topics selected for discussion are therefore closely related and overlap with each other. For example, the section on interdependence of theory and practice is actually almost inseparable from discussion of theory as a distillation of practice based upon actions.

Basic Approach to Accounting Theory

Very briefly, Littleton's basic approach to accounting theory and manner of thinking of accounting theory is presented as a foundation. Each of the brief points made appears to be basic to his approach to the study of and development of accounting theory.

Accounting is practical and the ideology of accountancy grew out of experience with using accounting methods.[2] Littleton adhered to the view that accounting is a practical art; as such, it is based upon a good deal of

----

[2]A. C. Littleton, "Significance of Invested Cost," The Accounting Review, XXVII, No. 2 (April, 1952), 170 (Hereinafter referred to as Littleton, "Significance of Cost"), and reprinted in A. C. Littleton, Essays on Accountancy (Urbana, Illinois: University of Illinois Press, 1961), p. 325 (Hereinafter referred to as Littleton, Essays).

objectivity. He said that accounting has a practical slant
which is based upon the necessity to serve business management. Related to the idea that accounting is practical is
the idea that accounting is action.[3] Accounting actions, in
turn, are based upon objectives. Accounting actions are
purposeful because they are based upon objectives, and the
actions become intelligible primarily through a relationship
to their foundation of objectives.[4]

Related to the idea that accounting ideology grew
out of experience with using accounting methods is the belief that accounting methodology came before accounting
theory. This leads to and is interrelated with the corresponding idea that the principles of accounting theory are
based upon practice and experience.[5] Based upon these
ideas, Littleton stressed that principles of accounting
theory and accounting practices are interdependent and each
is necessary to the other; neither can stand alone.[6] The
principles of accounting theory express significant

---

[3]A. C. Littleton, Structure of Accounting Theory
(Menasha, Wisconsin: George Banta Publishing Company for
American Accounting Association, 1953), p. 1 (Hereinafter
referred to as Littleton, Structure).

[4]Littleton, Structure, pp. 124-25, and Littleton,
Essays, p. 399.

[5]A. C. Littleton, "The Uses of Theory," The Journal
of Accountancy, LXVII, No. 4 (April, 1939), 227-29 (Hereinafter referred to as Littleton, "Uses of Theory"), and
reprinted in Littleton, Essays, pp. 375-76.

[6]Littleton, Structure, p. 1.

relationships between directed accounting action and the
reason(s) for that action.[7]

Theory is a body of doctrine made up of beliefs,
explanations, and justifications related to an area of practice; interrelated and consistent principles may or may not
act as headlines for the theory. This is a broad concept
of the nature of theory and involves the idea that the body
of doctrine can include principles but will stand without
them. Principles are the compact headlines of the body of
doctrine.[8] Principles are interrelated and must be consistent with each other. If principles are not consistent,
the body of doctrine will lack cohesiveness and be impossi-
ble to interpret.[9] Littleton used inductive reasoning to
derive accounting principles.[10] This inductive process is,
of course, connected with the view that accounting is based
upon practice, action, and experience. Deductive reasoning,

---

[7]A. C. Littleton, "Inductive Reasoning in Accounting," The New York Certified Public Accountant, XX, No. 8
(August, 1950), 450 (Hereinafter referred to as Littleton,
"Inductive Reasoning"), and reprinted in Littleton, Essays,
p. 385, and Littleton, Structure, p. 188.

[8]A. C. Littleton, "Three Audit Principles," The
Journal of Accountancy, LXXXIII, No. 4 (April, 1947), 280
(Hereinafter referred to as Littleton, "Three Principles"),
and reprinted in Littleton, Essays, p. 387, and Littleton,
Structure, p. 175.

[9]A. C. Littleton, "The Relation of Function to
Principles," The Accounting Review, XIII, No. 3 (September,
1938), 239 (Hereinafter referred to as Littleton, "Function
to Principles"), and reprinted in Littleton, Essays,
p. 306.

[10]Littleton, Structure, passim, Chapters 10-11.

said Littleton, can be used to test accounting principles. Important relationships can be traced deductively from an inductively derived primary concept back to the originating rules based upon particulars.[11] Littleton was convinced that principles of double entry bookkeeping form a part of the principles of accounting.[12]

This, briefly, is an overview of Littleton's basic approach to accounting theory and manner of thinking of accounting theory. These capsule thoughts form a basis for an expanded discussion.

Definitions and Uses of Terminology

There was a noticeable lack of consensus about accounting terminology at the time Littleton began his career. It is clear that Littleton was keenly aware of this deficiency. This section is devoted to a presentation of terms used by Littleton as well as the role of these terms in the expression of Littleton's views. It seems to be in order to introduce Littleton's statement concerning a definition. The statement is followed by his own illuminating examples:

---

[11]A. C. Littleton, "Classified Objectives," The Accounting Review, XXIV, No. 3 (July, 1949), 281 (Hereinafter referred to as Littleton, "Classified Objectives"), and reprinted in Littleton, Essays, p. 398.

[12]A. C. Littleton, "The Search for Accounting Principles," The New York Certified Public Accountant, XXVIII, No. 4 (April, 1958), 250 (Hereinafter referred to as Littleton, "Search"), and reprinted in Littleton, Essays, p. 181.

A _definition_ is a verbal statement distinguishing several attributes; a statement setting
limits to a category. Drawing up a definition
calls upon a strong sense of differences among
unlike things and of similarities among like
things. Both similarities and differences are
used in a well constructed definition: For a
definition tells us in effect, (1) that the thing
defined is part of a larger group (called genus)
and (2) that the thing defined is different from
other items in that group in certain designated
particulars (called differentiae).

Some examples will illustrate the idea. The
constituent elements are here separated by diago-
nals. Business capital / is property / invested
in an enterprise / by owners or lenders. Business
income / is property / derived from sales to
customers. Note that the following are not definitions: in accounting, capital means assets;
income is derived from customers.[13]

Concepts

Concepts are based upon broad assumptions which are
difficult to express in brief terms. In 1940, Paton and
Littleton wrote of concepts, or propositions. They said
that the fundamental concepts or propositions of accounting
are in themselves assumptions in considerable measure or are
based upon assumptions which cannot be conclusively demonstrated or proven.[14] Littleton elaborated upon concepts

---

[13]Littleton, _Structure_, pp. 144-45.

[14]W. A. Paton and A. C. Littleton, _An Introduction
to Corporate Accounting Standards_ (Chicago: American
Accounting Association, 1940), p. 21 (Hereinafter referred
to as Paton and Littleton, _Standards_). In 1958, Littleton
made a footnote comment concerning assumptions: " . ...
The present writer is beginning to wonder whether most, if
not all, of the accounting ideas usually labeled 'assumptions' would be more closely described as 'the better
choices among alternatives.'" Found in Littleton, "Search,"
250, and reprinted in Littleton, _Essays_, p. 181.

behind terminology at various times. He said that the concept behind a term is more important than the words used to state it. This is true because a concept involves purposes and limitations which cannot be suitably reflected by a phrase of a few words.[15]

A concept is a mental pattern of related ideas which finally become an integrated complex idea after many relevant instances become known. Concepts are much more inclusive than principles or definitions and include recognition of some aspects of what a thing is not. A concept could be viewed as a group of separate principles bound into a group.[16] Concepts constitute experience tested support, in the form of explanations and justifications, for fundamental principles.[17] Basic accounting concepts are ideas essential to understanding accounting functions and limitations.[18]

Convention

An accounting convention is an established fact of usage or a customary practice founded upon tradition. The term convention was not used in earlier accounting

[15]Littleton, "Significance of Cost," 171, and reprinted in Littleton, Essays, p. 321.

[16]Littleton, Structure, p. 148.

[17]A. C. Littleton, "'An Inventory of Principles,'" The Illinois Certified Public Accountant, XXVII, No. 4 (Summer, 1965), 15 (Hereinafter referred to as Littleton, "Inventory of Principles").

[18]A. C. Littleton, "The Significance of Interrelated Concepts in Accounting," The International Journal of Accounting Education and Research, II, No. 1 (Fall, 1966), 28.

literature. Convention did not appear as a listing in a 1931 publication on accounting terminology.[19] This term has gradually come to have a somewhat specialized meaning in accounting. Kohler's current definition is:

> A statement or rule of practice which, by common consent, express or implied, is employed in the solution of a given class of problems or guides behavior in a certain kind of situation. A convention as distinct from an _axiom_ (a general statement the truth of which is not questioned, Kohler, p. 50), may be said to exist when it is known that an alternative, equally logical rule or procedure is available but is not used because of considerations of habit, cost, time, or convenience. . . . Placing debits on the left and credits on the right of an account supplies [an] . . . example. The adoption of a particular convention may even be a historical accident, but once adopted, a convention acquires value as a means of communication and cooperation. . . .[20]

Littleton used the term convention as Kohler defines it. He said that the word effectively avoids the sense of universality attached to principle.[21] To Littleton, an accounting convention is an established fact of usage; a customary practice founded upon historical usage.[22] In addition, a convention is a customary rule which has been

---

[19]American Institute of Accountants, _Accounting Terminology_ (New York: The Century Co., 1931).

[20]Eric L. Kohler, _A Dictionary for Accountants_ (Third Edition; Englewood Cliffs, New Jersey: Prentice-Hall, Inc., 1963), p. 136.

[21]A. C. Littleton, "Inventory Variations," _The Journal of Accountancy_, LXXII, No. 1 (July, 1941), 9 (Hereinafter referred to as Littleton, "Variations"), and reprinted in Littleton, _Essays_, pp. 498-99.

[22]Littleton, "Inductive Reasoning," 450, and reprinted in Littleton, _Essays_, p. 384, and in Littleton, _Structure_, p. 189.

somewhat arbitrarily established by common consent. In
fact, said Littleton, sometimes a convention may merely pre-
serve a tradition which has lost its reason for being.[23]

Directive

Littleton said that a slight change in phraseology
will convert a statement of an accounting convention into
an accounting directive or instruction. This ties the definitions of convention and directive together. The directive is used to assure the achievement of the objective of
the convention. However, a directive alone lacks a stated
reason.[24]

Reason

Littleton defined reason as an aim or objective
that gives direction to action or provides an explanation
of some aspect of accounting. He viewed a reason as the
basis for accounting actions which are carried out in line
with conventions via directives.[25]

Rules

To Littleton, rules are a combination of directives
and justifying reasons; rules are authoritarian in nature
and form a basis for conformity by dictation of a

---

[23]Littleton, Structure, p. 142.

[24]Littleton, "Inductive Reasoning," 450, and reprinted in Littleton, Structure, p. 187, and Littleton,
Essays, p. 384.

[25]Littleton, Structure, p. 145.

procedure.[26] A fully stated rule of action should include
a statement of a directive plus its justifying or clearly
implied reason.[27] Littleton believed that reasons for accounting actions are like accounting objectives, ends, or
goals. The directed actions are the ways and means of
carrying out intentions. This joining of justification to
directives gives a rule a close relationship to a principle.[28] A fully stated accounting rule, said Littleton, is
often close to a phrasing suitable for compactly expressing
an accounting principle.[29] He expanded his idea somewhat in
an introductory paragraph added to the Essays on Accountancy
version of the article on "Inductive Reasoning in Accounting." He stated that the terms conventions, rules, and
principles have more similarities than differences in conno-
tation. A variation of phraseology could cause the idea
behind any one of the terms to be reflected in another of
the terms.[30]

---

[26]A. C. Littleton, "High Standards of Accounting,"
The Journal of Accountancy, LXVI, No. 2 (August, 1938), 99
(Hereinafter referred to as Littleton, "High Standards"),
and reprinted in Littleton, Essays, p. 380.

[27]Littleton, "Inductive Reasoning," 450, and reprinted in Littleton, Essays, pp. 384-85, and in Littleton,
Structure, pp. 187-88.

[28]Littleton, Structure, p. 169.

[29]A. C. Littleton, "Inductive Reasoning in Account-
ing - II," The New York Certified Public Accountant, XX,
No. 11 (November, 1950), 646 (Hereinafter referred to as
Littleton, "Inductive Reasoning, II"), and reprinted in
Littleton, Structure, p. 200.

[30]Littleton, Essays, p. 385.

Littleton believed that a rule could be converted into a principle. Littleton's concept of a principle, covered in a later section, was closely related to and dependent upon his views of conventions, rules, reasons, and directives. A principle can be derived, according to Littleton, by stating the directive portion of a rule in such a way that it represents a means or method of transforming an objective or aim into accounting action.[31]

Littleton believed that a principle should express a significant relationship. He said that there is a significant relationship discernible between any directed accounting action and the reason for that action. To be expressed in an accounting principle the significant relationship would usually have to be of the type that is maintained between a desirable end and/or result and an appropriate means to that result.[32]

Standards

Standards establish a high but attainable level of guideposts to truth, honesty, and fairness for accounting procedures and reports. Littleton wrote at considerable length at various times regarding standards. As early as 1938 he distinguished between rules and standards.

---

[31]Littleton, "Inductive Reasoning," 453, and reprinted in Littleton, Structure, p. 191.

[32]Littleton, "Inductive Reasoning," 450-51, and reprinted in Littleton, Structure, p. 188, and Littleton, Essays, p. 385.

Whereas rules establish a basis for conformity, standards provide a point of departure, when and if departure is clearly justifiable by circumstances and reported as such. Standards serve as guideposts to truth, honesty, and fair dealing in accounting practices and reports. A standard directs a high but attainable level of action without precluding justifiable variations. Littleton asserted that it should be understood that once an accounting standard is properly stated it becomes a guide, not a control. He stipulated that although a departure from standard is possible, it is the responsibility of the advocate of variations to justify such deviation. The mere desire of an individual or convenience for management do not constitute acceptable reasons for departure from standard. Vague conservatism, persuasiveness to investors, or timely expediency do not constitute a sufficiently sound basis for variation.[33] Littleton advocated an authoritative statement of accounting standards by professional organizations to aid and guide accounting practitioners.[34]

In Paton and Littleton's 1940 monograph, they also referred to accounting standards as guideposts to fair dealing in the midst of flexible rules and techniques. The term standards was used advisedly, they said, as the

---

[33]Littleton, "High Standards," 99-100, and reprinted in Littleton, _Essays_, pp. 380-81.

[34]Littleton, "High Standards," 103-4, and Littleton, "Uses of Theory," 231.

American Accounting Association committee had used the term advisedly in its 1936 Tentative Statement.[35] They reasoned that principles generally suggest a universality and degree of permanence unrealistic in an institution dedicated to the service of human beings. Their declared intention was to emphasize the usefulness of standards in the indication of an integrated conception of the function of accounting. They viewed this function of accounting to be the provision of a means of significantly expressing business financial facts.[36]

Paton and Littleton said that the essence of a scheme of accounting standards is the explanation of what the accounting reports are intended to tell of the financial position and results of operation. The standards should cover fundamental conceptions and general approaches to the report presentations rather than specific questions concerning precise captions, subdivisions, and estimating methods. Although standards are not accounting procedures, they guide toward such procedures or toward rules to apply to specific situations. Rules of procedure, according to Paton and Littleton, are authoritarian, inspire conformity, direct performance, apply to details, and provide for choice among alternative methods.[37]

---

[35]Littleton, "Function to Principles," 234.

[36]Paton and Littleton, Standards, pp. 2-5.

[37]Ibid., pp. 4-5.

170

There was a recognized need for a set of more precise and widely accepted standards to guide accountants in their practices and procedures. Paton and Littleton expressed the opinion that a codification of rules was unnecessary and fruitless; however, standards should be stated as useful guides to procedure over a wide area of application.[38] Their discussion echoed earlier statements by Littleton. In 1941, Littleton continued to promote the development of guiding standards which would be useful to all corporate accountants without standardizing methods, regimenting opinions, or injecting outside control over enterprise accounting practices.[39]

Littleton gave several reasons why the formulation of accounting standards or accounting principles ought to receive extensive consideration. He lamented the tendency to use the term principles loosely to describe procedures. He also was concerned about the unfortunate tendency to accept judicial dicta as an exposition of basic accounting ideas. He apparently believed there were too many different practical procedures applied to represent similar conditions. Finally, he thought the independent auditor could

[38]Ibid., passim, pp. 2-6.

[39]Littleton, "Variations," 7, and reprinted in Littleton, Essays, p. 497.

and should include a critical examination of financial
policy as a part of his duties.[40]

Littleton favored the use of standards, which
provides for possible variations, over the use of principles or rules. He recognized and stressed the standard as
a point of departure, a first preference, from which variations are possible. Littleton suggested that the possible
variations from the standard could be classified into a
graded sequence which could include necessary variations,
acceptable variations, questionable variations, and re-
jected variations. These variations would indicate the
limitations of acceptability inherent in a particular
standard.[41] A standard, said Littleton, provides a basis
for comparing the relative desirability of several lines of
action. Furthermore, the concept of accounting standards
includes a number of useful features. There is a recognition of the existence of exceptions as well as an indicated
sequence of preference among alternatives. Lastly, certain
alternatives are clearly indicated as undesirable.[42]

---

[40]Littleton, "Variations," 9, and reprinted in
Littleton, Essays, p. 498.

[41]Littleton, "Variations," passim, 9-12, 15, and
reprinted in Littleton, Essays, passim, pp. 499, 502-3.

[42]A. C. Littleton, "Questions on Accounting Standards," The Accounting Review, XVI, No. 4 (December, 1941),
331 (Hereinafter referred to as Littleton, "Questions"),
and reprinted in Littleton, Essays, pp. 378-79.

Littleton doubted that standards, which are not unchanging, could be established by authority. The acceptance or establishment of standards must come about by usage.[43] Standards do not confine practice, but they guide decisions toward the best practice without attaching penalties when the best cannot be reasonably attained.[44]

OBJECTIVES

Littleton was concerned about the objectives of accounting, and the topic appeared many times in the material written by him over the period of years. In 1937, he wrote of the chief problems of accounting. When the article was reprinted in 1961, he referred to the problems as objectives.[45]

The Pyramid of Objectives[46]

In July, 1949, Littleton wrote of a pyramid of objectives to portray in a graphic pattern the inductive approach to accounting thought. The pyramid has a broad base representing accounting actions and slopes sharply to

---

[43]Littleton, "Questions," 331-32, and reprinted in Littleton, Essays, pp. 379-80.

[44]Littleton, Structure, pp. 162-63.

[45]A. C. Littleton, "Concepts of Income Underlying Accounting," The Accounting Review, XII, No. 1 (March, 1937), 18-20 (Hereinafter referred to as Littleton, "Concepts of Income"), and reprinted in Littleton, Essays, p. 218.

[46]See Exhibit III, Pyramid of Accounting Objectives.

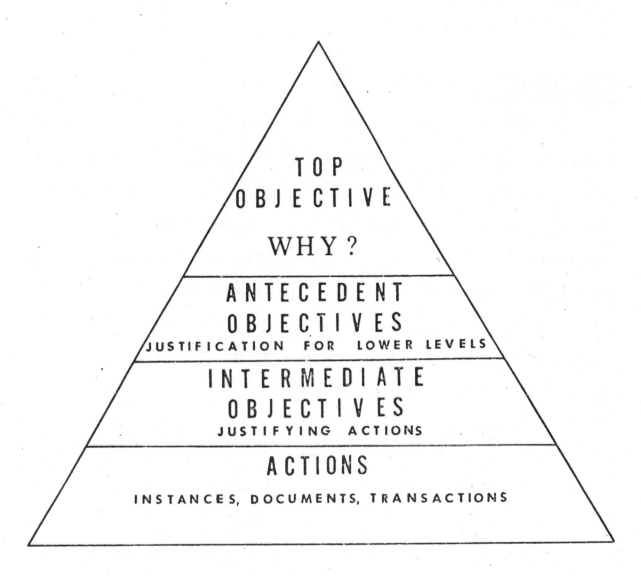

EXHIBIT III.   PYRAMID OF ACCOUNTING OBJECTIVES

Adapted from: A. C. Littleton, Structure of Accounting Theory (Menasha, Wisconsin: George Banta Publishing Company for Accounting Association, 1953), Chapter 7, pp. 116-31.

174

a peak which represents the top objective of accounting.

Above the action base are antecedent objectives which

gradually build up to the top focal objective, which justi-

fies all of the lower objectives and their related

actions.[47]

The Pyramid's Foundation--Business Transactions/Accounting Actions

The foundation of the pyramid proper is made up of

a broad foundation of enterprise transactions which support

the accounting actions. This broad foundation represents

the many particulars of business enterprise activities, the

actions, instances, documents, and transactions involving

properties, promises, and rights. These are the particulars

of business activities which must be molded by the purposes

and actions of accounting to provide an information service

of a primary nature to business.[48]

Littleton viewed accounting as an action process

which deals with the transaction data in order to portray

the breadth and depth of enterprise action. Accounting ac-

tions are made intelligible by their motivating objectives.

Littleton specified a clearly perceivable sequence of six

---

[47]A. C. Littleton, "Classified Objectives," The
Accounting Review, XXIV, No. 3 (July, 1949), 281 (Hereinafter referred to as Littleton, "Classified Objectives"),
and reprinted in Littleton, Essays, p. 398, and in
Littleton, Structure, p. 124.

[48]Littleton, "Classified Objectives," 282, and reprinted in Littleton, Essays, pp. 398-99, and in Littleton
Structure, p. 124.

areas of purposeful accounting action which progresses

toward the accounting objectives and purposes:

1. pricing business transactions
2. analyzing transactions into debits and credits
3. posting debits and credits into ledger accounts
4. making periodic adjusting and closing entries
5. preparing financial statements
6. auditing financial statements.[49]

Intermediate Objectives-- Justification for Actions

The next higher section of the pyramid represents

the objectives which justify the actions represented in the

lower sections. These intermediate objectives were listed

by Littleton as follows:

1. to reduce objects and events to price data
2. to transform price data into account data
3. to compress the mass of account data by using quasi-statistical means (categories)
4. to reassign, as between time periods, the data previously classified into accounts only as to qualitative characteristics
5. to organize periodic data into interpretative summary report statements
6. to examine into [sic] the adequacy of the disclosure made by accounting report statements.[50]

Antecedent Objectives--Reasons Justifying Intermediate Objectives

Littleton wrote also of the antecedent objectives

which make up the reasons for justifying intermediate

---

[49]Littleton, "Classified Objectives," 282, and reprinted in Littleton, Essays, pp. 398-99, and in Littleton Structure, p. 124.

[50]Littleton, "Classified Objectives," 282-83, and reprinted in Littleton, Essays, pp. 399-400, and in Littleton, Structure, p. 125.

176

objectives. The pyramid is built upward by a layer of antecedent objectives or reasons for the intermediate objectives below. Littleton listed these objectives as follows:

1. to represent greatly diversified economic events and objects (transactions) in a manner that will permit them to be marshaled into a variety of useful calculations
2. to prepare economic data to enter a particular pattern of quasi-statistical classification (double-entry accounts)
3. to substitute a small number of general categories (accounts) for a multitude of particular events (transactions)
4. to substitute segments of time (fiscal periods) for an unbroken flow of events and for the simple summaries by kinds initially accomplished by accounts
5. to communicate compactly and understandably the compressed mass of enterprise events
6. to create confidence in the dependability of the reported accounting data . . .[51]

The Objective at the Peak of the Pyramid

There remains only the question, said Littleton, concerning which objective stands at the peak of the pyramid. The peak or top objective of accounting is to assist readers via data to understand a business enterprise. This top objective is appropriate as the outcome of a pattern which connects the systematic features of accounting actions with a comparably systematic plan of related accounting objectives. Using the pyramid of objectives and actions as a basis it is possible to trace connections between actions,

[51]Littleton, Essays, p. 400, reprinted from Littleton, "Classified Objectives," 283, and Littleton, Structure, pp. 125-26.

and the several strata of objectives in either direction, upward or downward.[52]

Littleton advocated good objectives because they form the supporting piers of accounting actions and its service function. He said that the logic of good objectives is a more persuasive influence upon accounting practice than customary preferences. As new preferences or suggestions for altered actions appear they must be examined as to their relation to accounting objectives.[53] The basic objectives of accounting are the supporting piers of the accounting service function. Technical actions and influential objectives are inseparable and, therefore, good judgment concerning accounting must be based upon an understanding of both actions and objectives as well as their interrelationships.[54]

Littleton's discussions of accounting theory and principles were firmly supported by his own understanding of his terminology and his concern that others should also understand them. He was much concerned about the multiple interpretations sometimes given to terms; therefore, he was careful to make clear his interpretation.

---

[52]Littleton, "Classified Objectives," 283-84, reprinted in Littleton, Essays, pp. 400-1, and reprinted in Littleton, Structure, pp. 126-27.

[53]Littleton, Structure, pp. 215-16.

[54]A. C. Littleton, "The Heart of the Matter," The Illinois Certified Public Accountant, XXV, No. 4 (Summer, 1963), 2.

Need for Theory--Aid to Clear Thinking

Littleton viewed the development of theory as a necessary aid to clear thinking about accounting. It is the duty of accounting theory, he said, to set forth rules and reasons for making distinctions between assets and expenses and to establish reasonable connections between cost causes and revenue sources.[55] Theory can be an aid to understanding, and in combination with practical knowledge can guide toward good choices for the solution of problems. Theory should not direct or prescribe but help to analyze, to understand, and to persuade. To fulfill this role, theory must consist of explanations, definitions, reasons, justifications, persuasions, and principles.[56] Principles, as parts of accounting theory, must be elements of knowledge and bases of action which become unconscious, all-pervading ideas which form a part of the rational thinking processes regarding decisions.[57] Littleton said that perhaps the greatest usefulness of any stated principle could be found in its usefulness as an aid to clear thinking.[58] Littleton considered logic as an additional aid to clear thinking;

---

[55]Littleton, "Concepts of Income," 21, and reprinted in Littleton, Essays, p. 195.

[56]A. C. Littleton, "Fixed Assets and Accounting Theory," The Illinois Certified Public Accountant, X, No. 3 (March, 1948), 12 (Hereinafter referred to as Littleton, "Fixed Assets"), and reprinted in Littleton, Essays, p. 310.

[57]Littleton, Structure, pp. 178-79.

[58]Littleton, Essays, p. 387.

however, it is incomplete because it tests only validity
and not truth.[59]

What is Accounting Theory?

Littleton was much concerned to clarify the
question: What is accounting theory? Accounting theory,
he said, is not an exercise in abstract hair-splitting, it
is simply thinking focused upon doing. While practice is
fact and action, theory is made up of explanations and
reasons. Theory tells the reason why accounting action is
what it is, why it is not otherwise, and/or why it might be
otherwise. Accounting theory makes its principal contribution and justifies its existence by the help it can provide
to clear thinking in accounting.[60]

Littleton believed that a coordinated body of
accounting theory is dependent upon a consistent set of
principles.[61] Paton and Littleton also supported this view
of accounting theory and asserted that such a coherent,
coordinated, consistent body of doctrine could be compactly
expressed in the form of standards.[62] Although Littleton
believed that a coordinated body of accounting theory includes a group of coordinated and consistent principles as

---

[59]Littleton, "Uses of Theory," 230-32, and reprinted
in Littleton, Essays, p. 377.

[60]Littleton, Structure, p. 132.

[61]Littleton, "Function to Principles," 239, and reprinted in Littleton, Essays, p. 306.

[62]Paton and Littleton, Standards, preface, ix.

well as descriptions, definitions, arguments, explanations,
and reasons, he said that the other elements could make up
and be called a body of doctrine or theory even though principles are missing.[63]   Littleton said that theory shows what
to look for in experience as guidance and teaches how to
recognize significant and relevant experience.[64]   Accounting
theory cannot be expected to provide _scientific_ explanations
because immutable laws, laboratory tests, and controlled
experiments are not available in accounting.   However,
truths do exist which are based upon carefully defined
classifications, closely drawn distinctions, clearly perceived objectives, and a strong sense of relevance among
data.[65]

The chief characteristic of theory, as well as the
nature, intention, and use of theory, is explanation, and
ideally this explanation makes actions clear in a realistic
and rational manner.   The tools of theory (i.e., the explanations) are used to achieve this clarity.[66]   Relevance of
accounting data facts to known purposes and their suit-
ability for achievement of definite accounting objectives

---

[63]Littleton, "Three Principles," 280, and reprinted
in Littleton, _Essays_, p. 387, and Littleton, _Structure_,
p. 175.

[64]Littleton, _Structure_, p. 132.

[65]_Ibid._, pp. 135-36.

[66]_Ibid._, pp. 139, 144.

are best understood by the use of theory.[67] Accounting
theory is an explanation of ideas, intentions, and purposes
of accounting actions and justification of their limitations.[68] Theory can provide significance for accounting
practice as well as the means of choosing the better course
of action.[69]

Interdependence of Theory and Practice

Littleton said that good accounting practice and
sound accounting principles of theory are supplementary to
each other and are closely interrelated. He said that in
writing and practicing accounting the best results will be
achieved by a thorough understanding of sound, consistent
theory in combination with skilled judgment concerning the
necessity for practical deviations.[70] The integration of
expedient, individualistic, and customary practices with the
ideas, intentions, and objectives of good theory, which is
itself practice created and practice conditioning, builds

---

[67]Ibid., p. 150.

[68]A. C. Littleton, "Mission and Method," The Illinois Certified Public Accountant, XXIII, No. 4 (Summer,
1961), 3.

[69]A. C. Littleton, book review of Robert T. Sprouse
and Maurice Moonitz's A Tentative Set of Broad Accounting
Principles for Business Enterprises, Accounting Research
Study No. 3 (1962), in The Accounting Review, XXXVIII,
No. 1 (January, 1963), 222.

[70]A. C. Littleton, "Tests for Principles," The
Accounting Review, XIII, No. 1 (March, 1938), 24 (Herein-
after referred to as Littleton, "Tests"), and reprinted in
Littleton, Essays, p. 392.

into a system of coordinated explanations and justifications of accounting as it is and as it can become.[71] Littleton said that theory and practice provide mutual support as each supplies significance to and completes the other.[72]

Littleton considered the role of good accounting practice in the development of accounting theory as a beneficial one. Good practice, by the contribution of helpful ideas, varied experience, and constructive criticism, strengthens theory. On the other hand, good practice rests upon good theory made up of the orderly array of interrelated ideas and interconnected reasons that fit the facts. Theory, realistic by nature, can help practice to be sound as well as useful, and deliberately rational rather than accidently so. Accounting theory and practice thus condition each other. Practice conditions theory in the analysis of real situations and by requiring assistance as well as criticism. Accounting theory conditions practice by its explanations, justifications, and guidance toward good choices among alternatives.[73] In summary, neither theory nor practice outranks the other in importance or priority. They are so interrelated that they must always be used together.[74] The interdependence of the two is a given condition necessary to the consideration of either.

---

[71]Littleton, _Structure_, p. 131.

[72]_Ibid_., pp. 137-38.

[73]_Ibid_., pp. 139-40.

[74]_Ibid_., p. 149.

Theory as a Distillation of
Practice, Based Upon Actions

The argument that there is a strong interrelationship and interdependence between practice and theory is
supported by Littleton's basic view that accounting theory
has grown out of accounting practice, which it then
strengthens. Theory strengthens practice by analyzing customs and testing their justification by relating customary
ideas represented in practice to basic concepts and purposes
of theory.[75] Littleton believed that the actual historical
evolution of accounting led to the slow distillation of
accounting principles out of accounting actions.[76] In 1962,
Littleton and Zimmerman echoed and summarized this idea as
follows:

> Accounting theory is primarily a concentrate
> distilled from experience. Before intention (be-
> lief, hope) can become theory (explanation), it
> must be refined in the fire of trial-and-error
> use (experience). . . .[77]

Theory is Thinking Focused Upon Doing

A natural adjunct idea to the one that theory is a
distillation of practice is that accounting theory is simply

---

[75]Littleton, "Uses of Theory," 228, and reprinted
in Littleton, Essays, p. 376.

[76]Littleton, "Classified Objectives," 281, and reprinted in Littleton, Essays, p. 397, and Littleton,
Structure, p. 123.

[77]A. C. Littleton and V. K. Zimmerman, Accounting
Theory: Continuity and Change (Englewood Cliffs, N. J.:
Prentice-Hall, Inc., 1962), p. 10 (Hereinafter referred
to as Littleton and Zimmerman, Continuity and Change).

184

thinking focused upon doing. Practice is fact and action, while theory consists of explanations and reasons. Theory's explanation may be in the form of justification, persuasion, or supposition. All of the explanations of theory are not equally good. Littleton diagramed the several grades of theory explanations in the following stair step manner:

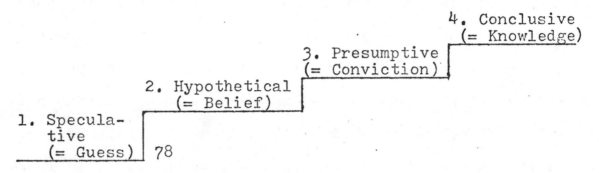

1. Specula-tive
(= Guess) | 78
2. Hypothetical
(= Belief)
3. Presumptive
(= Conviction)
4. Conclusive
(= Knowledge)

The Obligations of Accounting Theory

The obligations of accounting theory, according to Littleton, can be stated in several ways. All of these obligations of theory relate to its service to practice. Littleton's listing follows:

   1. Help us to examine what has been done so that we can see the reasons which direct that treatment or suggest another.
   2. Help us to find interconnecting threads, reasons and objectives between ideas and ideals.
   3. Help us to weigh alternative ideas, objectives and methods.
   4. Help us to be alert to relativity among ideas; to see that some ideas are more important than others; that some have strong ties to others while some are to be sharply distinguished.
   5. Help us to develop a capacity for working with ideas; to find ideas relevant to an issue, to resolve conflicts in ideas, to expand and amplify ideas.

---

[78]Littleton, Structure, passim, pp. 132-34.

6. Help us to recognize the places where principles apply as easily as we arrange procedures to suit the circumstances.

All this is but to say that theory exists to serve practice--even when it advances reasons against a familiar practice. . . .[79]

The obligations of accounting theory indicate the uses of theory. A knowledge of theory provides the equipment needed for confident exercise of judgment. Accounting theory is useful because it explains and offers justifications for accounting actions. This usefulness arises from thinking about practical experience and actions. Theory illuminates and makes understandable the practices from which it springs. It extends into the future only the best from the experience and criticism of the past, and thus theory extends the present toward the future in the way that the past became the present.[80]

Littleton emphasized that theory is developed as the outcome of conditions faced by practitioners, and its primary service is to aid these practitioners in meeting the impact of change. Theory is strongly influenced by surrounding conditions and the problems of the times. The events which cause deep concern for accounting practitioners also have a strong influence upon the beliefs and explanations which make up accounting theory.[81] Thus Littleton

---

[79]Ibid., pp. 133-34.

[80]Littleton and Zimmerman, Continuity and Change, pp. 10-11.

[81]A. C. Littleton, "Accounting Theory: 1933-1953," The Accounting Forum, XXIV (May, 1953), 11.

set forth his views as to the obligations of accounting
theory and its useful role as an explanation and justification of accounting actions. The obligations of accounting
theory explain its usefulness.

Principles as a Part of Theory

What Are Principles?

Principles are an important feature of theory. In
the section on Littleton's basic approach to accounting
theory, some statements were made regarding principles. To
repeat, principles of accounting are based upon accounting
practice and experience; they are interdependent with accounting practice and necessary to it, and practice is
necessary to the body of interrelated and consistent principles. Principles state significant relationships between
desirable ends (reasons for actions) and suitable means
(directed actions). Principles, according to Littleton, are
derived by inductive reasoning from practical experience.

This section on principles as a part of theory
includes discussion of principles as Littleton viewed them
over the period of years. As is true with the other sections, it is related to the earlier discussion and is
dependent upon it.

Fundamental Truths

The idea or theme that principles are fundamental
truths appears frequently in Littleton's writing. In
March, 1938, Littleton set forth the view that accounting

principles express fundamental truths about business enterprise. In his discussion of how these fundamental truths are recognized, Littleton indicated that the inductive generalization from experience is the best means of revealing such truths. Practical experience provides bases for generalizations to represent experience as well as points of departure for further search for truth. He then stated that the inductively derived principles can be tested by deduction. This involves logical analyses in which conclusions are tied into acceptable premises.[82] In summary, concerning the two ways of determining truths in accounting, Littleton wrote as follows:

> Fundamental truths of accounting (principles) may either be generalized out of practical experiences, or deduced from stated premises which are accepted as true in themselves or demonstrated true by convincing argument. . . .[83]

The combination of the two approaches to the determination of accounting truths, inductive and deductive, provides support for each and is the best over-all approach, according to Littleton. In the inductive approach the propositions are considered as truths because experienced men agree that out of various possibilities these are the most desirable, the most descriptive of best actions. In the deductive case the propositions are considered truths

---

[82]Littleton, "Tests," 17; this particular point is not included in the reprint in Littleton, Essays.

[83]Littleton, Essays, p. 391, reprinted from Littleton, "Tests," 17, and in Littleton, Structure, p. 181.

because logical analysis indicates that they follow prior propositions which are obviously true. When both methods yield similar results, an expression of fundamental truth can be assumed. According to Littleton, the two processes of generalizing from experience and inferring from premises work together. Convictions, which are derived inductively from the particulars of experience, can form the premises used deductively to derive additional convictions. Conclusions, which are reasonably inferred from acceptable truths, can become expressions representing acceptable standards of practice.[84]

Littleton wrote of principles at length and was concerned with the dilemma of defining a principle. He said a principle could be defined as an expression of a significant relationship or as a fundamental truth. The first definition is that a principle is an explanation concisely framed in words to compress an important relationship among accounting ideas into a few words. On the other hand, Littleton thought that the best dictionary meaning of principle is the one which considers a principle as a fundamental truth. Littleton concluded as follows:

> If the use of principle is to compact some aspect of theory, as a formula is used compactly to express some aspect of nature, then it is more important to know how the principle makes something clear than it is to prove that the statement can be called true and fundamental. If it does

---

[84]Littleton, "Tests," 17, and reprinted in Littleton, Essays, p. 391.

make clear something of importance, it can be
accepted as both true and fundamental. . . .[85]

Littleton said that principles express fundamental
truth because a significant relationship is revealed between
desirable ends and suitable means. This expression of fundamental truth acts as a highly useful instrument which is
an aid to better understanding.

Principles Compress Theory as Headlines

Expanding upon the idea that principles express
fundamental truths, Littleton said principles are tight
generalizations or headlines which compress a good deal of
theory into a few words. While principles are inadequate
alone, they serve a very useful purpose by compactly expressing fundamental relationships among the ideas which
make up the body of theory and practice which make up, in
turn, accounting doctrine. Every such idea is supported by
and lends support to every other idea in the accounting
theory structure.[86]

Principles Express a Significant Relationship

Littleton said that the expression of a significant
relationship between ends and means, in the form of a headline, is the chief and the necessary characteristic of a

---

[85]Littleton, Structure, pp. 146-47.

[86]Littleton, "Three Principles," 282, and reprinted
in Littleton, Essays, pp. 179, 390.

principle.[87] He stressed the idea that a principle must
express a significant relationship between directed accounting actions and reasons for actions.[88] In other words there
must be a significant relationship between the ends sought
and the accounting means used to achieve those ends.

Accounting Principles Are Not Immutable

Littleton expressed the opinion that accounting
principles could not be defined as scientific or immutable.
Accounting principles can only be man-made expressions of
man-made relationships; and these are not likely to be
immutable.[89]

Are There Principles of Accounting?

Over the years, Littleton addressed himself to the
recurrent question: Are there principles of accounting?
In August, 1938, Littleton was advocating the use of standards as a term superior to principles. He wrote that principles tend to be inflexible overgeneralizations which suggest undue universality. He stated at that time that the
word standard did not have these flaws.[90] In 1940, Paton

---

[87]Littleton, "Inductive Reasoning," 451, and reprinted in Littleton, Essays, p. 385.

[88]Littleton, Structure, p. 188.

[89]Littleton, "Classified Objectives," 284, and reprinted in Littleton, Structure, p. 127, and Littleton,
Essays, p. 401.

[90]Littleton, "High Standards," 99, and reprinted in
Littleton, Essays, p. 380.

and Littleton echoed this idea, and in 1941, Littleton continued to write of standards and principles. At that time, he said, "An accounting principle is a crystallization from careful theorizing, a distillation from accumulated experience."[91] He believed the word principle has much meaning and should not be abandoned; however, its meaning should be restricted. A principle says something important about some aspect of accounting; it is a verbalization of concepts, an expression of previously inarticulate thoughts. However, a principle is not a law, nor is it a rule or a convention.[92]

The dictionary definition of a principle as a fundamental truth was mentioned earlier. Littleton found the dictionary definitions inadequate for use in accounting. He wished to indicate the essence of the word in its accounting context, and suggested consideration of accounting principles simply as important accounting ideas that have been more or less compactly verbalized for convenient use. He cited two uses of such a view. Principles can serve as guideposts for extension of accounting knowledge and deepening understanding of accounting, and they can serve as

---

[91]Littleton, "Variations," 9, and reprinted in Littleton, Essays, p. 498.

[92]Littleton, "Variations," 9, and reprinted in Littleton, Essays, p. 498.

192

springboards for thinking toward appropriate accounting actions.[93]

Formulation of a Principle

Littleton believed that principles, as parts of theory, are based upon experience and accounting actions, and that the formulation of principles can be carried out within this framework. He also asserted that the distinctions between concepts, rules, and principles are important factors in the formulation of principles. Briefly: Concepts are assumptions or propositions concerning related ideas tested by experience with known actions. Rules include reasons and directives; they join justification to a directive. A convention is a customary rule or an established usage.

Accounting practice leads to accounting theory and also to the formulation of accounting principles. Experience which is good eventually leads to acceptance of similar actions. Verbal association of the action with a justifying reason of theory provides a framework of associated ideas for conversion into a statement of an end or objective in association with a means of attaining that end. This form of statement can be called a principle of accounting.[94]

---

[93]Littleton, "Search," 247, and reprinted in Littleton, Essays, p. 178.

[94]Littleton, Structure, p. 186.

In the phrasing of principles it was Littleton's belief that there should be an intentional incorporation of ends, objectives, and aims. The indication of such objectives distinguishes a principle from a rule. Littleton emphasized his own viewpoint concerning the derivation of a statement of principle in the following way:

> When well-known accounting actions have been clearly tied to appropriate justifying reasons, the way has been opened for converting that form of expression (a rule) into another (a principle). When this is acceptably done; . . . the line of derivation of that principle leads straight back to experience-tested actions; hence in origin that principle is an inductive generalization. In the forms of expression used herein for principles the aim is to phrase a desirable accounting end or objective and relate to it a suitable means or method of attaining that end. The two aspects of accounting thus joined are significantly relevant to each other. This is a highly important fact; if a significant relationship does not exist, the two ideas should not be joined. . . .[95]

The formulation of accounting principles led Littleton to develop what he called a working concept of a principle. This working concept was utilized to convert rules into principles.

Working Concept of a Principle

A working concept of a principle was developed to derive accounting principles by inductive reasoning about accounting actions and objectives. Littleton set forth the belief that accounting conventions, rules, and principles are more closely related in accounting usage than general

[95]Ibid., p. 198, Littleton, "Inductive Reasoning, II," 644, and reprinted in Littleton, Essays, p. 402.

dictionary definitions of these words indicate.. He believed the way could be opened to form a working concept of an accounting principle by showing the close relationship of the ideas represented by the words. This concept would join ideas from accounting theory with actions, and the union would support the belief that accounting principles are derived inductively out of accounting actions taken to achieve accounting objectives.[96]

Following the same line of thinking, Littleton wrote of the working concept of a principle in his Monograph No. 5. He said that the key links between principles and rules are the similarities (1) between a rule's directive and a principle's means to an end, and (2) between a rule's reason and a principle's objective. He set forth that the conversion of a fully stated rule from experience into a carefully phrased principle convincingly indicates how an accounting principle can originate in practical experience. In addition, it indicates how principles can lead one's thought from a known, desired objective to a thoughtful weighing of necessary alternative ways and means. This is necessary in order to choose the best practical action in view of the objective involved and the relevant circumstances. Littleton used his working concept of the principle to illustrate how theory ideas can be joined to typical

---

[96]Littleton, "Inductive Reasoning, II," 641, and reprinted in Littleton, Essays, p. 401.

practical accounting actions. Secondly, he illustrated the inductive derivation of accounting principles from accounting actions which are clearly relevant to given or known accounting objectives.[97]

Development of Principles--
Inductively or Deductively

Inductive reasoning to derive principles for accounting was a basic approach followed by Littleton; therefore, it is an important area of concern in this study. It has been mentioned earlier that Littleton believed that fundamental truths in accounting can be generalized out of practical experience. On the other hand, they may be deduced from stated premises which are accepted as true in themselves or demonstrated to be true by argument.[98]

Littleton explained the inductive and deductive approaches to the derivation of principles. He explained that the deductive approach considers propositions true from prior propositions known to be true. The inductive approach considers propositions true because experienced men agree that the given proposition is deemed the most suitable of the various possibilities. Induction, said Littleton, is not unrelated to the rational association of ends and means.[99]

---

[97]Littleton, Structure, p. 186.

[98]Littleton, "Tests," 17, and quoted by Littleton, Structure, p. 181.

[99]Littleton, Structure, p. 181.

Littleton suggested, as early as 1938, that the integration of induction and deduction may be the best way to learn of truth in accounting. He said this correlation of practice and theory would recognize the methods of science by looking for knowledge in experience and developing it by reflection. He pointed out that theory does not extend the boundaries of experience. Theory does widen and deepen reflection upon past and future experience.[100]

Littleton wrote that accounting has been developed inductively out of particulars, for the most part. A mass of rules and accumulated doctrine produced by experience form the basis for organization into a cohesive body of knowledge. Knowledge which is cohesive can be arranged into a clarifying order which reveals important relationships that can be arranged deductively downward from a top concept. This must be possible even though the varied aspects of the doctrine originated in rules about specifics. Littleton believed accounting thought can be explored profitably by both induction and deduction. The inductive approach can be expressed in the form of a pyramid standing on a broad base, and sloping sharply to a peak which represents the top objective of accounting.[101] This pyramid of

---

[100]Littleton, "Tests," 24, and reprinted in Littleton, Essays, p. 392.

[101]Littleton, "Classified Objectives," 281, and reprinted in Littleton, Essays, p. 398, and Littleton, Structure, pp. 123-24.

objectives which was discussed earlier might be called the inductive pyramid. After arrangement of the objectives and actions into a pattern, it is possible to move from actions upward through various levels of justifications. In addition, it is possible to trace the effects of the top objective downward through the several strata to sub-objectives until its influence on rules and actions can be discerned.[102]

Littleton wrote at length concerning inductive reasoning in accounting in two articles in 1950 and in Chapter 11 of <u>Structure of Accounting Theory</u>, which covers essentially the same material. Littleton used the process of induction to relate accounting conventions, rules, and principles. He pointed out that although there is a tendency to emphasize the differences between accounting conventions, rules, and principles they all stem from accounting actions which have been responses to recognized needs. Conventions, rules, and principles are generalized into words out of satisfactory experiences and actions by the process of induction. These terms are closely related because of common origins and similar objectives in the ideas behind them. This close relationship makes it possible to start with any of the three forms of expression and move to any other by a suitable change in phraseology.

---

[102]Littleton, "Classified Objectives," 284, and reprinted in Littleton, <u>Essays</u>, p. 401, and Littleton <u>Structure</u>, p. 127.

198

This relationship constitutes a good basis for believing
that a coordinated body of basic accounting doctrine can
be stated.[103]

Littleton's method involved the conversion of rules,
made up of directives and reasons, into principles by stating a significant relationship between ends and means to
those ends. Littleton's elaboration of the idea of the inductive generalization of the principle is quoted in the
section, Formulation of a Principle.[104] Littleton gave many
illustrations of the inductive method applied to the process
of deriving principles of accounting. The illustration presented here is a shortened version of his method:

> Beneath every revenue transaction is an
> enterprise action of rendering a service asked
> or of supplying goods chosen by a customer.
> This action is associated with performance by
> the enterprise. Accounting action is one of
> recognizing the account features of enterprise
> performance, i.e., (1) the time of performance
> objectively places the revenue transaction as to
> time, thereby fixing its relevance to a given
> fiscal period; (2) the dollar amount as agreed by
> the parties objectively determines the quantita-
> tive aspect of the revenue transaction. The ac-
> counting action may therefore be said to yield
> the following rule, consisting as usual of a
> directive and a justifying reason for the action:
> . . . Obtain objective evidence of services
> rendered and goods sold by the enterprise
> because an unobjective basis of assigning
> revenue to the present, or of postponing
> the recognition of it, will produce distorted
> periodic reports.

---

[103]Littleton, "Inductive Reasoning," 449-50, and
reprinted in Littleton, Essays, p. 383, and Littleton,
Structure, p. 186.

[104]Supra, p. 193.

A well established convention of accounting
can be expressed in this simple statement: Profit
is realized when sale is made. This may be a compressed bit of truth; but it would be better turn-
ed around: No profit can be realized unless a
sale is made. . . .
Another way of stating the accounting convention is this: Revenue is recognizable when a sale
is made to a solvent debtor. . . .
. . . The reason advanced in the above rule (to
avoid distorted periodic reports) is one that
justifies many different accounting actions. It
also constitutes an important general aim of accounting since any distortion of figures as between fiscal periods produces some degree of statistical mis-classification, and this is an accounting falsity as well as a statistical falsity.
It will be evident that revenue is more often
the leading clue to the assignment of applicable
costs, expenses, and losses than the latter are
clues to the recognition of revenue. It will also be noted in the following statement of principle that recognition, not realization, is the
key word of the objective:
Revenue Recognition: Objective evidence
of services performed and of benefits received
in return . . . afford the only acceptable
basis for periodically assigning revenue to
the present or of alternatively deferring
recognition into the future.[105]

Interrelationship of Principles

Littleton viewed good theory as that which is made

up of a group of interrelated principles which are consis-

tent with each other. In 1938, he said that principles can

be gathered into a single coordinated body of theory only

if they are consistent with each other.[106] Littleton looked

forward to the formulation of such an integrated body of

[105]Littleton, Structure, pp. 201-3, and Littleton,
"Inductive Reasoning, II," 647-48.

[106]Littleton, "Function to Principles," 239, and
reprinted in Littleton, Essays, p. 306.

principles. The formulation of such a body of doctrine must stress logic, coherence, consistency, and interrelationship as characteristics. He believed that even though this body of principles might not be perfect it would change and improve. He also believed that such a coherent body of accounting theory would provide a basis for distinguishing between necessary or useful variations from accepted practices and unnecessary or deceptive variations.[107]

In 1943, Littleton wrote of the similarity of basic accounting principles to the principles of war formulated by a military writer.[108] Littleton believed that by changing the word military to accounting in Wheeler-Nicholsen's formulation it could be converted into a statement with complete applicability to accounting. Littleton quoted as follows:

> . . . There is no occupation in which men engage that has not its basic principles. . . . It is the combined use of all the principles in skilled coordination that makes for (military) success. It is the use of any one of them without due regard to the others which makes for (military) failure.[109]

---

[107]Littleton, "Uses of Theory," 232-33, and reprinted in Littleton, Essays, p. 378.

[108]Littleton's reference was: Major Malcolm Wheeler-Nicholsen, "The Nine Principles of War," Harper's Magazine (August, 1942), p. 297.

[109]A. C. Littleton, "The Accounting Exchange: Principles of War," The Accounting Review, XVIII, No. 4 (October, 1943), 368 (Hereinafter referred to as Littleton, "Principles of War"), and reprinted in Littleton, Structure, pp. 170-71.

Littleton claimed that in order for principles to serve an accountant best their essence and their interrelationships must have been made so thoroughly a part of the accountant's thinking processes that statements as verbal propositions would become unnecessary. In other words, the principles, as an interrelated group, must be automatically included in the accountant's fund of knowledge.[110]

Littleton emphasized that the greatest of significance was to be attached to the factor of interdependence of the principles. He stressed the idea that all of the principles, patterned after the military plan, are interrelated and must be used in combination with all of the others. Much of the strength and usefulness of principles are dependent upon the tight interrelations among them. A material change of any important aspect of accounting affects all other aspects to some degree. This could conceivably destroy the internal adhesion of ideas and thus destroy much of the usefulness of accounting technology. Littleton believed the interdependence of basic ideas is so vital to clear thinking and right action that he used Wheeler-Nicholsen's statement of the interrelated principles of war to help discover interrelations among accounting principles. The military principles which Littleton discussed in detail are given here in summary form. Littleton

---

[110]Littleton, "Principles of War," 368, and reprinted in Littleton, Structure, pp. 170-71.

called attention to the circular effect created by linking
principles number 9 and number 1. The principles of of-
fense and security support each other, and finally the
principle of mobility is necessary as support to the principle of offensive. The principles listed were:

1. Principle of the Offensive
2. Principle of Security
3. Principle of Economy of Force
4. Principle of the Main Objective
5. Principle of Concentration of Force
6. Principle of Cooperation
7. Principle of Unity of Command
8. Principle of Surprise
9. Principle of Mobility.[111]

Littleton suggested a set of six headlines to
represent accounting principles which he designed to relate
as the military principles relate. Littleton chained the
six key ideas into a circle. The circular sequence is a,
c, d, e, b, f. In this manner the "a" transactions are converted into "b" financial statements by the "c, d, e" mech-
anism. The final link which ties the others into a circle
is the "f" auditing. The critical examination of the balance sheet and income statement leads back through the
sequence behind these statements into the basic transactions
data and the accounting process. Littleton's headlines were
listed as follows:

a. Principle of Invested Cost
b. Principle of Interpretative Summaries
c. Principle of Homogeneous Categories
d. Principle of Analysis of Categories

---

[111]Littleton, Structure, p. 171.

     e.   Principle of Periodic Accrual-deferment
     f.   Principle of Critical Review.[112]

Littleton thus used the set of interrelated military principles as a model to illustrate his conviction that accounting principles must be not only consistent with each other but also interrelated. His accounting model was set forth as depicting the accounting sequence as well as the integration of the system with the actual transactions. He stressed the essential point of interrelatedness. He pointed out that headlines of principles cannot tell the whole story and, of course, are inadequate alone. However, if they succeed in compacting expressive fundamental relationships among the ideas which constitute the body of accounting doctrine, they serve a very useful purpose. It is helpful to see how each idea is supported by and lends support to each other idea in the structure of theory and practice doctrine.[113]

Littleton stressed the inescapable incompleteness of a single principle without its companion principles. The usefulness of any statement of an important accounting relationship in the form of an accounting principle does not render it complete for use in isolation. Furthermore, it is incomplete because it is a highly compressed phrasing of

---

[112]Littleton, Structure, p. 174, based upon Littleton, "Principles of War," 369.

[113]Littleton, "Three Principles," 282, and reprinted in Littleton, Essays, p. 390, and Littleton, Structure, p. 179.

ideas which could be, and must be, much expanded and
intertwined with other accounting ideas. This dilemma,
Littleton concluded, is inevitable in a complex
technology.[114]

Uses of Theory and Princi-
ples as Theory Headlines

Littleton summarized the uses of theory and of
principles as theory headlines. These headlines express
Littleton's settled opinions in 1953, as follows:

> To view accounting as a whole.
> To penetrate into the premises of accounting.
> To relate principles to basic concepts.
> To provide a basis for examining trends in ideas.
> To measure the desirability of departures.
> To show how a principle may become untenable.
> To appraise new doctrines by contact with
> principles.
> To test neighbor principles by testing a related
> principle.
> In essence these uses say that theory helps
> us to have a better understanding of accounting
> thought and action; that theory can serve as a
> basis for appraising trends in accountants'
> thinking; that theory may at times be a means of
> systematically examining challenging suggestions.[115]

Nature of Theory

In 1953, Littleton summarized his views on the
Nature of Theory in the Structure of Accounting Theory.
His summary, which covered Elements of a Pattern, Tools of
Theory, Actions and Rules, Formulation of Principles,

---

[114]Littleton, Essays, pp. 404-5.

[115]Littleton, Structure, p. 230.

Inductively Derived Principles, and Uses of Theory, was

stated as follows:

(1) Accounting principles suitably founded upon prior experience (inductively derived) will necessarily be interrelated, because experience falls into patterns of related elements.

(2) Principles deductively considered are one means of putting to test the interrelation among ideas.

(3) Accounting principles may be further tested by being faced with challenging ideas.

(4) Accounting principles which by test show demonstrable interrelations can be accepted as indications of the existence of an underlying body of integrated accounting doctrines.

(5) If accounting doctrine is in fact integrated, the several ideas, concepts, principles, and the practices relevant thereto, give support to each other and strength to the whole.

(6) If ideas or concepts should be introduced into accounting which could not command the support of the other surrounding accounting ideas and did not contribute support to them, the integrating cement of this body of knowledge would to that extent lose its cohesive strength.

(7) To the extent that the factors of integration and interrelationship among the ideas in this area are weakened, distorted or destroyed, the integrity of subsequent accounting data would be shaken.

(8) If the integrity of accounting data should evaporate, the enterprise data taking its place would be subject to suspicion that the reported figures could then more easily be dressed up for propaganda effect to suit management's fancy of the moment.

(9) If investor confidence in management's reports of enterprise data should be seriously damaged, the flow of private capital into productive business would probably be correspondingly lessened, conceivably to the extent that self-governing, private business enterprise would then be charged with failing to serve the needs of the nation's economy.

(10) Supplementary data, using index numbers or other interpretative means and presented outside the structure of accounting, would not weaken the integration of accounting ideas, or change the methods of account keeping in terms of invested

206

cost, or alter the basis for professional audits
and certificates.[116]

Summary

Littleton said that accounting is practical. It is
dependent upon objectivity in order to perform its service
to business management. The ideology of accounting is based
upon practical experience. Actions (experience), which are
based upon objectives, are basic to accounting and therefore
accounting as well as action is purposeful. Accounting
methodology preceded theory, and it follows that principles
of accounting theory are based upon practice and experience.

Littleton believed there is a need for accounting
theory as an aid to clear thinking about accounting and
theory should aid understanding of accounting actions.
Littleton viewed accounting theory as a distillation of
practice, the outcome of conditions. Theory grows out of
accounting practice and strengthens practice by subjecting
customs to analysis and by testing justifications. The
principles which make up the body of accounting theory were
slowly distilled out of actions and are based upon thinking
about experience, thinking focused upon doing.

Accounting theory does not consist of scientific
explanations; there are no immutable laws of accounting. A
broad concept of the nature of accounting theory determines
its make-up of descriptions, definitions, arguments,

---

[116]Ibid., pp. 231-32.

inferences, explanations, reasons, and principles.

Littleton spoke of a body of doctrine which could be composed of all of these elements and which would stand alone even if the principles did not exist or were not expressed explicitly.

Theory is used to explain facts and to express ideas, intentions, and purposes behind accounting actions. Theory is useful in providing explanations of accounting actions to business management. Theory is not only practice oriented; it is practice conditioning. Good theory and practice complete and support each other. Good practice rests upon good theory. Theory should be realistic and practice should be rational.

Littleton distinguished carefully between a rule, a convention, and a principle. He said they are closely related and he related them to each other through the inductive method. Littleton used the inductive method to develop principles of accounting which, he said, could then be verified by the deductive method.

Earlier statements by Littleton indicated that he viewed principles as inflexible overgeneralizations and he advocated the use of standards instead of principles. Standards, he maintained, are guideposts to best or first preferences and points of departure which recognize and allow a sequence of justifiable variations and/or alternatives. Standards cover fundamental conceptions and general approaches to report presentations. Littleton advocated an official professional pronouncement covering standards.

Later, Littleton wrote of principles at greater length. He said principles are crystallizations derived from careful theorizing and a distillation of accumulated experience. They are fundamental truths about business enterprise condensed into carefully phrased sentences. The chief characteristic of a principle is that it compresses theory as a tight generalization or headline.

Littleton believed principles could be derived from rules by recognizing a significant relationship which links well-known accounting actions with appropriate justifying reasons. He viewed the principle as an inductive generalization based upon experience tested actions which are clearly relevant to known accounting objectives.

Littleton used his pyramid of objectives to illustrate his inductive approach. He viewed objectives as determinants of procedures. His pyramid includes a ranking of intermediate and antecedent objectives which are subsidiary to and coordinated with the top objective of the pyramid. The top objective answers the question of "Why do we have accounting?" We have accounting, Littleton proclaimed, to make enterprise transactions understandable via data.

The principles of accounting theory are interdependent with each other; they are interrelated and must be

consistent with each other. Isolated principles will not
be relevant to the whole. Littleton viewed good theory as
being composed of a group of interrelated and coordinated
principles which are consistent with each other. He used a
group of closely interrelated and interdependent military
principles as a model to illustrate his idea that it is
necessary to make a combination of principles into a
coordinated total.

Littleton, beginning his accounting career at a
time of somewhat dramatic change in the business and economic scene, was provided an opportunity to help solve some
of the related accounting problems. Littleton responded to
the challenges and opportunities in an enthusiastic and
thorough manner. Finally, it seems apparent that
Littleton's contributed works in the areas of terminology,
principles, and theory constitute a major element of the
total literature produced by writers of his period. He was
sincerely concerned about the lack of a commonly accepted
vocabulary of usage for accountants. He articulated his
careful and considered thoughts about acceptable terminology. He was equally interested in developing a set of interrelated and coordinated headlines (principles) to express in
meaningful form a framework of accounting theory. In short,
Littleton responded to needs which were evident in the
1920's and to those which emerged in the ensuing years.

CHAPTER VI

CONCLUSIONS

An analytical study of Littleton's major contributions to the literature of the selected areas of accounting theory has led to the foregoing exposition of his views. His views of income determination as a central purpose of accounting, of historical cost as the basic means of maintaining the integrity of the data, and his basic approach and views concerning principles have been, in fact, determined to be of major significance in his work. Furthermore, the nature, or inherent character, of his contributions in these areas has been determined to be significant as to his own productive period as well as the present.

In the early twentieth century, the demands from government, investors, and others for information regarding the earnings of the business entity created a pressing need for more accounting data. Littleton came into the accounting profession at a time when the discipline faced major problems. Although he chose accounting somewhat by chance, he emerged as a sound thinker, a prolific writer, and a major force in the development of accounting thought. It could be said that he was a product of his time and circumstances. Littleton, responsive to the needs, addressed himself to the intrinsic problems for accounting in the income determination methodology. Littleton resolutely defended and promoted the allocation of cost as an essential feature of the matching process. The allocation of costs is closely associated with the proper determination of depreciation, for one thing. Littleton confronted these problems with assurance and dealt with them positively.

Littleton wrote extensively over a time span of forty-five years. Certainly, by his highly expressive writing and his overall work in the field of accounting, he has contributed to the stature of the accounting profession. The constant flow of useful additions to the accounting literature of the period is an apparent facet of his total contribution. His meaningful relationship with other accountants, students, and other writers constitutes further evidence.

Style of Writing

Littleton wrote in a very lucid style which was not only scholarly but complete, comprehensive, and extremely effective. His clear statement of the topic of discussion, his explanations and examples, and his careful attention to clarifying detail and description all contributed to the overall effectiveness of his presentations. His early interest in and study of English composition no doubt contributed to his ability to use language to successfully convey precise meanings. Although he was not a particularly

colorful writer, Littleton was unstinting in his meticulous
attention to details of terminology, elaboration, and illustration. He was rigorous in his efforts to clearly set
forth and support his points. His statements reveal not
only clear thinking but conscientious attention to
exposition.

Response to Contemporary Influences

As a product of his times, Littleton was certainly
very much concerned with the issues which arose during his
productive period. The entire decade of the 1930's is probably unmatched as a period of development for present accounting practices. A pronounced interest in accounting
principles also became evident around 1930. The publication
of a report of the Special Committee of the American Institute of Accountants on cooperation with stock exchanges in
1934 and the creation of the Securities and Exchange
Commission in 1934, with authority to prescribe accounting
procedures, were significant events for the accounting profession in general. The production of literature concerning
accounting principles was extensive; the concept of accounting principles and ideas as to the manner of their formulation were developed during this period. The matching of
revenues and expenses through the cost allocation process
crystallized as the basic purpose of financial accounting.
The literature of this period prior to World War II
provided a basis for improvement of accounting practice as

well as a foundation for the development of a firmly established profession of accounting.[1]

It is evident that Littleton was concerned with the pressing problems of the time. His work provides ample evidence of his deep concern and interest in the issues and problems which were manifest during the period. He became deeply involved in these developing issues and problems. For example, he responded comprehensively to the issue of dividend legality which was important for an interval of time. He discussed the problem intensively and with insight. Although Littleton gave passing attention to temporary issues, his efforts were concentrated, in the main, upon the important, basic, continuing problems. He did not waste undue effort upon problems of a minor nature or ones with only a temporary impact. He demonstrated extraordinary insight in his selection of the most basic issues for serious concentration of effort.

The Development of Principles

Littleton's interest in the concept of accounting principles and the method of their formulation was unceasing. He devoted much effort to the study of the problem, and he developed his views carefully and thoughtfully.

---

[1]Reed K. Storey, The Search for Accounting Principles, Today's Problems in Perspective (New York: American Institute of Certified Public Accountants, Inc., 1964), pp. 4-5, 19-20 (Hereinafter referred to as Storey, Search).

The Terminology Problem

As a part of his effort in the area of principles, he demonstrated much thoughtfulness about accounting terminology. He endeavored to discourage the tendency on the part of different writers to establish new terms for ones already in use. He felt that the fact that accountants use a technical vocabulary consisting of, for the most part, words in common use is a handicap in itself without adding to the problem.[2] Littleton thought that the word _principles_ had been overworked; he proposed the substitution of standard for the more inflexible principle.[3] It has been noted by a researcher in the area that the rejection of a more precise terminology as a footing to the structure of accounting principles has hampered the development of meaningful principles.[4] The failure of the profession to respond to the call for a more uniform usage of terms has no doubt acted as a deterrent to progress in other areas of accounting.

---

[2]A. C. Littleton, "Accounting Exchange: Assets and Surplus," _The Accounting Review_, XXI, No. 3 (July, 1946), pp. 341-42, and reprinted in A. C. Littleton, _Essays on Accountancy_ (Urbana, Illinois: University of Illinois Press, 1961), p. 237 (Hereinafter referred to as Littleton, _Essays_).

[3]A. C. Littleton, "High Standards for Accounting," _The Journal of Accountancy_, LXVI (August, 1938), pp. 99-100.

[4]Storey, _Search_, p. 24.

The Inductive Approach or Integrated Approach

Littleton considered the inductive approach as the proper one to use in the development of accounting principles. He suggested that deductive reasoning, using logical analytical processes, could be used to test the principles which have been inductively derived from accounting practices. He illustrated his use of the approach carefully and supported it with clear explanations and defenses. He used this integrated approach involving both induction and deduction in his study of the correlation of accounting practice and theory.

Littleton's extensive concentration of effort regarding principles constitutes what can be considered as a significant contribution to the total literature of accounting. His reflections upon the composition of principles and their derivation were an important feature of his constant endeavors to resolve unsettled issues. The formulation of a consistent set of broad principles as the basis for a cohesive structure of accounting theory embodies the culmination of his efforts. As a whole, his undertakings in this area can be considered unique as well as significant.

The Acceptance of Historical Cost

In his advocacy of and adherence to the use of historical cost, Littleton crystallized a goal which became the accepted practice. In this manner he contributed to the unification and standardization of accounting ideas. He vehemently defended the use of the historical cost concept. Related to this was his belief in the integrity of the original data. He was not only staunch in his advocacy of the concept; he offered extensive support for his stand. Certainly, he was one of the most faithful advocates of the historical cost basis of accounting which was the subject of much discussion and debate.

At times, during the period involved, there was espoused the idea that cost was no longer useful information in financial statements. There was much pressure for injection of replacement values, appraisal values, and price-level adjustments into the accounts. Littleton continuously asserted that only transactions to which the accounting entity is a party can be justifiably recorded in the accounts. The integrity of the enterprise data must be maintained.

Littleton suggested, however, that the use of price-level adjusted figures presented in supplementary reports would certainly be unobjectionable and probably very useful for purposes of interpretation. This, he said, could be accomplished without inserting entries into the accounts. Although he could not have foreseen the extent of recent inflationary trends, Littleton was ahead of his time in advocating such a presentation. This presentation of supplementary information is now suggested as beneficial by the American Institute of Certified Public Accountants.

This suggestion of Littleton's is usually overlooked, and he is not credited with the insight indicated by his proposal. Time has served to substantiate Littleton's clear thinking about historical cost and the use of supplementary reports containing price-level adjustments.

It is noteworthy that Littleton has probably been unduly condemned as inflexible in his adherence to historical cost. It appears that he is not always properly credited with his actual perceptive insight with regard to the supplementary presentation of information reflecting price-level adjustments.

Further note should be made, however, that it is quite possible his adamant and consistent advocacy of historical cost may have delayed evolutionary improvements in accounting theory and practice. His emphasis of consistency may have eliminated possible responses to motivating economic forces which were present. The development of accounting thought concerning price-level adjustments may well have been delayed.

Income Determination and the Matching Concept

Littleton's stress upon income determination as the central purpose of accounting constitutes what appears to be a major contribution to the field of accounting. His emphasis upon income determination and its related matching concept as to revenues and costs appears to have been influential in the final acceptance of the concepts which are basic today. This question was certainly a dominant

one, particularly during the early years of Littleton's
literary efforts. He was in the midst of the evolution and
at the forefront of the development which led to the domi-
nance of the income statement over the balance sheet
information.

Overall Consistency of Treat-
ment of Areas of Concern

Consistency of One Viewpoint

Littleton's work is noteworthy for its consistency
of viewpoint over a lengthy period of time. His stated
views and position concerning an issue remained basically
unchanged with the passage of time. His thought processes,
as revealed in his writings, were consistent and evolutionary. Littleton set forth his considered views in early
materials. As time passed, he refined, expanded, and
clarified his earlier statements, without deviation from
his original exposition. He demonstrated that his original
statements were made and set forth only after careful study,
thought, and effort. As a result, the only changes made
were to achieve an improvement by repetitive and continuous
polishing, refinement, and elaboration.

Consistency of One Viewpoint with Others

Littleton, furthermore, demonstrated painstaking
effort to maintain a consistency of viewpoint concerning
related topics or related aspects of a given topic. He was
much concerned about maintaining the internal consistency

of a total body of thought. His view was that there must be a coordination of all aspects of a whole. The interrelationship of individual topics within the whole is vital to the validity of the total.

Littleton's adaptation of the set of military principles of warfare as a model for a set of interrelated, coordinated, consistent accounting principles is an overt illustration of this characteristic view. Littleton followed this same approach in his treatment of various topics related to accounting theory. His idea of the integration of the accounts in the accounting system is an example of this viewpoint.

Possible Limitations

As mentioned earlier, Littleton's unyielding support of the consistent use of historical cost may have prevented his consideration of possible responses to economic change. If Littleton had been more flexible in his view, it is possible that certain changes which are taking place today might have already been an integral part of today's body of accounting theory and practice.

Possible Permanent Impact

There are numerous illustrations of Littleton's possible permanent impact upon the contemporary accounting scene. His selection as one of the four pioneers of accounting is a positive illustration of the recognition of his contributions. The selection was made upon the basis of major contribution to the profession's literature during the first sixty years of the twentieth century. Understandably, this sixty-year period is viewed by the authors of the book which honors the four pioneers as the most interesting and dynamic in the history of accounting.[5]

An Introduction to Corporate Accounting Standards, coauthored with W. A. Paton and published in 1940, has been noted as the single most significant contribution of its period to the development of accounting theory.[6] It is likely that no single accounting publication in the United States has been cited so often or esteemed so highly. It has been a staple in courses on accounting theory since its publication and has thereby influenced accounting teaching and research. There have been fourteen printings which have sold 55,000 copies in the United States. Annual sales amount to about 2,000 copies. The book was translated into Japanese by Seigo Nakajima in 1953 and 14,000 copies have been distributed.[7] It should be noted that dissemination of this publication to the entire membership of both the American Accounting Association and the American Institute

---

[5]James Don Edwards and Roland F. Salmonson, Contributions of Four Accounting Pioneers, Kohler, Littleton, May, Paton (East Lansing: Bureau of Business and Economic Research, Michigan State University, 1961), preface vii.

[6]Eldon S. Hendriksen, Accounting Theory (Revised edition; Homewood, Illinois: Richard D. Irwin, Inc., 1970), pp. 68-69.

[7]Stephen A. Zeff, The American Accounting Association, Its First 50 Years (Evanston, Illinois: American Accounting Association, 1966), pp. 55-57.

of Accountants, in 1940, provided an initial impetus toward making this an accounting best seller. The Structure of Accounting Theory was never distributed on a similar basis.

Structure of Accounting Theory, published in 1953, grew out of Littleton's seminars, thinking, and writing over a twenty-year period. In 1966, there had been six printings or a total of 11,300 copies sold. In 1955, it also was published in a Japanese translation by Toshiro Otsuka, Kobe University; by 1966, 4,000 copies had been sold.[8]

Another interesting indication of the far-reaching influence of Littleton's writings is contained in a Japanese article written by Professor Ichiro Katana for a special issue of The Hitotsubashi Review. The issue contained articles about the life and works of nine selected international scholars.[9]

It is apparent that 302 articles, editorials, comments, discussions, bulletins, and book reviews written and presented in the various accounting journals from 1926 to 1966 constitute a conspicuous contribution to the literature of accounting. It is worth repeating that the articles covered a broad spectrum of topics in total although the bulk covered basic and continuing topics of

---

[8]Ibid., p. 58.

[9]Ichiro Katana, "A. C. Littleton and His Accounting Thought," The Hitotsubashi Review, LIII, No. 4 (April, 1965), Special Issue: Eminent Scholars--Notes on Their Life and Work (translated by Yukio Fujita).

interest and importance to the field of accounting. Con-temporaries took careful note of Littleton's views. He furnished guidance, inspiration, and thought-provoking ideas to accountants during the four-decade period.

Littleton served as director of research and later as editor of The Accounting Review for the American Ac-counting Association for a total of eight years. It appears that he used the editorial section and "The Accounting Ex-change" column of The Accounting Review as sounding boards for his views.

Littleton's recognition by various groups and or-ganizations is indicative of his impact. He received the American Accounting Association's Alpha Kappa Psi Award in 1955 for his contributions to the profession. He was selected for the Accounting Hall of Fame in 1956. In 1967, he was presented with an honorary doctor of laws degree by the University of Illinois.[10] In 1969, he was honored as the first recipient of the Weldon Powell Memorial Profes-sorship grant at the University of Illinois. This grant is awarded upon the basis of the following qualifications:

> (1) truly stimulating and influential as a teacher, (2) an unusual capacity for research amply supported by publications, (3) a substan-tial record of professional services, and (4) a high order of support of the university's and

---

[10]V. K. Zimmerman, unpublished interview recorded by K. T. Current, July 9, 1969: ". . . in our system this is a rare honor. Few faculty are honored in that way, and certainly few alumni faculty . . . and to be so honored after fifteen years of retirement is very unique."

department's total program in teaching, research and public contacts.[11]

Other Recurrent Themes

Certain themes are recurrent in all of Littleton's writings. Littleton was ever conscious of the role of history and its influence in the development of accounting ideas. He looked to history as a source of support for present practices and ideas. He saw change as a continuing element in the evolutionary development of accounting as a discipline responsive to change and need. He emphasized continuously the interrelationship between theory and practice. The theory of accounting, he said, is rooted in transactions reflecting actions and experiences. Theory and practice are inseparably connected, and it is not possible for either to stand alone. It follows that accounting is a practical art. In his continuing discussions of the historical cost concept, Littleton repeatedly referred to the choice among alternatives which must be faced. This choice lay between the use of cost or value in income determination.

Littleton's Philosophy--
His Beliefs and Attitudes

Littleton's beliefs and attitudes are illustrated in his written works. His meticulous care directed toward

---

[11]"From Public Information Office," January 23, 1969, Biographical File of A. C. Littleton, Office of President, University of Illinois, Urbana, Illinois.

224

clear, concise, and understandable presentations has already been mentioned. It is indicated that he read prodigiously, not only in accounting, but in other areas as well. He taught himself German, Italian, and enough French to be able to translate articles and make book reviews. There is repeated evidence that he exerted efforts to be well-grounded in the background and current material related to any subject upon which he wrote.

There are indications that his breadth of vision and keen analytical ability were exerted unstintingly in the consideration of accounting problems. Littleton developed a pictorial diagram to represent his views concerning the importance of analytical ability and analytical techniques as communication skills.[12] This diagram is presented in Appendix III to illustrate his idea of the necessity for not only a facility in manipulating figures but also an ability to communicate ideas via figures in order to use analytical ability in accounting. Littleton advanced the belief that analytical ability in association with a wide knowledge of accounting should result in technical competence. In his characteristically thorough manner, Littleton pointed out that the proper analytical ability and technique must be accompanied by additional qualities. He listed these as physical capacity for

---

[12]A. C. Littleton, "Accounting Exchange: Analytical Ability, Analytical Technique," The Accounting Review, XIX, No. 2 (April, 1944), pp. 196-98, and reprinted in Littleton, Essays, pp. 550-51.

concentrated work, capacity for continuing to grow with experience, a personality for friendliness and leadership, pride in professional craftmanship, resourceful adaptability, and common sense. Again, characteristically, he quoted Webster's _Dictionary of Synonyms_ in his explanation of common sense. He viewed common sense as a native capacity for seeing things as they are and without illusion or emotional bias, a capacity for making practical choices or decisions that are sane, prudent, fair, reasonable, and that convey themselves to the normal or average good mind.[13] It can be reasonably assumed that Littleton endeavored, at all times, to fulfill these qualifications as set forth.

The analytical scheme appears to forecast many points made by the recent _Horizons for a Profession_ study concerning the necessary skills of communication. It seems that Littleton should be properly recognized for this demonstration of foresight. The emphasis upon these elements of the professional accountant's necessary skills and preparation is another illustration of Littleton's own perception of the needs.

Summation

In conclusion, Littleton should be granted a place among the major contributors to accounting development during the first half of the twentieth century. The weight of

---

[13]Littleton, _Essays_, p. 550.

evidence clearly indicates his stature. His advocacy of the historical cost concept was recognized by contemporaries, and his influence has continued in this area. The historical cost concept is the basic one followed today in accounting for business enterprise transactions. His development of income determination concepts in conjunction with the cost allocation procedure to assist in the matching process was a major contribution of lasting significance. Again, the matching concept is a major concept today, and the income statement continues to be the report of primary significance. His continued and repetitive concern for the development of a structure of accounting theory based upon inductively derived principles rooted in experience and action has no doubt marked significantly the developments of the period. These areas of influence do not represent an all-inclusive picture of his total contribution. His impact should be viewed as a total consisting of these and other interrelated concepts; however, the areas covered by this study are, in fact, dominant themes.

APPENDIXES

APPENDIX I[1]

THE PUBLISHED WORKS OF A. C. LITTLETON

Introduction to Elementary Accounting. Cincinnati, Ohio: Southwestern Publishing Co., 1919.

Lectures on Retail Merchandising: A Short Course in Business for Retail Merchants. Champaign, Illinois: The Chamber of Commerce, 1920.

"Discussion: Karl F. McMurry's 'Graduate and Research Work in Accounting,'" The American Association of University Instructors in Accounting, Papers and Proceedings, Fourth Annual Meeting, Chicago, 1919, IV, No. 1. n.p., March, 1920.

"Adjusting Inventories," System, XXXVII, No. 6 (June, 1920), 1153-57.

Review of Kemper Simpson's Economics for the Accountant, Administration, III, No. 4 (April, 1922), 497-501.

"Discussion: To What Extent, If Any, Should Part-time Outside Paid Employment of Full-time University Instructors Be Encouraged?" The American Association of University Instructors in Accounting, Papers and Proceedings, Sixth Annual Meeting, Pittsburgh, 1921, VI, No. 1. n.p., April, 1922.

"An Appraisal of the Balance Sheet Approach." The American Association of University Instructors in Accounting, Papers and Proceedings of the Seventh Annual Meeting, Chicago, Illinois, 1922, II, No. 1. n.p., April, 1923.

---

[1]These works are arranged in chronological order.

(With) Adams, J. P. and Stevenson, R. A. "Report of the Committee on Standardization." The American Association of University Instructors in Accounting, Papers and Proceedings, Eighth Annual Meeting, Columbus, Ohio, 1923, VIII, No. 1. n.p., June, 1924.

"Discussion: Roy B. Kester's 'Principles of Valuation as Related to the Functions of the Balance Sheet,'" The American Association of University Instructors in Accounting, Papers and Proceedings, Eighth Annual Meeting, Columbus, Ohio, 1923, VIII, No. 1. n.p., June, 1924.

"The Relation of Accounting to the Business Cycle," The American Association of University Instructors in Accounting, Papers and Proceedings of the Ninth Annual Meeting, Chicago, 1924, IX, No. 1. n.p., February, 1925.

"A Study of the Costs of Retailing Nursery Stock," American Nursery, XXXXI, No. 4 (April, 1925), 99-105.

"The Development of Accounting Literature," Publications of the American Association of University Instructors in Accounting, IX, No. 2. Urbana, Illinois: n.p., December, 1925.

"The Cost of Doing Business," Farm Machines and Hardware, 1704 (1926), 46.

"Know Your Costs," Farm Machines and Hardware, 1706 (1926), 92.

"Research Work at the University of Illinois," The Accounting Review, I, No. 1 (March, 1926), 31-38.

"Italian Double Entry in Early England," The Accounting Review, I, No. 2 (June, 1926), 60-71.

The Current Ratio in Public Utility Companies, Bulletin No. 9. Urbana, Illinois: University of Illinois, College of Commerce and Business Administration, Bureau of Economic and Business Research, June 29, 1926.

"The 2 to 1 Ratio Analyzed," The Certified Public Accountant, VI, No. 8 (August, 1926), 244-46.

The Productivity Ratios of Public Utility Companies, Bulletin No. 10. Urbana, Illinois: University of Illinois, College of Commerce and Business Administration, Bureau of Economic and Business Research, September 14, 1926.

"The Current Ratio in Prosperity and Depression, Utilities Show Great Stability," The Annalist, XXVIII, No. 718 (October 22, 1926), 531-32.

"Evolution of the Ledger Account," The Accounting Review, I, No. 4 (December, 1926), 12-23.

"Two Pioneers of Accountancy," The Certified Public Accountant, VII, No. 2 (February, 1927), 35-37.

"Effects of Graduate Work," Pamphlet Conference on Graduate Work, Urbana, Illinois (May, 1927).

"The Antecedents of Double-Entry," The Accounting Review, II, No. 2 (June, 1927), 140-49.

"Thomas Jones -- Pioneer," The Certified Public Accountant, VII, No. 6 (June, 1927), 183-86.

(With) Winaker, A. H. Illinois Appropriations for Social and Educational Purposes, Research Bulletin No. 14. Urbana, Illinois: University of Illinois, College of Commerce and Business Administration, Bureau of Economic and Business Research, July 26, 1927.

"Two Fables of Bookkeeping," The Accounting Review, II, No. 4 (December, 1927), 388-96.

"University Education for Accountancy," The Certified Public Accountant, VII, No. 12 (December, 1927), 361-65, 369.

"The Accountant's Personal Library," Illinois Alumni News, V, No. 10 (1927), 374.

"Earning Power Ratios: A Statistical Comparison of Utilities and Industrials," The Annalist, XXXI, No. 795 (April 13, 1928), 645-46.

Property Investments in Public Utility Companies, Research Bulletin No. 18. Urbana, Illinois: University of Illinois, College of Commerce and Business Administration, Bureau of Economic and Business Research, April 17, 1928.

"Paciolo and Modern Accounting," The Accounting Review, III, No. 2 (June, 1928), 131-40.

"Pioneers of Accountancy," The Certified Public Accountant, VIII, No. 7 (July, 1928), 201-2, 217.

"What is Profit?" The Accounting Review, III, No. 3
(September, 1928), 278-88.

"The Evolution of the Journal Entry," The Accounting Review,
III, No. 4 (December, 1928), 383-96.

"The Ancient History of Accounting at Illinois," Enterpriser,
VIII, No. 2 (1928).

Review of Grimes and Caigue, "Principles of Valuation,"
Tax Bulletin, XIV (1928-1929), 1.

"Chartered Accountants for Germany," The Certified Public
Accountant, IX, No. 7 (July, 1929), 198.

Review of Franz Josef Dusemund's Der Betriebswirtschaftliche
Gewinnbegriff in seiner historischen Entwicklung
(Evolution of the Concept of Profit), (C. E. Poeschel,
1929), The Accounting Review, IV, No. 3 (September,
1929), 207.

"Value and Price in Accounting," The Accounting Review, IV,
No. 3 (September, 1929), 147-54.

Review of The International Congress on Accounting, 1929,
"Balance Sheet Theory and Practice," The Accounting
Review, IV, No. 4 (December, 1929), 234-41.

"The Fifth Year in Accounting," The Enterpriser, X, No. 2
(February, 1930), 11, 20.

"Comments on: 'A Symposium on Appreciation,'" The Accounting
Review, V, No. 1 (March, 1930), 57-59.

Review of The International Congress on Accounting, 1929,
"Education for the Profession," The Accounting Review,
V, No. 1 (March, 1930), 70-74.

Review of Hereward T. Price's, Volkswirtschafliches
Wörterbuch (Economic Dictionary), (Julius Springer,
Berlin. G. E. Steckert, New York). Vol. I, English-
German, 1927; Vol. II, German-English, 1929, The
Accounting Review, V, No. 1 (March, 1930), 79-81.

"Comments on the Definition of Earned Surplus," The
Accounting Review, V, No. 2 (June, 1930), 1970-71.

"Accounting for Appreciation in Two Typical Cases Described,"
The American Accountant, XV, No. 7 (July, 1930), 302-3.

"The Accounting Exchange: Foreign Accounting Terms," The
Accounting Review, V, No. 3 (September, 1930), 262-63.

"The Accounting Exchange: Foreign Accounting Terms," The
    Accounting Review, V, No. 4 (December, 1930), 320-22.

Die Ursachen der Trustbildung unter Vereinigten Staaten
    von Amerika. Zeits.f. Betriebswirtschaft. VIII,
    No. 1 (1930), 1-11.

Der heutige Stand des berufsmaessegen Revisionswesens in
    dem Vereinigten Staaten. Betriebswirtschaft. XXIII,
    No. 6 (1930), 171-75.

Die Entwicklung des Rechnungswesens in den Vereinigten
    Staaten. Zeitschrift für Handelswissenschaft und
    Handelspraxes. Stuttgart, XXII, No. 4 (1930).

"The Accounting Exchange: Foreign Accounting Terms,"
    The Accounting Review, VI, No. 1 (March, 1931), 64-65.

"A Cost Approach to Elementary Bookkeeping," The Accounting
    Review, VI, No. 1 (March, 1931), 33-37.

"The Accounting Exchange: Foreign Accounting Terms," The
    Accounting Review, VI, No. 2 (June, 1931), 147-49.

(Editorial). "Overburdened Terms," The Accounting Review,
    VI, No. 2 (June, 1931), 142-43.

"Early Transaction Analysis," The Accounting Review, VI,
    No. 3 (September, 1931), 179-83.

(Editorial). "Modernizing Certificates," The Accounting
    Review, VI, No. 3 (September, 1931), 231-32.

"More About Best Words to Use in Certificates," The
    American Accountant, XVI, No. 9 (September, 1931), 720.

(Editorial). "Social Significance of Accounting," The
    Accounting Review, VI, No. 3 (September, 1931), 230-32.

(Editorial). "Terminology for Accountants," The Accounting
    Review, VI, No. 3 (September, 1931), 232.

(Editorial). "Dispraise of Appreciation," The Accounting
    Review, VI, No. 4 (December, 1931), 305-7.

Review of Fritz Henzel's Erfassung und Verrechnung der
    Gemeinskosten in der Unternehmung, (Spaeth and Linde,
    1931), The Accounting Review, VI, No. 4 (December,
    1931), 324-25.

Review of Henrich Horn's Tendenzen zur Aussonderung von Vermögenswertänderungen in Betriebswirtschaftslehre, Wirtschaftspaxis und Steuerrecht, (Spaeth, & Linde, 1931), The Accounting Review, VI, No. 4 (December, 1931), 324-25.

Review of Werner Rusche's Die Nennwertlose Aktie, (Emil Pilgram, 1931), The Accounting Review, VI, No. 4 (December, 1931), 324-25.

"Die Ausbildung des Revisors in der Vereinigten Staaten von Amerika," Die Betriebswirtschaft (periodical), (Stuttgart), XXV, No. 10 (1932), 235-73.

(With) Hatfield, H. R. "A Check-List of Early Bookkeeping Texts," The Accounting Review, VII, No. 3 (September, 1932), 194-206.

"Capital and Surplus," The Accounting Review, VII, No. 4 (December, 1932), 290-93.

Accounting Evolution to 1900. New York: Russell & Russell, Reissued, 1966 (American Institute Publishing Co., Inc., 1933).

Review of Dr. H. Nicklisch's Die Betriebswirtschaft (Business Administration, 7th edition), (Stuttgart: C. E. Poeschel, 1932), The Accounting Review, III, No. 1 (March, 1933), 88-89.

Review of Dr. R. Ruth and Dr. K. Schmaltz's Bilanz der Aktiengesellschaft, (Berlin: Franz Vahlen, 1932), The Accounting Review, III, No. 1 (March, 1933), 88-89.

Review of Wirtschaftsprufung und Revisionswesen. Special, double number of Die Betriebswirtschaft (periodical), (Stuttgart: C. E. Poeschel, 1932), The Accounting Review, III, No. 1 (March, 1933), 88-89.

"Creditors' Interest in Surplus," Certified Public Accountant, XIII, No. 4 (April, 1933), 199-202.

"The Accounting Exchange: Independent Study," The Accounting Review, VIII, No. 2 (June, 1933), 160-61.

"Capital Flexibility," The Journal of Accountancy, LVI, No. 2 (August, 1933), 102-8.

"Social Origins of Modern Accountancy," The Journal of Accountancy, LVI, No. 4 (October, 1933), 261-70.

Book Review of Balduin Penndorf's Abhandlung uber die
Buchhaltung (Luca Pacioli's Summa . . . interpreted
in German), (Stuttgart: C. E. Poeschel Verlag), The
Accounting Review, VIII, No. 4 (December, 1933),
359-60.

"Socialized Accounts," The Accounting Review, VIII, No. 4
(December, 1933), 267-71.

Book Review of John Briggs, Jr. and Stewart Lunch's
(Editors) Delaware Laws Affecting Business Combinations,
Annotated, (United States Corporation Company, 1933),
The Accounting Review, IX, No. 1 (March, 1934), 101-2.

Book Review of Proceedings of the Fourth International
Congress on Accounting, (Gee & Co., 1933), The
Accounting Review, IX, No. 1 (March, 1934), 102-3.

"Socialized Accounts (II)," The Accounting Review, IX,
No. 1 (March, 1934), 69-74.

"The Dividend Base," The Accounting Review, IX, No. 2
(June, 1934), 140-48.

Book Review of Willard J. Graham's Public Utility
Valuations, (University of Chicago Press, 1934), The
Accounting Review, IX, No. 2 (June, 1934), 186-88.

Book Review of Public Service Commission of Wisconsin's
Depreciation, A Review of Legal and Accounting
Problems, (New York: State Law Reporting Co., 1933),
The Accounting Review, IX, No. 2 (June, 1934),
186-188.

"Some Later Problems of Economic Planning," Illinois
Journal of Commerce, XVI, No. 6 (June, 1934), 8-9;
and XVI, No. 7 (July, 1934), 15-16.

"The Accounting Exchange: The Income Approach," The
Accounting Review, IX, No. 4 (December, 1934), 342-46.

"Dividends Presuppose Profits," The Accounting Review, IX,
No. 4 (December, 1934), 304-11.

Book Review of Florence Elder's Glossary of Mediaeval
Terms of Business - Italian Series 1200-1600. (The
Mediaeval Academy of America, 1934), The Accounting
Review, X, No. 1 (March, 1935), 119-21.

"Auditor Independence," The Journal of Accountancy, LIX,
No. 1 (April, 1935), 283-91.

"Educational Browsing," The Journal of Accountancy, LIX, No. 5 (May, 1935), 330-38.

"Value or Cost," The Accounting Review, X, No. 3 (September, 1935), 269-73.

Book Review of Harry C. Bentley and Ruth S. Leonard's Bibliography of Works on Accounting by American Authors, (H. C. Bentley, Vol. I, 1934 and Vol. II, 1935), The Journal of Accountancy, LX, No. 4 (October, 1935), 309-11.

"An Inevitably Mediocre Bureaucracy," The Journal of Accountancy, LX, No. 4 (October, 1935), 264-69.

Book Review of Gabriel A. D. Preinreich's The Nature of Dividends, (Lancaster Press, Inc., 1935), The Accounting Review, X, No. 4 (December, 1935), 413-14.

"Contrasting Theories of Profit," The Accounting Review, XI, No. 1 (March, 1936), 10-18.

"The Professional College," The Accounting Review, XI, No. 2 (June, 1936), 109-16.

Book Review of Henry W. Sweeney's Stabilized Accounting, (Harper's, 1936), The Accounting Review, XI, No. 3 (September, 1936), 296-99.

"Concepts of Income Underlying Accounting," The Accounting Review, XII, No. 1 (March, 1937), 13-22.

"Business Profits as a Legal Basis for Dividends," Harvard Business Review, XVI, No. 1, (Autumn, 1937), 51-61.

"The Accounting Exchange: Accounting Theses - A List Compiled," The Accounting Review, XII, No. 3 (September, 1937), 313-15.

Book Review of Raymond de Roover's La Formation et l'Expansion de la Comptabilite' à partie double (The Formation and Expansion of Double-entry Bookkeeping), (Paris: Librairie Armand Colin, 1937), The Accounting Review, XII, No. 4 (December, 1937), 440-41.

"Tests for Principles," The Accounting Review, XIII, No. 1 (March, 1938), 16-24.

"High Standards of Accounting," The Journal of Accountancy, LXVI, No. 2 (August, 1938), 99-105.

"The Relation of Function to Principles," The Accounting
    Review, XIII, No. 3 (September, 1938), 233-41.

"A Substitute for Stated Capital," Harvard Business Review,
    XVII, No. 1 (Autumn, 1938), 75-84.

Book Review of W. A. Hosmer's Problems in Accounting,
    Second Edition, (McGraw-Hill Book Company, Inc., 1938),
    The Accounting Review, XIII, No. 4, Part I (December,
    1938), 432-33.

"Suggestions for the Revision of the Tentative Statement of
    Accounting Principles," The Accounting Review, XIV,
    No. 1 (March, 1939), 57-64.

"Thesis Research," The Accounting Forum, (March, 1939).

"The Uses of Theory," The Journal of Accountancy, LXVII,
    No. 4 (April, 1939), 227-33.

"Accounting Research," Accounting Forum, XI (November, 1939),
    21-22.

(With) Paton, W. A. An Introduction to Corporate Accounting
    Standards, Monograph No. 3. Chicago, Illinois:
    American Accounting Association, 1940.

"The Integration of Income and Surplus Statements," The
    Journal of Accountancy, LXIX, No. 1 (January, 1940),
    30-41.

"A Genealogy for 'Cost or market,'" The Accounting Review,
    XVI, No. 2 (June, 1941), 161-67.

"Inventory Variations," The Journal of Accountancy, LXXII,
    No. 1 (July, 1941), 7-16.

"Questions on Accounting Standards," The Accounting Review,
    XVI, No. 4 (December, 1941), 330-40.

"The Meaning of Accounting Education," The Accounting Review,
    XVII, No. 3 (July, 1942), 215-21.

"Auditing Techniques," The Journal of Accountancy, LXXIV,
    No. 2 (August, 1942), 106-10.

Directory of Early American Public Accountants, Bulletin
    No. 62. Urbana, Illinois: University of Illinois,
    College of Commerce and Business Administration,
    Bureau of Economic and Business Research, October 13,
    1942.

"The Accounting Exchange: Costs Under Government Contracts,"
The Accounting Review, XVIII, No. 2 (April, 1943),
164-67.

"The Accounting Exchange: Fund Statement Terminology,"
The Accounting Review, XVIII, No. 2 (April, 1943),
159-64.

"The Accounting Exchange: Liberal Education," The
Accounting Review, XVIII, No. 2 (April, 1943), 156-57.

"The Accounting Exchange: Practitioners' Responsibilities,"
The Accounting Review, XVIII, No. 2 (April, 1943),
157-58.

"The Accounting Exchange: Vigorous Exploration," The
Accounting Review, XVIII, No. 2 (April, 1943), 156.

"The Accounting Exchange: Words and Figures," The
Accounting Review, XVIII, No. 2 (April, 1943), 158-59.

"A Message from the Incoming President," The Accounting
Review, XVIII, No. 2 (April, 1943), 185-87.

Book Review of Walter A. Staub's Accounting Developments
During the Present Century, (Harvard University Press,
1942), The Accounting Review, XVIII, No. 2 (April,
1943), 178-80.

"The Accounting Exchange: Aptitudes," The Accounting
Review, XVIII, No. 3 (July, 1943), 272-73.

"The Accounting Exchange: Attributes of a Profession," The
Accounting Review, XVIII, No. 3 (July, 1943), 269-70.

"The Accounting Exchange: Educational Compromise," The
Accounting Review, XVIII, No. 3 (July, 1943), 270-71.

"The Accounting Exchange: The Social Sciences," The
Accounting Review, XVIII, No. 3 (July, 1943), 271-72.

"Association Reports - Memorandum from the President," The
Accounting Review, XVIII, No. 3 (July, 1943), 288-90.

"The Accounting Exchange: Accounting Principles," The
Accounting Review, XVIII, No. 4 (October, 1943),
369-70.

"The Accounting Exchange: Examination Horoscope," The
Accounting Review, XVIII, No. 4 (October, 1943),
370-71.

"The Accounting Exchange: Final Professional Examinations,"
The Accounting Review, XVIII, No. 4 (October, 1943),
372-73.

"The Accounting Exchange: Intermediate Examinations," The
Accounting Review, XVIII, No. 4 (October, 1943),
371-72.

"The Accounting Exchange: Principles of War," The Accounting
Review, XVIII, No. 4 (October, 1943), 368-69.

"Association Reports - Representative College Programs,"
The Accounting Review, XVIII, No. 4 (October, 1943),
382-91.

"Examinations in Auditing," The Accounting Review, XVIII,
No. 4 (October, 1943), 307-16.

"The Accounting Exchange: Categories of Accountants,"
The Accounting Review, XIX, No. 1 (January, 1944),
81-82.

"The Accounting Exchange: Counsels of Perfection," The
Accounting Review, XIX, No. 1 (January, 1944), 86.

"The Accounting Exchange: Qualities Classified," The
Accounting Review, XIX, No. 1 (January, 1944), 83-85.

"The Accounting Exchange: Qualities of Conduct," The
Accounting Review, XIX, No. 1 (January, 1944), 85.

"The Accounting Exchange: Qualities of Mentality," The
Accounting Review, XIX, No. 1 (January, 1944), 85.

"The Accounting Exchange: Qualities of Personality," The
Accounting Review, XIX, No. 1 (January, 1944), 85.

"The Accounting Exchange: Qualities Related to Aptitude,"
The Accounting Review, XIX, No. 1 (January, 1944),
85-86.

"The Accounting Exchange: Traits Underlying Success," The
Accounting Review, XIX, No. 1 (January, 1944), 82-83.

"Association Reports - Representative College Programs,"
The Accounting Review, XIX, No. 1 (January, 1944),
99-108.

"The Accounting Exchange: Analytical Ability," The
Accounting Review, XIX, No. 2 (April, 1944), 196-97.

"The Accounting Exchange: Analytical Technique," The Accounting Review, XIX, No. 2 (April, 1944), 197-98.

"The Accounting Exchange: The Junior Assistant," The Accounting Review, XIX, No. 2 (April, 1944), 194-95.

"The Accounting Exchange: Mathematics," The Accounting Review, XIX, No. 2 (April, 1944), 195-96.

"The Accounting Exchange: Selection of Personnel," The Accounting Review, XIX, No. 2 (April, 1944), 193-94.

"Association Reports for the Year 1943," The Accounting Review, XIX, No. 2 (April, 1944), 221-30.

"Association Reports - Representative College Programs," The Accounting Review, XIX, No. 3 (July, 1944), 347-60.

"The Accounting Exchange: Cultural Economics," The Accounting Review, XIX, No. 3 (July, 1944), 319-22.

"The Accounting Exchange: Culture in Accountancy," The Accounting Review, XIX, No. 3 (July, 1944), 322-23.

"The Accounting Exchange: Economic Literacy," The Accounting Review, XIX, No. 3 (July, 1944), 319.

"The Accounting Exchange: Educational Theory," The Accounting Review, XIX, No. 3 (July, 1944), 315-16.

"The Accounting Exchange: Hypothetical Programs," The Accounting Review, XIX, No. 3 (July, 1944), 317-19.

"The Accounting Exchange: Mixed Program," The Accounting Review, XIX, No. 3 (July, 1944), 316-17.

"The Accounting Exchange: Social Significance," The Accounting Review, XIX, No. 3 (July, 1944), 315.

Book Review of Margaret E. Broadley's Square Pegs in Square Holes, (New York: Doubleday, Doran & Co., 1943), The Accounting Review, XIX, No. 3 (July, 1944), 340-41.

"The Accounting Exchange: Claims Upon Income," The Accounting Review, XIX, No. 4 (October, 1944), 452-53.

"The Accounting Exchange: Educational Director," The Accounting Review, XIX, No. 4 (October, 1944), 451-52.

"The Accounting Exchange: Fifteenth Century Reserves,"
The Accounting Review, XIX, No. 4 (October, 1944),
457-59.

"The Accounting Exchange: Interacting Forces," The
Accounting Review, XIX, No. 4 (October, 1944), 453-55.

"The Accounting Exchange: Internal Auditing," The
Accounting Review, XIX, No. 4 (October, 1944), 456-57.

"The Accounting Exchange: Interpreter - Moderator," The
Accounting Review, XIX, No. 4 (October, 1944), 455-56.

"The Accounting Exchange: Statistical Accounting," The
Accounting Review, XIX, No. 4 (October, 1944), 457.

"The Accounting Exchange: Technology of Profession," The
Accounting Review, XIX, No. 4 (October, 1944), 455.

"The Accounting Exchange: Traveling Auditor," The
Accounting Review, XIX, No. 4 (October, 1944), 459.

"Association Reports - Annual Meeting," The Accounting
Review, XIX, No. 4 (October, 1944), 469-76.

"Occupational Levels in Public Accounting," The Journal of
Accountancy, LXXVIII, No. 6 (December, 1944), 470-76.

"The Accounting Exchange: Counselling Service," The
Accounting Review, XX, No. 1 (January, 1945), 104.

"The Accounting Exchange: CPA Legislation," The Accounting
Review, XX, No. 1 (January, 1945), 106-7.

"The Accounting Exchange: Delayed Certification," The
Accounting Review, XX, No. 1 (January, 1945), 110-11.

"The Accounting Exchange: Examination Statistics," The
Accounting Review, XX, No. 1 (January, 1945), 104-6.

"The Accounting Exchange: Mixed Candidates," The Accounting
Review, XX, No. 1 (January, 1945), 111-12.

"The Accounting Exchange: Satisfactory Experience," The
Accounting Review, XX, No. 1 (January, 1945), 107-8.

"The Accounting Exchange: Substitutes for Education," The
Accounting Review, XX, No. 1 (January, 1945), 108-9.

"The Accounting Exchange: Trends in Certification," The
Accounting Review, XX, No. 1 (January, 1945), 109-10.

"The Accounting Exchange: Bank Reconciliation," The Accounting Review, XX, No. 2 (April, 1945), 233-34.

"The Accounting Exchange: Coordinated Research," The Accounting Review, XX, No. 2 (April, 1945), 231-32.

"The Accounting Exchange: Federal Accounting," The Accounting Review, XX, No. 2 (April, 1945), 232-33.

"The Accounting Exchange: Grade Consistency," The Accounting Review, XX, No. 2 (April, 1945), 239-40.

"The Accounting Exchange: Measuring the Quality of Teaching," The Accounting Review, XX, No. 2 (April, 1945), 239.

"The Accounting Exchange: Raising the Sights," The Accounting Review, XX, No. 2 (April, 1945), 235-36.

"The Accounting Exchange: Student Achievement Tests," The Accounting Review, XX, No. 2 (April, 1945), 238.

"The Accounting Exchange: Trained Powers of Observation," The Accounting Review, XX, No. 2 (April, 1945), 236-38.

"The Accounting Exchange: Why and How," The Accounting Review, XX, No. 2 (April, 1945), 235.

"The Accounting Exchange: Auditing Progress," The Accounting Review, XX, No. 3 (July, 1945), 349-50.

"The Accounting Exchange: Balance Sheet Prominence," The Accounting Review, XX, No. 3 (July, 1945), 352-54.

"The Accounting Exchange: Capacities," The Accounting Review, XX, No. 3 (July, 1945), 354-56.

"The Accounting Exchange: Classroom Screening," The Accounting Review, XX, No. 3 (July, 1945), 356-57.

"The Accounting Exchange: Committees on Education," The Accounting Review, XX, No. 3 (July, 1945), 348-49.

"The Accounting Exchange: The Indispensable," The Accounting Review, XX, No. 3 (July, 1945), 350-52.

The Accounting Exchange: Professional Qualities," The Accounting Review, XX, No. 3 (July, 1945), 357-59.

"The Accounting Exchange: Technical Monographs," The
   Accounting Review, XX, No. 3 (July, 1945), 350.

"Association Reports - Representative College Programs,"
   The Accounting Review, XX, No. 3 (July, 1945), 380-89.

"The Accounting Exchange: Admission to Examinations," The
   Accounting Review, XX, No. 4 (October, 1945), 466-67.

"The Accounting Exchange: Creation of Concepts," The
   Accounting Review, XX, No. 4 (October, 1945), 469.

"The Accounting Exchange: Leadership for Legislation,"
   The Accounting Review, XX, No. 4 (October, 1945),
   465-66.

"The Accounting Exchange: Recognition of Schools," The
   Accounting Review, XX, No. 4 (October, 1945), 467-69.

"The Accounting Exchange: Some Questions About Regulations,"
   The Accounting Review, XX, No. 4 (October, 1945),
   469-71.

"The Accounting Exchange: Group Education," The Accounting
   Review, XXI, No. 2 (April, 1946), 219.

"The Accounting Exchange: Help from the Larger Firms,"
   The Accounting Review, XXI, No. 2 (April, 1946),
   213-14.

"The Accounting Exchange: Provide for All Losses," The
   Accounting Review, XXI, No. 2 (April, 1946), 216-17.

"The Accounting Exchange: The Smaller Practitioner," The
   Accounting Review, XXI, No. 2 (April, 1946), 212-13.

"The Accounting Exchange: Statistical Truth," The
   Accounting Review, XXI, No. 2 (April, 1946), 215-16.

"The Accounting Exchange: Theory Can Be Useful," The
   Accounting Review, XXI, No. 2 (April, 1946), 214-16.

"The Accounting Exchange: The Valuationist," The Accounting
   Review, XXI, No. 2 (April, 1946), 217-19.

"Correspondence: Inventory Pricing," The Journal of
   Accountancy, LXXXI, No. 4 (April, 1946), 333-34.

"Correspondence: November, 1945, CPA Examination," The
   Journal of Accountancy, LXXXI, No. 6 (June, 1946),
   513-14.

Book Review of George O. May's Financial Accounting,
(Macmillan Company, 1943), The Accounting Review,
XXI, No. 3 (July, 1946), 352-56.

"The Accounting Exchange: Assets and Surplus," The
Accounting Review, XXI, No. 3 (July, 1946), 341-43.

"The Accounting Exchange: Balance-Sheet Headings," The
Accounting Review, XXI, No. 3 (July, 1946), 343-44.

"The Accounting Exchange: Effects and Debts," The
Accounting Review, XXI, No. 3 (July, 1946), 340-41.

"The Accounting Exchange: Surplus in the Law," The
Accounting Review, XXI, No. 3 (July, 1946), 338-40.

"The Accounting Exchange: 'Surplus' Terminology,"
The Accounting Review, XXI, No. 3 (July, 1946), 337-38.

"The Accounting Exchange: Accounting Courses," The
Accounting Review, XXI, No. 4 (October, 1946), 452-53.

"The Accounting Exchange: Accounting Limitations," The
Accounting Review, XXI, No. 4 (October, 1946), 455-56.

"The Accounting Exchange: Collateral Courses," The
Accounting Review, XXI, No. 4 (October, 1946), 452.

"The Accounting Exchange: Early Accounting Machines,"
The Accounting Review, XXI, No. 4 (October, 1946),
460-62.

"The Accounting Exchange: Field Training," The Accounting
Review, XXI, No. 4 (October, 1946), 453.

"The Accounting Exchange: Foundation Courses," The
Accounting Review, XXI, No. 4 (October, 1946), 451-52.

"The Accounting Exchange: The Horizontal Ledger," The
Accounting Review, XXI, No. 4 (October, 1946), 459-60.

"The Accounting Exchange: Qualifications of Trainees,"
The Accounting Review, XXI, No. 4 (October, 1946), 451.

"The Accounting Exchange: Sixteenth Century Systems," The
Accounting Review, XXI, No. 4 (October, 1946), 462-63.

"The Accounting Exchange: Toward a Broad Course," The
Accounting Review, XXI, No. 4 (October, 1946), 453-55.

"The Accounting Exchange: Towards a Professional Course,"
    The Accounting Review, XXI, No. 4 (October, 1946),
    456-59.

"Guidance Tests for Accounting Students," The Accounting
    Review, XXI, No. 4 (October, 1946), 404-9.

"The Accounting Exchange: Post-CPA Education," The
    Accounting Review, XXII, No. 1 (January, 1947), 85-86.

"The Accounting Exchange: Public Opinion," The Accounting
    Review, XXII, No. 1 (January, 1947), 84-85.

"The Accounting Exchange: Serving the Public Interest,"
    The Accounting Review, XXII, No. 1 (January, 1947),
    81-84.

"The Accounting Exchange: Upper Staff School," The
    Accounting Review, XXII, No. 1 (January, 1947), 86-88.

"The Accounting Exchange: What Auditors Do," The Accounting
    Review, XXII, No. 1 (January, 1947), 80-81.

"Three Audit Principles," The Journal of Accountancy,
    LXXXIII, No. 4 (April, 1947), 280-82.

"Vocabulary of Auditing Technique," The New York Certified
    Public Accountant, XVII, No. 10 (October, 1947),
    639-44.

"Fixed Assets and Accounting Theory," The Illinois CPA, X,
    No. 3 (March, 1948), 11-18.

"Extension of Accrual Principles Would Help Depreciation
    Accounting," The Journal of Accountancy, LXXXVI, No. 1
    (July, 1948), 21-22.

"Inventory Disclosures," The New York Certified Public
    Accountant, XVIII, No. 11 (November, 1948), 807-10.

Book Review of Raymond de Roover's The Medici Bank, (New
    York University Press, 1948), The Accounting Review,
    XXIV, No. 2 (April, 1949), 229-30.

"Classified Objectives," The Accounting Review, XXIV, No. 3
    (July, 1949), 281-84.

Book Review of Lybrand, Ross Bros. & Montgomery's Fiftieth
    Anniversary, 1898-1948, (Philadelphia: privately
    printed, 1949), The Accounting Review, XXIV, No. 3
    (July, 1949), 330-31.

"Correspondence: Leo Schmidt's Premises Could Be Called
    Broad Generalizations, and Out of Context They Could
    Be Dangerous," The Journal of Accountancy, LXXXIX,
    No. 3 (March, 1950), 16.

"The Teachers' Clinic: A Third Use Value of Accounting,"
    The Accounting Review, XXV, No. 2 (April, 1950), 192-93.

"The Teachers' Clinic: The Social Service of Accounting,"
    The Accounting Review, XXV, No. 3 (July, 1950), 320-21.

"Inductive Reasoning in Accounting," The New York Certified
    Public Accountant, XX, No. 8 (August, 1950), 449-60.

"Inductive Reasoning in Accounting - II," The New York
    Certified Public Accountant, XX, No. 11 (November,
    1950), 641-51.

"Educational Theory in Accountancy," Collegiate News and
    Views, IV, No. 4 (May, 1951), 5-9.

"The Teachers' Clinic: Removing the Mysteries from
    Accounting," The Accounting Review, XXVI, No. 3 (July,
    1951), 418-20.

"Preparation for the CPA, Technical or Liberal Education,"
    The Illinois CPA, XIV, No. 2 (December, 1951), 50-53.

"Characteristics of a Profession," The New York Certified
    Public Accountant, XXII, No. 4 (April, 1952), 207-11.

Significance of Invested Cost," The Accounting Review,
    XXVII, No. 2 (April, 1952), 167-73.

Book Review of Brian Magee's Dicksee's Auditing, Seven-
    teenth Edition, (London: Gee and Co., 1951), The
    Accounting Review, XXVII, No. 3 (July, 1952), 405-6.

Structure of Accounting Theory, Monograph No. 5. Urbana,
    Illinois: American Accounting Association, 1953.

"A Reply," The Accounting Review, XXVIII, No. 1 (January,
    1953), 8-11.

"Conflicting Ideas," Hermes (Quebec), (Spring, 1953).

"The Trust Fund Doctrine," Hermes (Quebec), (Spring, 1953).

"Accounting Theory: 1933-1953," The Accounting Forum,
    XXIV (May, 1953), 11-15, 21.

246

"Formal Education for Accountants," The Illinois Certified
Public Accountant, XV, No. 4 (June, 1953), 43-47.

"Variety in the Concept of Income," The New York Certified
Public Accountant, XXIII, No. 7 (July, 1953), 419-24.

"Principles Under Challenge," The New York Certified Public
Accountant, XXIV, No. 1 (January, 1954), 24-28.

"The Principle of Irrelevant Effects," The Illinois
Certified Public Accountant, XVI, No. 3 (March, 1954),
21-24.

"Old and New in Management and Accounting," The Accounting
Review, XXIX, No. 2 (April, 1954), 196-200.

"But Is It Accounting?" The New York Certified Public
Accountant, XXIV, No. 11 (November, 1954), 688-92.

"The Logic of Accounts," The Accounting Review, XXX, No. 1
(January, 1955), 45-47.

Book Review of Nicholas A. H. Stacey's English Accountancy,
1800-1954, (London: Gee & Co., 1954 and Staples Press,
Inc., New York), The Accounting Review, XXX, No. 1
(January, 1955), 160-63.

Book Review of Norman E. Webster's (compiler) The American
Association of Public Accountants, Its First Twenty
Years, (New York: American Institute of Accountants,
1954), The Accounting Review, XXX, No. 1 (January,
1955), 160-63.

"Prestige for Historical Cost," The Illinois Certified
Public Accountant, XVII, No. 3 (March, 1955), 23-27.

"Some Thoughts on Accounting Instruction at the University
of Illinois." Unpublished article, University of
Illinois, 1956.

(With) Yamey, B. S., Editors. Studies in the History of
Accounting. Homewood, Illinois: Richard D. Irwin, Inc.,
1956.

"Towards Understanding Accountancy," The Australian
Accountant, XXVI, No. 2 (February, 1956), 81-84.

"Two Professions in Contact," American Business Law
Association Bulletin, I (March, 1956), 21-26.

"Economists and Accountants," The Illinois Certified Public Accountant, XVIII, No. 4 (Summer, 1956), 18-24.

"Choice Among Alternatives," The Accounting Review, XXXI, No. 3 (July, 1956), 363-70.

"Learning to Write," The New York Certified Public Accountant, XXVI, No. 10 (October, 1956), 608-12.

"Do-It-Yourself Writing," The Illinois Certified Public Accountant, XIX, No. 4 (Summer, 1957), 46-48.

Book Review of F. Sewell Bray's The Interpretation of Accounts, (New York and London: Oxford University Press, 1957), The Accounting Review, XXXIII, No. 1 (January, 1958), 157-59.

"Education for Professional Accounting," Western Business Review, II, No. 1 (February, 1958), 50-53.

"Accounting Rediscovered," The Accounting Review, XXXIII, No. 2 (April, 1958), 246-53.

Book Review of Louis Goldberg's An Outline of Accounting, Fourth Edition, (Melbourne: Law Book Co. of Australasia, Ltd., 1957), The Accounting Review, XXXIII, No. 2 (April, 1958), 347-48.

"The Search for Accounting Principles," The New York Certified Public Accountant, XXVIII, No. 4 (April, 1958), 247-56.

"The Interpretative Function," The Illinois Certified Public Accountant, XXII, No. 2 (Winter, 1959-60), 3-7.

Essays on Accountancy. Urbana, Illinois: University of Illinois Press, 1961.

Book Review of James Don Edwards' History of Public Accounting in the United States, (Bureau of Business and Economic Research, Michigan State University, 1960), The Journal of Accountancy, CXI, No. 5 (May, 1961), 93-94.

"Mission and Method," The Illinois Certified Public Accountant, XXIII, No. 4 (Summer, 1961), 1-5.

(With) Zimmerman, V. K. Accounting Theory: Continuity and Change. Englewood Cliffs, New Jersey: Prentice-Hall, Inc., 1962.

"The Purpose of Accounting Education," Proceedings of International Conference on Accounting Education, 1962. Urbana: Center for International Education and Research in Accounting, 1962, 12-20.

Book Review of Maurice Moonitz's The Basic Postulates of Accounting, Accounting Research Study No. 1, (American Institute of Certified Public Accountants, 1961), The Accounting Review, XXXVII, No. 3 (July, 1962), 602-5.

Book Review of Robert T. Sprouse and Maurice Moonitz's A Tentative Set of Broad Accounting Principles for Business Enterprises, Accounting Research Study No. 3, (American Institute of Certified Public Accountants, 1962), The Accounting Review, XXXVIII, No. 1 (January, 1963), 220-22.

"The Heart of the Matter," The Illinois Certified Public Accountant, XXV, No. 4 (Summer, 1963), 1-9.

"Appraising the Knowns," The Illinois Certified Public Accountant, XXVII, No. 2 (Winter, 1964), 7-11.

"Integrity," The Illinois Certified Public Accountant, XXVI, No. 3 (Spring, 1964), 6-9.

"Reporting the Financial Effects of Price-Level Changes'- A Commentary," The Illinois Certified Public Accountant, XXVI, No. 4 (Summer, 1964), 1-7.

(With) Moonitz, Maurice, Editors. Significant Accounting Essays. Englewood Cliffs, New Jersey: Prentice-Hall, Inc., 1965.

Book Review of Eric L. Kohler's Accounting for Management, (Englewood Cliffs, New Jersey: Prentice-Hall, Inc., 1965), The Journal of Accountancy, CXXI, No. 1 (January, 1966), 93-94.

"'An Inventory of Principles,'" The Illinois Certified Public Accountant, XXVII, No. 4 (Summer, 1965), 14-16.

"The Continuing Importance of Basic Concepts," The International Journal of Accounting, I, No. 1, Fall, 1965. Edited by V. K. Zimmerman. Urbana: Center for International Education and Research in Accounting, 1965, 55-65.

"The Significance of Interrelated Concepts in Accounting,"
The International Journal of Accounting, II, No. 1,
Fall, 1966. Edited by V. K. Zimmerman. Urbana:
Center for International Education and Research in
Accounting, 1966, 25-34.

Book Review of R. J. Chambers, L. Goldberg, and R. L.
Mathews' (Editors) The Accounting Frontier, (Melbourne,
Australia: F. W. Cheshire, 1966), The Accounting
Review, XLII, No. 2 (April, 1967), 421.

"Factors Limiting Accounting," The Accounting Review, XLV,
No. 3 (July, 1970), 476-80.

APPENDIX II

BIOGRAPHICAL SKETCH

Ananias Charles Littleton was born December 4, 1886, at Bloomington, Illinois, in the United States of America. After finishing high school in the class of 1905 at Bloomington,[1] Littleton worked for two years as a telegrapher on the Chicago and Alton Railroad to earn funds for college.[2] The Study of railroad administration, at the University of Illinois, seemed a reasonable program in conjunction with his part-time employment as a railroad telegrapher. However, as a sophomore he learned of the relatively new Illinois Certified Public Accountant statute and decided to prepare for the profession of public accounting.[3]

---

[1]"Request for Information, August 6, 1915," Biographical File of A. C. Littleton, Office of the President, University of Illinois, Urbana, Illinois (Hereinafter referred to as "Request, August 6, 1915," Biographical File, Office of the President).

[2]Newspaper clipping, December 5, 1925, "Littleton Has Birthday Today," Biographical File of A. C. Littleton, Alumni Office, University of Illinois, Urbana, Illinois (Hereinafter referred to as "Birthday," Biographical File, Alumni Office).

[3]V. K. Zimmerman, "The Long Shadow of a Scholar," The International Journal of Accounting Education and Research, II, No. 2 (Spring, 1967), pp. 2-3 of reprint.

As a senior in 1912, Littleton was elected to Delta Kappa Chi which later became one of the charter chapters of Beta Gamma Sigma in 1913.[4] Concentration on economics and accounting subjects led to an undergraduate degree in business administration in 1912.[5]

During the year of 1913 Littleton compiled a history of Delta Kappa Chi for use by the newly organized Beta Gamma Sigma.[6] After graduation from the University of Illinois, Littleton took a position with a public accounting firm in Chicago, Illinois. From 1912-1915, he worked with this firm, Deloitte, Plender, Griffith and Co.[7] In September, 1915, an invitation was received to return to the University of Illinois as an instructor of accounting. The invitation was extended by Hiram T. Scovill, who had been Littleton's senior accountant and associate at the public accounting firm. Scovill had later returned to the University to teach and

---

[4]Fayette H. Elwell, The First 50 Years of Beta Gamma Sigma (Homewood, Illinois: Richard D. Irwin, Inc., 1963), pp. v, 10.

[5]"Request, August 6, 1915," Biographical File, Office of the President.

[6]Elwell, The First 50 Years of Beta Gamma Sigma, p. v.

[7]J. McKeen Cattell, Jaques Cattell, and E. E. Ross, eds., Leaders in Education, a Biographical Directory (2nd edition; New York: The Science Press, 1941), p. 619.

was increasing the accounting staff by 100 percent in 1915.[8]

Littleton served as an instructor of accounting at the

University from 1915-1919.[9]

On August 21, 1916, Miss Bonnie Ray of Terre Haute,

Indiana became his bride.[10] The Littletons were the parents

of two children, Barbara and Robert Scott.[11]

Littleton continued a course of graduate study and

received a Master of Arts degree in economics in 1918.[12]

One year later a Certified Public Accountant Certificate

(Number 229) was issued to him by the State of Illinois.[13]

In January, 1920, Littleton was appointed assistant

Dean of the College of Commerce by the University of

Illinois Board of Trustees. The first person to be named

---

[8]Hiram T. Scovill, "A. C. Littleton: Sound Theory is Necessary," unpublished article, April 25, 1956, Biographical File of A. C. Littleton, Department of Accountancy, College of Commerce and Business Administration, University of Illinois, Urbana, Illinois (Hereinafter referred to as Scovill, "Sound Theory," Biographical File, Department of Accountancy).

[9]"Permanent Academic and Professional Record," Biographical File of A. C. Littleton, Office of the President, University of Illinois, Urbana, Illinois.

[10]Cattell, Cattell, and Ross, eds., Leaders in Education, A Biographical Directory, p. 619.

[11]Newspaper clipping, Gazette, May 9, 1952, and Illinois Alumni News, July, 1952, Biographical File of A. C. Littleton, Alumni Office, University of Illinois, Urbana, Illinois.

[12]"Request for Information, March 17, 1926," Biographical File of A. C. Littleton, Office of the President, University of Illinois, Urbana, Illinois.

[13]"Birthday," Biographical File, Alumni Office.

to this position,[14] he served until 1922 when he was made assistant director of the bureau of business research.[15] Littleton served as assistant director of the bureau of business research for twenty years before his resignation, in 1941, in order to devote more time to teaching.[16]

Promotion to associate professor of accounting came in 1925.[17] Continued study and research led to a Doctor of Philosophy degree in economics in June, 1931. A thesis entitled "The Historical Foundations of Modern Accounting"[18] was written which later was developed into Accounting Evolution to 1900. Promotion to the rank of professor of accounting came in the same year.[19]

Graduate Degree Development

Littleton is widely credited as a primary force in the development of the graduate program at the University of

---

[14]Newspaper clipping, January 21, 1920, "Littleton Chosen Assistant Dean in Commerce College," Biographical File of A. C. Littleton, Alumni Office, University of Illinois, Urbana, Illinois.

[15]"Birthday," Biographical File, Alumni Office.

[16]"University Notes," The Accounting Review, XVI, No. 3 (September, 1941), 319.

[17]"University of Illinois News," Publications of the American Accounting Association of University Instructors in Accounting, IX, No. 2 (December, 1925), 174.

[18]"University Notes," The Accounting Review, VI, No. 2 (June, 1931), 158.

[19]"University Notes," The Accounting Review, VI, No. 3 (September, 1931), 245.

Illinois under which the first Doctor of Philosophy degree in accounting in the United States was conferred. Littleton, at the request of the head of the accounting department, Professor Hiram T. Scovill, had prepared graduate accounting courses in the 1920's. The development of these courses came at the same time he undertook his own advanced education at the doctoral level. He personally initiated and developed materials for a significant proportion of the graduate course offerings. Up to the time of his retirement, his imprint, both apparent and real, was reflected in the graduate curriculum. His tested course material is also reflected in his writings. He has been referred to as a one-man seminar.[20]

Effective September, 1936, authority was granted by the executive faculty of the Graduate School of the University of Illinois to offer work leading to a Doctor of Philosophy degree in accounting.[21] Littleton directed the ensuing development of the first doctoral level program in accounting in the United States.[22] In June, 1939, the

---

[20]V. K. Zimmerman, unpublished interview recorded by K. T. Current, July 9, 1969, Department of Accountancy, College of Commerce and Business Administration, University of Illinois, Urbana, Illinois and V. K. Zimmerman, "The Long Shadow of a Scholar," The International Journal of Accounting Education and Research, II, No. 2 (Spring, 1967), 3-4 (Hereinafter referred to as Zimmerman, "Shadow of a Scholar").

[21]"University Notes," The Accounting Review, XI, No. 2 (June, 1936), 207.

[22]"A. C. Littleton: Accounting Ideas Are Fun," The Journal of Accountancy, CI (June, 1956), 6 (Hereinafter referred to as "Accounting Ideas Are Fun").

first Doctor of Philosophy degree in accountancy was awarded. The total enrollment in the graduate program in 1939
was fifty-two.[23] The Dean of the College of Commerce and
Business Administration noted that this was, in fact, the
first Doctor of Philosophy degree in accountancy to be
awarded in the United States. This statement was made in
recognition of Littleton's efforts to inaugurate graduate
education in the field of accountancy.[24]

Littleton's creative efforts are demonstrated by
the statistics concerning supervision of graduate theses in
accountancy at the University of Illinois. University
records reveal the following facts for the years 1913-1952:

	Total Written at the University	Supervised by Littleton
Master's Theses	225	76 or 34%
Doctoral Theses	26	24 or 92%[25]

The list of graduate students who wrote their
master's theses or doctoral dissertations under the supervision of Littleton is impressive not only for its length.
The list includes the names of many who have become notable
writers in various areas of accounting. It includes the

---

[23]"University Notes," The Accounting Review, XIV,
No. 3 (September, 1939), 330.

[24]Paul M. Green, "Award of the Honorary Degree of
Doctor of Laws to A. C. Littleton," May 12, 1967, remarks
printed in "Newsletter, July, 1967," Center for International
Education and Research in Accounting, College of Commerce
and Business Administration, Department of Accountancy,
University of Illinois.

[25]Zimmerman, "Shadow of a Scholar," 4.

names of many who have become academicians and educators, as
well. Littleton necessarily exercised lasting influences
upon these graduate students. His deep and sincere interest
in the students and their work cannot be questioned. The
magnitude of his total impact upon accounting as it has been
and is being exerted through the efforts, contacts, and publications of his former students can only be the subject of
speculation. It would seem conservative to estimate that it
has been of quite considerable magnitude.

Hiram T. Scovill, the head of the Department of
Accountancy for the thirty-seven years Littleton spent at
the University of Illinois, noted in 1956, that Littleton's
influence was far-reaching. He made the following
observation:

> His impression on graduate students can be
> observed as his keen analysis of contemporary
> topics from time to time reflects itself through
> teachers in universities coast to coast.[26]

Retirement

At the age of 66, Littleton decided to retire. In a
letter to H. T. Scovill, head of the Department of
Accountancy, he said,

> . . . I grow tense and tired and irritable so
> easily these days that I have come to believe this
> has changed (and will increasingly reduce) my
> ability to do, satisfactorily to myself, the work
> which I find so absorbing. I have been most happy
> in my work and in my associations. It all has
> been more than I deserved; more than I have earned.

---

[26]Scovill, "Sound Theory." Biographical File,
Department of Accountancy.

The graduate work we have been building so long will not suffer if I fade out of the picture a few years early. You can have high confidence in the staff you have assembled. Some of them, without realizing it clearly, have been tested in various ways as understudies for my principal courses and other responsibilities. They are experienced teachers now, Ph.D.'s and C.P.A.'s; they will build well on the foundations we have laid, as many indications already show they can do. Sincerely and gratefully yours,[27]

Scovill forwarded Littleton's retirement request to the Dean with the following comments:

Professor A. C. Littleton has presented his request for retirement as of September 1, 1952 under Section 30 of the . . . I recommend that his request be granted.

My recommendation is made with regret because we would be very glad to have Professor Littleton serving on our staff until he reaches the maximum retiring age limit of 68. His services in the last 36 or 37 years have been invaluable in the development of our accountancy courses, and especially at the graduate level. . . . [28]

A dinner was held upon the occasion of Littleton's retirement. More than 100 colleagues honored him at this dinner held to recognize his thirty-seven years of service to the University.[29]

Retirement did not halt Littleton's interest in accountancy. Thinking and writing about his profession

[27]Biographical File of A. C. Littleton, Department of Accountancy, College of Commerce and Business Administration, University of Illinois, Urbana, Illinois.

[28]Letter dated February 27, 1952, Biographical File of A. C. Littleton, Department of Accountancy, College of Commerce and Business Administration, University of Illinois, Urbana, Illinois.

[29]Courier, Urbana, Illinois, May 27, 1952, Biographical File of A. C. Littleton, Alumni Office, University of Illinois, Urbana, Illinois.

258

continued to occupy his time. In 1956, he did not have
a hobby and explained it as follows: "Teaching and writing
about accounting were such engaging activities that, like
the tuba player, my work was play."[30] Littleton noted his
retirement pastimes as writing down accounting ideas and
painting. Both activities were absorbing and nontiring.
". . . And best of all, the results of both can be thrown
away if, the next day, they seem something less than
professional."[31]

The Illinois Society of
Certified Public Accountants

Littleton received a Certified Public Accountant
Certificate in 1919. Admitted as a member of the Illinois
Society of Certified Public Accountants in December, 1925,
he is listed in various issues of the Bulletin of the Society as a member from 1925-1932 and 1937-1950. Membership
listings for the years 1933-1936 do not show his name.[32]

Littleton was a member of the educational committee
of the society in 1939.[33] In 1940-1941, he was the chairman of the same committee.[34] Also, in 1940, he served as

---

[30]"Accounting Ideas Are Fun," 6.

[31]Ibid.

[32]The Bulletin of Illinois Society of Certified
Public Accountants, various issues.

[33]"University Notes," The Accounting Review, XIV,
No. 4, Part I (December, 1939), 464.

[34]Bulletin of Illinois Society of Certified Public
Accountants, Vol. II (December, 1940), 5.

a member of a committee to study the history of accounting
in Illinois. Littleton outlined the various topics and
chapters to be included in the book covering the entire history of accounting in Illinois following 1890. The topics
were then assigned to various members of the group for
completion.[35]

Littleton frequently appeared on the programs given
by the Illinois Society of Certified Public Accountants.
For example: A talk on the problems of instruction in a
graduate program was presented at a 1927 meeting.[36] In May,
1942, he participated in a presentation of a program along
with Samuel J. Broad, George Ellis, and Howard Greer, on
auditing standards.[37] On December 10, 1947, a paper on

---

[35]"History of Accounting in Illinois," Bulletin of
Illinois Society of Certified Public Accountants, II, No. 4
(September, 1940), 5.

[36]"Graduate Instruction in Accountancy," Program,
Illinois Society of Certified Public Accountants,
November 12, 1927, University of Illinois. Hiram T. Scovill
Papers, 1915-1959, Box No. 10, University Archives, College
of Commerce and Business Administration, University of Illi-
nois, Urbana, Illinois.

[37]"The Need for a Statement of Auditing Standards,"
Program, Illinois Society of Certified Public Accountants,
Annual Down-State Meeting, Illini Union Building, Urbana,
May 14-15, 1942. Hiram T. Scovill Papers, 1915-1959, Box
No. 10, University Archives, College of Commerce and Busi-
ness Administration, University of Illinois, Urbana,
Illinois.

"Property Accounting" was presented at the annual meeting of the Illinois Society.[38]

The American Institute of
Certified Public Accountants

Littleton served as a member of three different committees for the American Institute of Accountants. These memberships were on the Committee on Accounting Procedure from 1939-1941; the Committee on Selection of Personnel, 1943-1947; and the Committee on Accounting History, 1946-1947.[39] He continued on the Committee on Accounting History during the year 1948-1949.[40]

American Accounting Association

Littleton's most extensive work with professional organizations was undoubtedly with the American Association of University Instructors in Accounting and its successor organization, the American Accounting Association. The membership list of the organization first contained his name

---

[38]"Property Accounting," Program, Illinois Society Of Certified Public Accountants, Sixth Annual Accounting Conference, December 10, 1947. Hiram T. Scovill Papers, 1915-1959, Box No. 10, University Archives, College of Commerce and Business Administration, University of Illinois, Urbana, Illinois.

[39]"Biographical Sketch, October 4, 1957," Biographical File of A. C. Littleton, Department of Accountancy, College of Commerce and Business Administration, University of Illinois, Urbana, Illinois.

[40]"Committee on History," American Institute of Accountants, Officers and Committees, Proceedings of 1948 Annual Meeting, By-Laws of the Institute, Rules of Professional Conduct, for the Year 1948-1949 (New York: American Institute of Accountants, 1948), 16.

in 1918, when there were a total of 122 members.[41] Active participation in the meetings and programs of the organization is evident. Papers were presented at a number of the annual meetings. In 1919, he took part in a discussion of a paper which was presented on graduate and research work in accounting.[42] In 1921, the question of outside employment for full-time instructors was discussed.[43] In 1922, a topic concerning methods of teaching the principles course in accounting was covered.[44] In 1923, Littleton discussed a paper which was presented on principles of valuation.[45] In

---

[41]The American Association of University Instructors in Accounting, Papers and Proceedings of the Third Annual Meeting, December, 1918, III, No. 1 (n.p., January, 1919), p. 46.

[42]A. C. Littleton, "Discussion: Karl F. McMurry's 'Graduate and Research Work in Accounting,'" The American Association of University Instructors in Accounting, Papers and Proceedings Fourth Annual Meeting, Chicago, 1919, II, No. 1 (n.p., March, 1920), pp. 83-86.

[43]A. C. Littleton, "Discussion: To What Extent, If Any, Should Part-time Outside Paid Employment of Full-time University Instructors Be Encouraged?" The American Association of University Instructors in Accounting, Papers and Proceedings Sixth Annual Meeting, Pittsburgh, 1921, VI, No. 1 (n.p., April, 1922), pp. 55-57.

[44]A. C. Littleton, "An Appraisal of the Balance Sheet Approach," The American Association of University Instructors in Accounting, Papers and Proceedings Seventh Annual Meeting, Chicago, Illinois, 1922, VII, No. 1 (n.p., April, 1923), pp. 85-92.

[45]A. C. Littleton, "Discussion: Roy B. Kester's 'Principles of Valuation as Related to the Functions of the Balance Sheet,'" The American Association of University Instructors in Accounting, Papers and Proceedings Eighth Annual Meeting, Columbus, Ohio, 1923, VIII, No. 1 (n.p., June, 1924), pp. 14-15.

1924, a paper concerning the need to study business cycles
in conjunction with the study of accounting constituted his
contribution to the program.[46] In 1925, Littleton presented
a paper concerning the development of accounting literature,[47] and in 1926, he took part in the third program
session.[48]

At the meeting in 1929, Littleton presented a
"Symposium on Appreciation," in which graduate students reported upon their research efforts at the University of Illinois under his guidance.[49] At the meeting held in 1930,
"A Cost Approach to Elementary Accounting" was the topic of
his paper.[50] In 1933, at the 18th annual convention,
Littleton was again on the program. He gave an address at

---

[46]A. C. Littleton, "The Relation of Accounting to
the Business Cycle," The American Association of University
Instructors in Accounting, Papers and Proceedings, Chicago,
1924, IX, No. 1 (n.p., February, 1925), pp. 108-16.

[47]A. C. Littleton, "The Development of Accounting
Literature," Publications of The American Association of
University Instructors in Accounting, IX, No. 2 (Urbana,
Illinois, December, 1925), pp. 7-17.

[48]A. C. Littleton, "Discussion: H. T. Scovill, 'The
Proper Treatment of Distribution Costs,'" Proceedings of
11th Annual Convention, The American Association of University Instructors in Accounting, The Accounting Review, II,
No. 1 (March, 1927), 74.

[49]Stephen A. Zeff, The American Accounting Association, Its First 50 Years, Commemorative Document of the 50th
Anniversary Meeting, 1966 (n.p., American Accounting Association, 1966), p. 33 (Hereinafter referred to as Zeff,
50th Anniversary).

[50]"Program of Fifteenth Annual Convention, American
Association of University Instructors in Accounting,
December 29-30, 1930," The Accounting Review, V, No. 4
(December, 1930), 341.

the Thursday evening session on December 28, entitled

"Accounting Evolution: Third Stage."[51] H. T. Scovill noted

that this was one of the major talks at the convention.[52]

In 1935, Littleton was again on the program at the

annual meeting as a major speaker. "Changing Themes of In-

come," was his topic.[53] This meeting was an important one

at which a real effort was made to revive membership inter-

est, to promote research efforts, and to merge the American

Association of University Instructors in Accounting with a

newly formed American Accounting Association. Pro-merger

speeches were made by Littleton and others. Littleton was

also nominated and elected as vice president of the new

organization for the following year.[54]

In 1936, Littleton read a paper entitled, "Concepts

of Capital and Income Underlying Accounting."[55] This paper

appeared in the next issue of The Accounting Review.[56] In

---

[51]"Convention Report," The Accounting Review, IX, No. 1 (March, 1934), 90.

[52]Biographical File of A. C. Littleton, Department of Accountancy, College of Commerce and Business Administration, University of Illinois, Urbana, Illinois.

[53]"Convention Report, Twentieth Annual Convention, New York, December 27-28, 1935," The Accounting Review, XI, No. 1 (March, 1936), 74.

[54]Zeff, 50th Anniversary, pp. 38-39.

[55]"American Accounting Association, 21st Annual Meeting, Stevens Hotel, Chicago, Illinois, December 28-29, 1936," The Accounting Review, XI, No. 4 (December, 1936), 410.

[56]A. C. Littleton, "Concepts of Income Underlying Accounting," The Accounting Review, XII, No. 1 (March, 1937), 13-22.

1938, his addition to the program was a paper on "Revision of the Tentative Statement of Accounting Principles,"[57] which also appeared as an article in The Accounting Review.[58] In 1940, Littleton presented one of three papers which were given on the subject of inventories.[59]

An open forum on accounting principles at the meeting in 1941 was presided over by Littleton.[60] There were no national annual meetings held by the American Accounting Association in 1942, 1943, or 1945. In 1946, when meetings were resumed after the war years, Littleton presented a paper at the Chicago meeting under the general topic of "Problems in Education." This paper, also, appeared later in The Accounting Review.[61] "The Meaning of

---

[57]"Convention Report, American Accounting Association, Proceedings of the Twenty-Third Annual Convention, Detroit, Michigan, December 28-30, 1938," The Accounting Review, XIV, No. 1 (March, 1939), 76.

[58]A. C. Littleton, "Suggestions for the Revision of the Tentative Statement of Accounting Principles," The Accounting Review, XIV, No. 1 (March, 1939), 57-64.

[59]"Convention Report, Proceedings of the Twenty-Fifth Annual Convention of the American Accounting Association, Chicago, Illinois, December 27-28, 1940," The Accounting Review, XVI, No. 1 (March, 1941), 87.

[60]"Convention Report, Proceedings of the Twenty-Sixth Annual Convention of the American Accounting Association, New York, New York, December 29-30, 1941," The Accounting Review, XVII, No. 1 (January, 1942), 67.

[61]A. C. Littleton, "Guidance Tests for Accounting Students," The Accounting Review, XXI, No. 4 (October, 1946), 404-9.

Historical Cost," was Littleton's topic at the 1951 meeting,[62] which formed the basis for an article in the April, 1952 issue of The Accounting Review.[63]

Littleton served as Vice President, as well as Assistant Director of Research under William A. Paton, during 1936-1937. He was Acting Director of Research during 1938 and co-director of research from 1939 through 1942. From 1943 through 1946 he served as chairman of the editorial board for The Accounting Review and was virtually the only active member. Littleton also served as president of the Association in 1943,[64] when officers were selected by a special committee of seven past presidents for the year 1943. This procedure was necessitated because no annual meeting was held in 1942 due to war-time transportation difficulties.[65]

Honors and Awards

In 1912, Littleton was elected to Delta Kappa Chi as a senior at the University of Illinois. In 1913, when Delta Kappa Chi became a charter chapter of Beta Gamma Sigma,

---

[62]"Announcing 1951 Annual Convention of the American Accounting Association, September 6 and 7, Denver, Colorado," The Accounting Review, XXVI, No. 3 (July, 1951), 446.

[63]A. C. Littleton, "Significance of Invested Cost," The Accounting Review, XXVII, No. 2 (April, 1952), 167-73.

[64]Zeff, 50th Anniversary, passim, pp. 91-92.

[65]Ibid.

Littleton supplied material for an early history of the chapter.[66] Littleton was appointed the chairman of a committee, in 1921, to revise the Beta Gamma Sigma fraternity ritual which was approved and adopted in 1923.[67]

Littleton was the third national president (1927-1929) of Beta Alpha Psi, the national professional accounting fraternity which was founded in 1919.[68] In January, 1935, he was awarded a scroll by the Grand Chapter of Beta Alpha Psi for the most noteworthy contribution to accounting literature during the preceding year. The book which won the award for Littleton was Accounting Evolution to 1900.[69] This book has been referred to in the ensuing years as a well-known historical study.[70]

At the time of his retirement in 1952, after 37 years at the University of Illinois, Littleton was honored at a recognition dinner attended by 100 persons.[71] At the

---

[66]Elwell, The First 50 Years of Beta Gamma Sigma, pp. v, 10.

[67]Ibid., p. 52.

[68]"Past Presidents of Beta Alpha Psi, 1919-1969," Newsletter, Beta Alpha Psi, VIII, No. 4 (50th Anniversary Edition, Spring, 1969), 4.

[69]"University Notes," The Accounting Review, X, No. 1 (March, 1935), 130.

[70]"Contributors to the March Issue," The Accounting Review, XIII, No. 1 (March, 1938), i, and others.

[71]Courier, May 27, 1952, Biographical File of A. C. Littleton, Alumni Office, University of Illinois, Urbana, Illinois.

50th anniversary exercises to celebrate the founding of courses in business at the University of Illinois, on November 7, 8, and 10, 1952, Littleton was one of a group of seven teachers honored as responsible for the initiation, development, and growth of courses in business.[72]

On August 31, 1954, Professor Emeritus Littleton was presented the annual award of Alpha Kappa Psi. Many contributions to accounting education were cited as constituting the reason for the award by the accounting and commerce honorary society.[73] This award was presented at the annual convention of the American Accounting Association.[74] At the time of presentation, Littleton remarked that his professional work had been far more satisfying than he could have imagined it would be.[75]

In 1956, Littleton was the sole nominee to the Ohio State University Accounting Hall of Fame.[76] The Accounting Hall of Fame was established in 1950 to honor living North

---

[72]"Accounting Review Notes, 12/5/52," Hiram T. Scovill Papers, 1915-1959, Box 8, University Archives, College of Commerce and Business Administration, University of Illinois, Urbana, Illinois.

[73]Newspaper clipping, Illinois Alumni News, September, 1954, Biographical File of A. C. Littleton, Alumni Office, University of Illinois, Urbana, Illinois.

[74]"Notes About the Author," The Illinois Certified Public Accountant, XVII, No. 3 (March, 1955), 23.

[75]"Accounting Ideas Are Fun," 6.

[76]"Accounting Hall of Fame," The Journal of Accountancy, CI (June, 1956), 6.

Americans who have made outstanding contributions to the field of accounting.[77]

An honorary degree of doctor of laws was awarded by the University of Illinois to Littleton on May 12, 1967, at a banquet held in conjunction with a Seminar on International Accounting sponsored by the Center for International Education and Research in Accounting.[78] The award of such an honorary doctorate by the University of Illinois in this manner occurs rarely. Few faculty members are honored in this way and certainly very few alumni faculty. This makes the award to Littleton, fifteen years after his retirement, very unique.[79] At the same meeting, Littleton was awarded a certificate in recognition of his past and continuing contributions to the educational program of the Center for International Education and Research in Accounting.[80]

---

[77] J. Brooks Heckert, "Accounting Hall of Fame," The Journal of Accountancy, XXV, No. 3 (July, 1950), 260.

[78] "Newsletter, July, 1967," Center for International Education and Research in Accounting, Department of Accountancy, College of Commerce and Business Administration, University of Illinois, Urbana, Illinois.

[79] V. K. Zimmerman, unpublished interview recorded by K. T. Current, July 9, 1969, Department of Accountancy, College of Commerce and Business Administration, University of Illinois, Urbana, Illinois.

[80] "Newsletter, July, 1967," Center for International Education and Research in Accounting, Department of Accountancy, College of Commerce and Business Administration, University of Illinois, Urbana, Illinois.

Littleton was named the first Weldon Powell
Memorial Professor at the University of Illinois for the
year 1968-1969. His selection resulted from the Awards
Committee's consideration of the requisite qualifications
stipulated by the Board of Trustees of the University of
Illinois. The recipient must be a truly stimulating and
influential teacher. He must have displayed unusual capacity for research amply supported by publications. A substantial record of professional services is required.
Finally, a high order of support of the University's and
Department of Accountancy's total program in teaching, research, and public contacts must have been evident. The
award was made on May 15, 1969, in conjunction with an International Seminar on accounting held at the Center for
International Education and Research in Accounting on the
campus at the University of Illinois.[81]

The Individual

Littleton, as an individual, was dedicated to and
absorbed by his professional work. He was exceedingly thorough. He taught a heavy teaching load in addition to his
research and writing efforts. He read prodigiously, not
only in accounting, but in other areas as well. He taught
himself German, Italian, and enough French to be able to

[81]"Weldon Powell Memorial Professorship, First
Recognition Lecture and Banquet, May 15, 1969," Department
of Accountancy, University of Illinois, Urbana, Illinois.

translate articles and make book reviews. He was virtually a "one-man seminar," a "sparkling graduate teacher."[82]

Littleton had a summer cabin in Wisconsin and he liked to camp there and in the Rocky Mountain National Park. He was not especially interested in sports, but he did enjoy the out-of-doors life. He spent many vacations in the woods near Lake Superior fishing, tramping, and paddling a canoe.[83] Littleton himself claimed he had no hobbies because his work of teaching and writing was his play.[84]

Publications

Littleton contributed an almost continuous flow of articles, reviews, editorials, and comments to the various professional journals in addition to the books with which he added to the store of scholarly professional literature in accounting. His Accounting Evolution to 1900 published in 1933, and reprinted in 1966, has been translated into Japanese. An Introduction to Corporate Accounting Standards, coauthored with William A. Paton, and Structure of Accounting Theory have also been translated into Japanese.

Appendix I includes a chronological listing of Littleton's articles and books. The list is impressive.

---

[82]Zimmerman, unpublished interview.

[83]Scovill, "Sound Theory," Biographical File, Department of Accountancy.

[84]"Accounting Ideas Are Fun," p. 6.

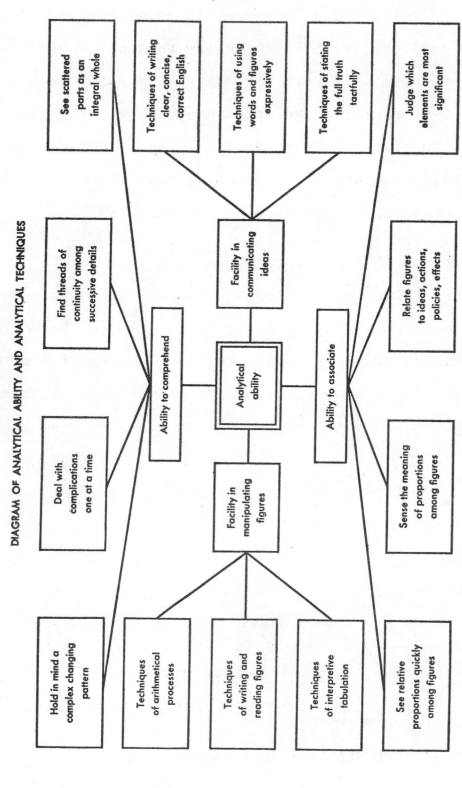

APPENDIX III[1]

DIAGRAM OF ANALYTICAL ABILITY AND ANALYTICAL TECHNIQUES

See scattered parts as an integral whole

Techniques of writing clear, concise, correct English

Techniques of using words and figures expressively

Techniques of stating the full truth tactfully

Judge which elements are most significant

Find threads of continuity among successive details

Facility in communicating ideas

Deal with complications one at a time

Ability to comprehend

Analytical ability

Ability to associate

Relate figures to ideas, actions, policies, effects

Facility in manipulating figures

Sense the meaning of proportions among figures

Hold in mind a complex changing pattern

Techniques of arithmetical processes

Techniques of writing and reading figures

Techniques of interpretive tabulation

See relative proportions quickly among figures

[1] A. C. Littleton, "Accounting Exchange: Analytical Ability and Analytical Techniques," The Accounting Review, XIX, No. 2 (April, 1944), pp. 196-98, and reprinted in A. C. Littleton, Essays on Accountancy (Urbana, Illinois: University of Illinois Press, 1961), p. 550-51.

BIBLIOGRAPHY

BIBLIOGRAPHY

Books

Accounting Terminology. New York: The Century Co., 1931,
    for American Institute of Accountants.

Anyon, James T. Recollections of the Early Days of American
    Accountancy, 1883-1893. New York: By the Author,
    1925.

Backer, Morton, ed. Handbook of Modern Accounting Theory.
    Englewood Cliffs, N. J.: Prentice-Hall, Inc., 1955.

Backer, Morton, ed. Modern Accounting Theory. A Revision
    of Handbook of Modern Accounting Theory. Englewood
    Cliffs, New Jersey: Prentice-Hall, Inc., 1966.

Bentley, H. C., and Leonard, R. S. Bibliography of Works
    on Accounting by American Authors, 1796-1934, Vol. 1
    (1796-1900) and Vol. 2 (1901-1934). Boston:
    Harry C. Bentley, 1934.

Bower, James B., and Welke, William R. Financial Informa-
    tion Systems. Boston: Houghton Mifflin Company,
    1968.

Brown, Richard. A History of Accounting and Accountants.
    New York: Reissued by Augustus M. Kelley Publishers,
    1968. Originally issued: London: Frank Cass and
    Company Limited, 1905.

Bursk, Edward C.; Clark, Donald T.; and Hidy, Ralph W., eds.
    The World of Business, Four Volumes. New York:
    Simon and Schuster, 1962.

Carey, John L. The Rise of the Accounting Profession.
    Vol. I: From Technician to Professional, 1896-1936.
    New York: American Institute of Certified Public
    Accountants, 1969.

Cattell, J. McKeen; Cattell, Jaques; and Ross, E. E., eds.
    Leaders in Education, & Biographical Directory, 2nd
    Edition. New York: The Science Press, 1941.

273

274

Cole, William Morse. Accounts, Their Construction and Interpretation. Revised and Enlarged Edition. Boston, New York, Chicago, San Francisco: Houghton Mifflin Company, 1915.

Cole, William Morse. The Fundamentals of Accounting. Boston: Houghton Mifflin Company, 1921.

Deinzer, Harvey T. Development of Accounting Thought. New York: Holt, Rinehart and Winston, Inc., 1965.

Edwards, James Don. History of Public Accounting in the United States. MSU Business Studies, 1960. East Lansing: Bureau of Business and Economic Research, Michigan State University, 1960.

Edwards, James Don, and Salmonson, Roland F. Contributions of Four Accounting Pioneers: Kohler, Littleton, May, Paton. MSU Business Studies, 1961. East Lansing: Bureau of Business and Economic Research, Michigan State University, 1961.

Elwell, Fayette H. The First 50 Years of Beta Gamma Sigma. Homewood, Illinois: Richard D. Irwin, Inc., 1963.

Goldberg, Louis. An Inquiry Into The Nature of Accounting. Menasha, Wisconsin: George Banta Company, Inc. for the American Accounting Association, 1965.

Gras, N. S. B., and Larson, Henrietta M. Casebook in American Business History. New York: Appleton-Century-Crofts, Inc., 1939.

Green, Wilmer L. History and Survey of Accountancy. Brooklyn, N. Y.: Standard Text Press, 1930.

Hatfield, Henry Rand. Modern Accounting, Its Principles and Some of Its Problems. New York and London: D. Appleton and Company, 1915 (Copyright in 1909).

Hatfield, Henry Rand. Accounting, Its Principles and Problems. New York: Appleton-Century-Crofts, Inc., 1927. (Revision of Modern Accounting, Copyright 1909).

Hendriksen, Eldon S. Accounting Theory. Revised edition. Homewood, Illinois: Richard D. Irwin, Inc., 1970.

Higgins, John A., Jones, Charles W., and Williams, Paul D., eds. The First Fifty Years, 1913-1963. Chicago: Arthur Andersen & Co., 1963.

Kester, Roy B. Accounting Theory and Practice, Volume I.
Second Edition. New York: The Ronald Press Company,
1922.

Kohler, Eric L. A Dictionary for Accountants. 3rd Edition.
Englewood Cliffs, N. J.: Prentice-Hall, Inc., 1963.

Lafrentz & Co., F. W. A Half Century of Accounting, 1899-
1949. New York: Privately Printed by The John B.
Watkins Company, 1949.

Littleton, A. C. and Yamey, B. S., eds. Studies in the
History of Accounting. Homewood, Illinois:
Richard D. Irwin, Inc., 1956.

Littleton, A. C. and Zimmerman, V. K. Accounting Theory:
Continuity and Change. Englewood Cliffs, N. J.:
Prentice-Hall, Inc., 1962.

Lybrand, Ross Bros. & Montgomery. Fiftieth Anniversary,
1898-1948. n.p.: Privately Printed by Lybrand, Ross
Bros. & Montgomery, n.d.

Moonitz, Maurice. The Basic Postulates of Accounting,
Accounting Research Study No. 1. New York: American Institute of Certified Public Accountants, Inc.,
1961.

Moonitz, Maurice, and Littleton, A. C., eds. Significant
Accounting Essays. Englewood Cliffs, New Jersey:
Prentice-Hall, Inc., 1965.

Murphy, Mary E. Advanced Public Accounting Practice.
Homewood, Illinois: Richard D. Irwin, Inc., 1966.

1971 Federal Tax Course. New York: Commerce Clearing
House, Inc., 1970.

Paton, W. A. Paton on Accounting, Selected Writings of
W. A. Paton. Edited by Herbert F. Taggart. Ann
Arbor, Michigan: Bureau of Business Research,
Graduate School of Business Administration, The
University of Michigan, 1964.

Paton, W. A., and Littleton, A. C. An Introduction to
Corporate Accounting Standards, Monograph No. 3.
Chicago, Illinois: American Accounting Association,
1940.

Paton, William Andrew. *Accounting Theory, With Special Reference to the Corporate Enterprise*. Chicago, Illinois: A. S. P. Accounting Studies Press, Ltd., Reprinted 1962 (Originally published in 1922).

Salmonson, R. F. *Basic Financial Accounting Theory*. Belmont, California: Wadsworth Publishing Company, Inc., 1969.

Sprague, Charles E. *The Philosophy of Accounts*. 4th Edition. New York: The Ronald Press, 1920.

A Statement of Basic Accounting Theory. Evanston, Illinois: American Accounting Association, 1966.

Storey, Reed K. *The Search for Accounting Principles, Today's Problems in Perspective*. New York: American Institute of Certified Public Accountants, Inc., 1964.

Who's Who in America, a Biographical Dictionary of Notable Living Men and Women, Vol. 24. Chicago: The A. N. Marquis Company, 1946-1947.

Zeff, Stephen A. *American Accounting Association: Fiftieth Anniversary 1916-1966*. Evanston, Illinois: American Accounting Association, 1966.

Zeff, Stephen A., and Keller, Thomas F., eds. *Financial Accounting Theory, Issues and Controversies*. New York: McGraw-Hill Book Company, 1964.

Periodicals

"Accounting Errors in Corporation Tax Bill," Editorial, *The Journal of Accountancy*, VIII (July, 1909), 213.

"Accounting Hall of Fame," *The Journal of Accountancy*, CI (June, 1956), 6.

"A. C. Littleton: Accounting Ideas Are Fun," *The Journal of Accountancy*, CI (June, 1956), 6.

Allen, C. E. "The Growth of Accounting Instruction Since 1900," *The Accounting Review*, II, No. 2 (June, 1927), 150-66.

"American Accounting Association, 21st Annual Meeting, Stevens Hotel, Chicago, Illinois, December 28-29, 1936," *The Accounting Review*, XI, No. 4 (December, 1936), 410.

"Announcing 1951 Annual Convention of The American
        Accounting Association, September 6 and 7, Denver,
        Colorado," The Accounting Review, XXVI, No. 3
        (July, 1951), 446.

"Association Notes," The Accounting Review, XVIII, No. 1
        (January, 1943), 89.

"Bright Prospects of Accountancy," Editorial, The Journal
        of Accountancy, XVI, No. 6 (December, 1913), 459-60.

Brummer, Leon. "The Inception and Foundation of the School
        of Commerce, Accounts, and Finance," The Journal of
        Accountancy, XI, No. 4 (February, 1911), 252-55.

Brundage, P. F. "Milestones on the Path of Accounting,"
        Harvard Business Review, XXIX, No. 4 (July, 1951),
        71-81.

Chambers, R. J. "Blueprint for a Theory of Accounting,"
        Accounting Research, VI (1955), 17-25.

Chambers, R. J. "Detail for a Blueprint," The Accounting
        Review, XXXII, No. 2 (April, 1957), 206-15.

"Comments on the Capital Principle," A. C. Littleton,
        chairman of open forum. The Accounting Review,
        XVII, No. 1 (January, 1942), 41-60.

"Contributors to the March Issue," The Accounting Review,
        XIII, No. 1 (March, 1938), i.

"Convention Report," The Accounting Review, XII, No. 1
        (March, 1937), 68-75.

"Convention Report, American Accounting Association,
        Proceedings of the Twenty-Third Annual Convention,
        Detroit, Michigan, December 28-30, 1938," The
        Accounting Review, XIV, No. 1 (March, 1939), 76.

"Convention Report, Proceedings of the Twenty-Fifth Annual
        Convention of the American Accounting Association,
        Chicago, Illinois, December 27-28, 1940," The
        Accounting Review, XVI, No. 1 (March, 1941), 87.

"Convention Report, Proceedings of the Twenty-Sixth Annual
        Convention of the American Accounting Association,
        New York, December 29-30, 1941," The Accounting
        Review, XVII, No. 1 (January, 1942), 67-70.

"Convention Report, Twentieth Annual Convention, New York,
        December 27-28, 1935," The Accounting Review, XI,
        No. 1 (March, 1936), 74.

278

Edwards, James Don. "The Antecedents of American Public Accounting." Contemporary Studies in the Evolution of Accounting Thought. Edited by Michael Chatfield. Belmont, California: Dickenson Publishing Company, Inc., 1968, 144-66.

Edwards, James Don. "Some Significant Developments of Public Accounting in The United States." Contemporary Studies in the Evolution of Accounting Thought. Edited by Michael Chatfield. Belmont, California: Dickenson Publishing Company, Inc., 1968, 196-209.

Green, David, Jr. "A Moral to the Direct-Costing Controversy." The Journal of Business, XXXIII, No. 3 (July, 1960), 218-26.

Greer, Howard C. "Benchmarks and Beacons." The Accounting Review, XXXI, No. 1 (January, 1956), 3-14.

Hatfield, H. R., and Littleton, A. C. "A Check-List of Early Bookkeeping Texts," The Accounting Review, VII, No. 3 (September, 1932), 194-206.

Hawkins, David F. "The Development of Modern Financial Reporting Practices Among American Manufacturing Corporations," The Business History Review, XXXVII (Autumn, 1963), 135-68.

Heckert, J. Brooks. "Accounting Hall of Fame," The Accounting Review, XXV, No. 3 (July, 1950), 260-61.

Irish, R. A. "The Evolution of Corporate Accounting." Contemporary Studies in the Evolution of Accounting Thought. Edited by Michael Chatfield. Belmont, California: Dickenson Publishing Company, Inc., 1968, 57-85.

Jucius, M. J. "Historical Development of Uniform Accounting," Journal of Business, XVI (1943), 219-29.

Katano, Ichiro. "A. C. Littleton and His Accounting Thought," The Hitotsubashi Review, Vol. 53, No. 4 (April, 1965), Special Issue: Eminent Scholars—Notes on Their Life and Work. Translated by Yukio Fujita, unpublished in translation. Found in: Biographical File of A. C. Littleton. Department of Accountancy, College of Commerce and Business Administration, University of Illinois, Urbana, Illinois.

Lockwood, Jeremiah. "Early University Education in Accountancy," The Accounting Review, XIII, No. 2 (June, 1938), 131-44.

Masters, J. Edward. "The Accounting Profession in the United States," The Journal of Accountancy, XX, No. 5 (November, 1915), 349-55.

Montgomery, Robert H. "What Have We Done, and How?" The Journal of Accountancy, LXIV, No. 5 (November, 1937), 333-48.

Moyer, C. A. "Early Developments in American Auditing." Contemporary Studies in the Evolution of Accounting Thought. Edited by Michael Chatfield. Belmont, California: Dickenson Publishing Company, Inc., 1968, 188-95.

"Notes About the Author," The Illinois Certified Public Accountant, XVII, No. 3 (March, 1955), 23.

Parker, R. H. "Accounting History: A Select Bibliography." Contemporary Studies in the Evolution of Accounting Thought. Edited by Michael Chatfield. Belmont, California: Dickenson Publishing Company, Inc., 1968, 389-423.

"Program of Fifteenth Annual Convention, American Association of University Instructors in Accounting, December 29-30, 1930," The Accounting Review, V, No. 4 (December, 1930), 341.

Ross, T. Edward. "Random Recollections of an Eventful Half Century," The Journal of Accountancy, LXIV, No. 4 (October, 1937), 256-78.

Sampson, Roy J. "American Accounting Education, Textbooks and Public Practice Prior to 1900," Business History Review, XXXIV, No. 4 (Winter, 1960), 459-66.

Scovill, Hiram T. "Comments on Some Tentative Propositions Underlying Consolidated Reports," The Accounting Review, XIII, No. 1 (March, 1938), 73-77.

Scovill, Hiram T. "Reflections of Twenty-Five Years in the American Accounting Association," The Accounting Review, XVI, No. 2 (June, 1941), 167-75.

Sears, Marian V. "The American Businessman at the Turn of the Century," The Business History Review, XXX (December, 1956), 382-443.

Sells, E. W. "The Accountant of 1917," The Journal of Accountancy, III, No. 4 (February, 1907), 297-99.

280

Sells, Elijah W. "The Accounting Profession: Its Demands and Its Future," The Journal of Accountancy, XX No. 5 (November, 1915), 325-33.

Sells, Elijah Watt. "President Sells' Inaugural Address," The Journal of Accountancy, III, No. 1 (November, 1906), 39-41.

Sorter, George H. and Horngren, Charles T. "Asset Recognition and Economic Attributes--The Relevant Costing Approach," The Accounting Review, XXXVII, No. 3 (July, 1962), 391-99.

Staubus, George J. "Revenue and Revenue Accounts," Accounting Research, VII (January, 1956), 284-94.

Sterrett, J. E. "Education and Training of a Certified Public Accountant," The Journal of Accountancy, I, No. 1 (November, 1905), 1-15.

Sterrett, J. E. "The Present Position and Probable Development of Accountancy as a Profession," The Journal of Accountancy, VII, No. 4 (February, 1909), 265-73.

Sterrett, Joseph E. "Progress of the Accounting Profession," The Journal of Accountancy, IX (November, 1909), 11-16.

Storey, Reed K. "Revenue Realization, Going Concern, and Measurement of Income," Contemporary Studies in the Evolution of Accounting Thought. Edited by Michael Chatfield. Belmont, California: Dickenson Publishing Company, Inc., 1968, 297-306.

Suffern, Edward L. "Twenty-Five Years of Accountancy," The Journal of Accountancy, XXXIV, No. 3 (September, 1922), 174-81.

Trumbull, Wendell P. "The All-Inclusive Standard," The Accounting Review, XXVII, No. 1 (January, 1952), 3-14.

"University Notes," The Accounting Review, II, No. 4 (December, 1927), 425.

"University Notes," The Accounting Review, VI, No. 2 (June, 1931), 158.

"University Notes," The Accounting Review, VI, No. 3 (September, 1931), 245.

"University Notes," The Accounting Review, X, No. 1 (March, 1935), 130.

"University Notes," The Accounting Review, XI, No. 2 (June, 1936), 207.

"University Notes," The Accounting Review, XIV, No. 3 (September, 1939), 330.

"University Notes," The Accounting Review, XIV, No. 4, Part I (December, 1939), 464.

"University Notes," The Accounting Review, XVI, No. 3 (September, 1941), 319.

Vatter, William J. "Origins of the Fund Theory," Contemporary Studies in the Evolution of Accounting Thought. Edited by Michael Chatfield. Belmont, California: Dickenson Publishing Company, Inc., 1968, 95-112.

Webster, Norman E. "Early Movements for Accountancy Education," The Journal of Accountancy, LXXI, No. 5 (May, 1941), 441-50.

Wilkinson, George. "The Accounting Profession in the United States," The Journal of Accountancy, X, No. 5 (September, 1910), 339-47.

Wilkinson, George. "Organization of the Profession in Pennsylvania," The Journal of Accountancy, XLIV, No. 3 (September, 1927), 161-79.

Zimmerman, V. K. "The Long Shadow of a Scholar," The International Journal of Accounting Education and Research, II, No. 2 (Spring, 1967), 1-20.

Proceedings, Newsletters, and Other

Adams, J. P., Littleton, A. C., and Stevenson, R. A. "Report of the Committee on Standardization," The American Association of University Instructors in Accounting, Papers and Proceedings Eighth Annual Meeting, Columbus, Ohio, 1923, VIII, No. 1. n.p., June, 1924.

The American Association of University Instructors in Accounting. Papers and Proceedings of the First Annual Meeting, Columbus, Ohio, December, 1916, I, n.p., May, 1917.

282

The American Association of University Instructors in
        Accounting. _Papers and Proceedings of the Third
        Annual Meeting_, Richmond, Virginia, December,
        1918, III, No. 1. n.p., January, 1919.

The American Association of University Instructors in
        Accounting. _Proceedings of 11th Annual Convention_,
        St. Louis, 12/28 & 29, 1926, II, No. 1. Ann Arbor,
        March, 1927.

Biographical File of A. C. Littleton. Alumni Office,
        University of Illinois, Urbana, Illinois.

Biographical File of A. C. Littleton. Department of Ac-
        countancy, College of Commerce and Business
        Administration, University of Illinois, Urbana,
        Illinois.

Biographical File of A. C. Littleton. Office of President,
        University of Illinois, Urbana, Illinois.

Books and Articles Published by the Corps of Instruction,
        University of Illinois, University Archives and
        Library, 1917-1926.

Books and Articles Published by the Corps of Instruction,
        University of Illinois, University Archives and
        Library, 1926-1931.

Books and Articles Published by the Corps of Instruction,
        University of Illinois, University Archives and
        Library, 1931-1939.

_Bulletin of Illinois Society of Certified Public Account-
        ants_, II (December, 1940), and various other issues.

"Chronology of Beta Alpha Psi," _Keys of Beta Alpha Psi_
        (September, 1930), 23.

"Committee on History," _American Institute of Accountants,
        Officers and Committees, Proceedings of 1948 Annual
        Meeting, By-Laws of the Institute, Rules of Profes-
        sional Conduct; For the Year 1948-1949._ New York:
        American Institute of Accountants, 1948, 16.

Green, Paul M. "Award of the Honorary Degree of Doctor of
        Laws to A. C. Littleton," May 12, 1967. Remarks
        printed in "Newsletter, July, 1967," Center for
        International Education and Research in Accounting,
        College of Commerce and Business Administration,
        Department of Accounting, University of Illinois.

"History of Accounting in Illinois," Bulletin of Illinois Society of Certified Public Accountants, II, No. 4 (September, 1940), 5.

Littleton, A. C. and Winakor, A. H. Illinois Appropriations for Social and Educational Purposes, Research Bulletin No. 14. Urbana, Illinois: University of Illinois, College of Commerce and Business Administration, Bureau of Economic and Business Research, July 26, 1927.

"Littleton Receives Accounting Award," Diary of Alpha Kappa Psi, XLIV (Autumn, 1954), 17.

"Newsletter, July, 1967," Center for International Education and Research in Accounting, College of Commerce and Business Administration, Department of Accountancy, University of Illinois, Urbana, Illinois.

"Past Presidents of Beta Alpha Psi, 1919-1969," Newsletter, Beta Alpha Psi, VIII, No. 4 (50th Anniversary Edition, Spring, 1969), 4-16.

Scovill Papers, Hiram T. 1915-1959, Boxes 8, 9, 10. University Archives, Commerce and Business Administration, University of Illinois.

Scovill, Hiram T. "A. C. Littleton: Sound Theory Is Necessary." Unpublished comments, April 25, 1956, Biographical File of A. C. Littleton, Department of Accountancy, College of Commerce and Business Administration, University of Illinois, Urbana, Illinois.

Treleven, John E. "The Present Status of Instruction in Accounting in Colleges and Universities," The American Association of University Instructors in Accounting, Papers and Proceedings of the First Annual Meeting, 1916, I, No. 1. Columbus, May, 1917, 7-19.

University of Illinois Annual List of Publications of the Faculty, 1939-1949. University of Illinois, University Archives and Library.

University of Illinois Bulletin: Graduate Programs in Accountancy. Urbana: University of Illinois Press, 1968.

"University of Illinois News," Publications of the American Accounting Association of University Instructors in Accounting, IX, No. 2 (December, 1925), 174.

284

"Weldon Powell Memorial Professorship, First Recognition
Lecture and Banquet, May 15, 1969," (printed
program), Department of Accountancy, University of
Illinois, Urbana, Illinois.

Zimmerman, V. K. Unpublished interview, recorded by
K. T. Current, July 9, 1969, Department of Account-
ancy, College of Commerce and Business
Administration, University of Illinois, Urbana,
Illinois.

INDEX

    see Income Statement,
    Profit)

    accrual and deferral, 101-
    104

        cost allocation funda-
        mental, 105, 114

        essence of accrual ac-
        counting, 114

        objective, income truth,
        103

        relation to time periods,
        101-102

        to determine income,
        101, 113

        to make matching possi-
        ble, 104

    all-inclusive, 92

    cause and effect, 11

    central feature of double-
    entry, 81

    central purpose, 11, 75,
    78, 83-85

        dependent upon central
        problem of business,
        57, 75-85, 112-14

        supported by enterprise
        principles pyramid, 64

    central theme, 56, 75-85

        consistently emphasized,
        56, 75, 83, 111-14

        emphasis upon, 54

    cost allocation necessity,
    54, 115, 122

    earning power, 57, 84-85

    of enterprise, 89-90,
    92-93, 114

    effort and accomplish-
    ment, 11, 57-72, 100

        accomplishment as reve-
        nues, 58

        as arrow to accounting,
        64-65

        effort as cost, 58

        Littleton's consistent
        treatment, 68, 226

        measured by attaching
        costs, 149

        to measure is account-
        ing goal, 68, 75

    emphasis on, 54, 108-111,
    122

        historically, 42

    enterprise actions, 76

    matching, 57, 58, 66, 76-
    79, 81, 88, 97-100,
    122, 140-42

        accrual and deferral
        (See Accrual and
        deferral), 104

        as focal center of ac-
        counting, 81-82, 97,
        100, 127

        as integral to accrual
        accounting, 97

        mating, more than com-
        parison, 99, 113

        objectivity necessary,
        97-98

        of relevant elements,
        102